L. J. Henderson

ON THE SOCIAL SYSTEM

THE HERITAGE OF SOCIOLOGY

A Series Edited by Morris Janowitz

L. J. Henderson

ON THE SOCIAL SYSTEM

Selected Writings

Edited and with an Introduction by

BERNARD BARBER

THE UNIVERSITY OF CHICAGO PRESS

CHICAGO AND LONDON

Standard Book Number: 226-32689-6 (Clothbound)
226-32691-8 (Paperbound)
Library of Congress Catalog Card Number: 79-99484

THE UNIVERSITY OF CHICAGO PRESS, CHICAGO 60637
The University of Chicago Press, Ltd., London

Printed in the United States of America

Contents

Preface

WHEN I WAS an undergraduate student at Harvard College, I took L. J. Henderson's course, Sociology 23, the first time it was offered, in the spring of 1938. Both Henderson's character and his ideas made a powerful impression on me—an impression which persists to this day. So effective a teacher, in the largest sense, was Henderson that whenever I re-read his Sociology 23 lectures (published for the first time in this book)[1] I can see and hear him as I saw and heard him over thirty years ago. His ideas, always lucidly and forthrightly expressed, have made essential contributions to my sociological work, even when I felt I had to modify or reject them. Henderson's ideas were especially influential because they often confirmed or supplemented basic ideas I was learning, at the time I took his course, from some of my other undergraduate sociology teachers—particularly Talcott Parsons, but also P. A. Sorokin and Robert K. Merton. The editing of this book has been an exercise in remembering and rediscovering a past which, I hope, will be useful for other sociologists who can come, through this book, to see Henderson's place in the heritage of sociology.

Nearly all of Henderson's social science writings and the essential statements of his philosophy of science are contained in the work published in this book. The pieces are printed in chronological order except for Henderson's "Sociology 23 Lectures," which are by far the longest, the most comprehensive, and the most systematic of all Henderson's sociological writings. The lectures

[1]   See p. 57 of this volume.

are placed first to give an overview of his work, and the subsequent pieces expand and supplement what is contained in them. Although the other pieces might have been grouped under headings which express some of the main focuses of Henderson's work, such as "the concept of system," "the philosophy of science," or "the sociology of medicine," I have chosen not to make such groupings. As the reader will soon see, Henderson's writings overlap, interpenetrate, and supplement one another in ways which make any grouping artificial and disturbing.

I have retained the original titles of all Henderson's essays because it seems to me that these often reveal something of the context in which they were published. But in a few instances, even though the titles may suggest the context, they are unfortunately not adequate guides to the contents. I have therefore inserted brief headnotes to all the essays to enlighten the reader about their contents and about additional aspects of the context.

It is a rare privilege for an editor to bring into print for the first time a document like Henderson's "Sociology 23 Lectures." The version printed here is not the one I myself used, as a student, in 1938, but the amended and expanded version of 1942, kindly furnished me by Professor George C. Homans, Henderson's student and associate. This is the last version, since Henderson died in 1942. It is gratifying to know that Henderson himself wanted these lectures published as they stood. In the preface to the lectures, he indicates that they are part of a larger book which he intended to have published. Unfortunately, he died before he could see to this himself, and his close associates, who would otherwise probably have taken on this enterprise, left to serve in World War II. When they returned, four or five years later, they apparently were occupied with other matters and the publication of Henderson's book was not taken up again.

For generous permission to publish his father's writings, I am much indebted to Mr. Lawrence J. Henderson, Jr. For help in searching for Henderson's writings, I am grateful to the late Professor Crane Brinton and to Mrs. Bernard DeVoto. To George Homans I have the most debts of all: for helping me find Henderson's writings, for discovering the last version of the Sociology 23 lectures, and for making a useful critique of my introduction to this book. I should also like to thank my good friend Morris Janowitz, editor of the Heritage of Sociology series, for his general moral and intellectual guidance and for his specific comments on the introduction. Finally, as with all my work, I must thank Elinor G. Barber for her help, although I regret that we could not edit this book together as we had originally planned. It would have been a much better book.

L. J. Henderson: An Introduction

Was Henderson a Sociologist?

IT IS PROBABLE that nine out of ten sociologists, on first learning of this book or otherwise hearing about L. J. Henderson, would respond with the question, "Who *is* L. J. Henderson?" His name occurs very rarely in sociological texts, and only a little more frequently in monographs. In a recent citation study, the names of twenty-three sociologists were found to have been cited five times or more in at least four of the ten introductory sociology textbooks, published between 1963 and 1967, that were selected for study.[1] The number of citations ran from 27 for A. B. Hollingshead to 148 for Robert K. Merton. Those twenty-three were: R. Bendix, E. W. Burgess, C. H. Cooley, K. Davis, E. Durkheim, S. Freud, A. B. Hollingshead, G. Homans, P. F. Lazarsfeld, R. Linton, S. M. Lipset, R. K. Merton, C. W. Mills, W. E. Moore, G. P. Murdock, T. Newcomb, T. Parsons, E. Shils, S. Stouffer, W. L. Warner, M. Weber, W. F. Whyte, and R. Williams; but nowhere is L. J. Henderson's name to be found. Yet Henderson had at least some influence on Davis, Homans, Merton, Moore, Parsons, Warner, Whyte, and Williams, and some of them were greatly affected by him. Henderson's influence on present-day sociology was large, but it was indirect—through other people. Himself not a professional

---

[1]   Mark Jay Oromaner, "The Most Cited Sociologists: An Analysis of Introductory Text Citations," *The American Sociologist* 3 (1968) : 124–26.

sociologist but a biochemist, he influenced sociology by influencing some influential sociologists.

How did it happen that as late as the 1930s a professional bio-chemist earned a place in the heritage of sociology? That it happened reminds us of something significant about this heritage. It has been built by many amateur sociologists and by different kinds of professional specialists. Only gradually, with accelerating pace over the last forty years, has the role of professional specialist in sociology emerged in stable and institutionalized form in the university and scientific worlds. More and more, mature sociologists practice their specialty full time, in university, government, and business corporation roles especially established for them, after specific graduate and even undergraduate training as sociologists. Even today, however, some recognized professional sociologists have entered their specialty as mature men, coming from other fields; and there is also much "brain gain" into sociology at the graduate and postgraduate levels. A generation ago, there were many nonsociologists who were making full-time or part-time contributions to sociology, and among them Henderson was a notable and not atypical figure.

Biographical Sketch

Lawrence Joseph Henderson was born in Lynn, Massachusetts, near Boston, in 1878 and died in Boston sixty-four years later, in 1942. He was the son of a ship chandler, a dealer in supplies and equipment for ships. His father's headquarters were in the old port of Salem, Massachusetts, near Lynn, and he also had business interests in the French islands of Saint Pierre and Miquelon, off the coast of Canada. Henderson did not follow in his father's footsteps, but spent his life in an academic career at Harvard.[2]

Henderson graduated from Harvard College in 1898 and from the Harvard Medical School in 1902. He immediately went to the University of Strasbourg for further study and research in chem-

[2]   No full-scale biography of Henderson has been written. There is a short article by one of his earliest and most outstanding students in social science, George C. Homans, in the *International Encyclopedia of the So-*

istry, especially in the newly emerging field of biochemistry, which was by then his special area of interest. After returning from Strasbourg, Henderson was first a lecturer, then a regular instructor, and successively an assistant, associate, and full professor of biological chemistry in both Harvard College and the Harvard Medical School. He never practiced medicine, but he had a great knowledge of and influence on the scientific medicine that was rapidly developing in his lifetime. Although Henderson was a scientist rather than a medical practitioner, he always admired a certain kind of medical man—the decisive therapeutist who bases his judgments on a combination of science, experience, and intuition and who is reflective about his own behavior. He felt that there were many such men among his colleagues and friends in the Harvard-Boston medical community. As we shall see, Henderson invited such men to help him instruct his students in his sociology course at Harvard.

In biochemistry and in natural science generally, Henderson was a researcher and original discoverer, a methodologist, and a philosopher. As a researcher, Henderson soon became interested in the mechanisms of neutrality regulation in the animal organism; he brought to these physiological problems the knowledge and techniques of chemistry and shed a great new light on them. In 1908, as part of his work in this area, Henderson presented a precise mathematical formulation of the acid-base equilibrium. In his later work, he applied his concepts of equilibrium, of regulation, of "homeostasis" mechanisms, as his great colleague at the Medical School, W. B. Cannon, came to call them, to the chemistry of blood. Henderson was active in his biochemical and physiological research until the late 1920s, and his work culminated in the publication of *Blood: A Study in General Physiology* in 1928. Homans, on the authority of specialists in this field, calls Henderson "one of the most original and distinguished biological chemists of his time."[3]

---

cial Sciences (New York: Macmillan and Free Press, 1968). For an excellent account of some of his work in social science, with bits of biographical data, see Cynthia Eagle Russett, *The Concept of Equilibrium in American Social Thought* (New Haven: Yale University Press, 1966).

[3]   Russett, *The Concept of Equilibrium.*

Russett, in her book on the concept of equilibrium in American social thought, says of Henderson's scientific work, again on the authority of the relevant specialists: "The rearing of general physiology came about through the efforts of men like Pavlov, L. J. Henderson, J. B. S. Haldane, and Walter B. Cannon, who established beyond doubt the validity of the idea of an internal environment; and others like Joseph Barcroft, who specified what was meant by [Claude] Bernard's 'free and independent life.' "[4] Russett's statement provides the specifics for Homans's more general one; this is distinguished scientific company indeed. Henderson was great in his chosen field.

Henderson was also a methodologist and a philosopher of science. He expressed these interests in seminars in the philosophy department at Harvard and in two general books, one on the relationship between the organism and its environment, the other on the relationship between teleology and determinism: *The Fitness of the Environment: An Inquiry into the Biological Significance of the Properties of Matter* (1913) and *The Order of Nature: An Essay* (1917). He carried his methodological and philosophical interests over into the social sciences, when he came to them toward the end of his life, and it was through them that he had his greatest influence on social scientists.

Although Henderson himself was never an active administrator in scientific or other organizations, he was friend and confidant to very powerful administrators, especially at Harvard. He knew President Charles W. Eliot and later was very close to Eliot's successor, A. Lawrence Lowell. As Homans and Bailey put it, "The professor and the president were friends, not just colleagues. They saw one another; they talked, especially on long and fast walks back to Cambridge after meetings of the Medical School faculty."[5] In addition, as the footnotes to his Sociology 23 lectures and to other articles clearly show, Henderson read very widely in historical and protosociological books about human affairs. He

---

[4]   Ibid., p. 21.
[5]   G. C. Homans and Orville T. Bailey, "The Society of Fellows, Harvard University, 1933–1947," in *The Society of Fellows*, ed. Crane Brinton (Cambridge, Mass.: Harvard University Press, 1939), pp. 3–4.

seemed always to be looking for a satisfactory sociology with which to counsel his powerful friends about the social systems in which they were all involved.

In the late 1920s (Homans says "about 1926," Russett says "in 1928"), Henderson was encouraged to read Pareto's *Sociologie générale* (1917) by his Harvard colleague William Morton Wheeler, whose own classic studies of insect societies had led him to become interested in Pareto's analysis of human societies. Henderson was immediately and enormously impressed; it was just what he had been looking for. He became an enthusiast of Pareto, and for the rest of his life he devoted more and more of his time and activities to Pareto and to social science. Yet, curiously enough, it was not mainly Pareto's ideas that Henderson passed on to some of the young social scientists of the 1930s, who are themselves very influential today. (Who now uses the Paretan notions of "residues" and "derivations"?) His influence consisted more in teaching his own methodological ideas about such essential matters as system, equilibrium, mutual dependence, and the functions of conceptual schemes. "Henderson," says Russett, "may have given greater impetus to the diffusion of equilibrium concepts among American social scientists than any other single individual. To a whole generation of Harvard students he passed on his conception of scientific method, of social science methodology, and specifically of the place of equilibrium analysis in social science."[6]

We have spoken of Henderson's work in physiology and in social science. In one area of activity, these two kinds of work were directly related. In 1927, Harvard University set up the Fatigue Laboratory to study physical and mental stress in workers. The laboratory was at the Harvard Business School and sponsored both physiological and social research. Henderson was the first director of the Fatigue Laboratory. As a physiologist, he took an interest in and influenced the physiological work of Dr. David Dill; as a social scientist he took an interest in and influenced the social research of Elton Mayo, Fritz J. Roethlisberger, and T. North Whitehead, especially their now famous work at the Haw-

[6]   Russett, *The Concept of Equilibrium*, p. 117.

thorne Plant of the Western Electric Company.[7] In its turn, this "industrial relations" research had a considerable influence on American sociology in the period after World War II.[8]

Because Henderson spent his whole academic life at Harvard, one might assume that he is the archetype of what sociologists, in describing local communities and academic communities, have come to call a "local" rather than a "cosmopolitan." But Henderson, though taking great pride in Harvard, was by no means a "local." He was a cosmopolitan in several different ways. First, he was very much a devotee of French culture and spent some of his summers in France. Second, he had nearly universal cultural interests and read widely in several languages. He knew philosophy, literature, general history, social science, the history of medicine and science, and theology, among other matters. Henderson also participated in several national and international medical, scientific, and learned societies. For a number of years he was the foreign secretary of the National Academy of Sciences.

Indeed, even at Harvard, Henderson was what may be called a "cosmopolitan local." In the complex and universalistic structure of a great modern university, he was very much a citizen of the whole. In his career at Harvard, he was from the beginning a member of both the Medical School and the Arts and Sciences faculties, thus bridging the applied and the pure sides of biochemical science. As a friend of President Lowell, he not only counseled him about many aspects of university affairs but came to know many professors in the professional schools, such as the

---

7   See F. J. Roethlisberger and W. J. Dickson, *Management and the Worker* (Cambridge, Mass.: Harvard University Press, 1939); T. N. Whitehead, *The Industrial Worker* (Cambridge, Mass.: Harvard University Press, 1938); Elton Mayo, *The Human Problems of an Industrial Civilization* (New York: Macmillan, 1933); and Elton Mayo, *The Social Problems of an Industrial Civilization* (Cambridge, Mass.: Harvard University Graduate School of Business Administration, 1945).

8   For a summary and critique of the Harvard work and its influence, see Clark Kerr and Lloyd H. Fisher, "Plant Sociology: The Elite and the Aborigines," in *Common Frontiers of the Social Sciences*, ed. Mirra Komarovsky (Glencoe, Ill.: The Free Press, 1957); and for a defense, see Conrad M. Arensberg and Geoffrey Tootell, "Plant Sociology: Real Discoveries and New Problems," in Komarovsky, *Common Frontiers*.

Law School and the Business School, as well as in the specialized departments within each faculty. As we shall see later, in the first run of his Sociology 23 course, in the spring of 1938, he invited twenty-five different guest lecturers, from almost every major section and subsection of the university.

Nowhere in his Harvard activities was Henderson more the cosmopolitan local than in his connection with the Society of Fellows.[9] The society, which Henderson started thinking about as early as 1924, was finally established in 1933, with an endowment from President Lowell, to provide a prestigious place and adequate resources in the university for young men of exceptional talent and independence in any field of science and scholarship.[10] In the small group responsible for founding the society—Henderson, Lowell, the philosopher A. N. Whitehead, the English literature scholar John Livingston Lowes, and the lawyer and author Charles P. Curtis—Henderson took the lead: his conception of the society was scientifically cosmopolitan, if somewhat elitist, and he was the organizer of the founding committee, the author of its founding report, and, finally, the first chairman of the Senior Fellows of the society, who were responsible for the selection and minor guidance of the Junior Fellows. In the society, Henderson, his founder colleagues, and their successors have succeeded in creating an institution in which diversity of talent and independence help make each specialist at least a little broader in his work and in his general cultural interests. Henderson had also hoped that the society would encourage not only "isolated geniuses, but men who will do the work of the world."[11] The society has been less successful in this aim, although it has produced at least a few leaders as well as many scholars and scientists.

Although we lack much of what we would like to know about Henderson, we have a few scraps of information. Homans and Bailey tell us that "Henderson's beard was red but his politics were vigorously conservative."[12] Readers of his work will note

9   See Brinton, ed., *The Society of Fellows* (Cambridge, Mass.: Harvard University Press, 1959).
10   See Homans and Bailey, "The Society of Fellows."
11   Ibid., p. 26.
12   Ibid., p. 3.

many points at which his conservative social views reveal them-selves, although he tried very hard to overcome them in his scien-tific discourse. We get another important glimpse of Henderson from Homans and Bailey when they say, "His method in discus-sion is feebly imitated by the pile-driver. His passion was hottest when his logic was coldest."[13] Nowhere, as my own experience as a student of Henderson showed, was this more evident than in his teaching. Yet it made him a great teacher. Whether he agreed or disagreed, a student could never forget Henderson's words because of the passion so clearly expressed in them. Finally, Homans and Bailey let us see something of the reason for Henderson's great influence on his colleagues and students. "If he felt a man had something in him, no one could be more patient than he in helping it come to light. He had the gift of taking a scholar's raw data, no matter how far they might be from his own field of biochemistry, and bringing out the pattern that lay in them."[14] In somewhat the same way, Henderson helped bring out patterns not fully mani-fested in Pareto's work, particularly in the concept of a social system.

Leading Themes

For the social scientist, there are at least five leading themes in Henderson's work. Their importance is signalized both by their constant recurrence and by various of Henderson's ex-plicit statements and latent cues, such as the passion with which he discusses them. These themes overlap and interpenetrate in Henderson's writings: for example, his critique of positivism and excessive rationality is mixed with his admiration for Pareto's work. But we shall discuss the themes separately, as far as possible, because they do stand out from one another. These are the five leading themes:

1. The methodology and philosophy of science
2. A critique of positivism and excessive rationality
3. The concept of system and social system

13   Ibid.
14   Ibid.

4. The usefulness of Pareto's work
5. Medical sociology

THE METHODOLOGY AND PHILOSOPHY OF SCIENCE

Social scientists have taken considerable interest in the methodology and philosophy of science, because they have felt that knowledge in this area would be a key aid to moving from adolescence or novitiate in science to mature scientific status. In this area, perhaps because he himself had helped the maturation of biochemistry, Henderson read and wrote a great deal and has much to say to social scientists. Among the essential and relevant topics he discussed are the role of theory in science; the role of observation and experiment; the role of the trivial, the obvious, and the vulgar in scientific research; the probability character of scientific statements; and the social process of scientific discovery.

THE ROLE OF THEORY IN SCIENCE   At a time when both empiricism (the view that theory is not important in science) and ontological realism (the view that science only discovers rather passively the reality that is "really" out there) were widespread in natural science, Henderson was what we might call an ardent constructivist, taking the view that without theory any thought is impossible and that the scientist actively constructs the theory that shapes men's ideas about "reality." This constructivism is expressed in several different ways. For example, Henderson speaks of scientific concepts and theories as "abstractions"—as aspects of reality drawn out by the searching mind of the scientist.[15] He repeatedly emphasizes how arbitrary all conceptual definitions are; a favorite phrase he used to indicate this active and arbitrary character when he was offering a definition was "as we choose to say."[16] Further, when he is discussing the notion of waves of social change, he says, "For such waves are, like the conceptual schemes of the physicists, partly constructions of our own minds that go beyond the mere facts."[17] As this last statement indicates, Hender-

---

[15]   See p. 59 of this volume.
[16]   See p. 61.
[17]   See "What Is Social Progress?" p. 251 of this volume.

son was no absolutist in his constructivism; yet the limits of active scientific theory construction were apparently rather broad for him. He could say, when he was laying out a conceptual scheme for the social system, "I shall endeavor to construct one among an *infinite* number of possible conceptual schemes in which a part of my experience will be contained and made useful."[18] Henderson's most explicit statement on this matter probably is a short sentence from his Sociology 23 lectures, which are a mature and concise presentation of his ideas on many problems: "Without a conceptual scheme, thinking seems to be impossible."[19] Henderson asserts explicitly that so-called common-sense thinking involves conceptual schemes as much as science does. At this point in the lectures he continues, "In general, the conceptual schemes of the sciences are simpler and more clearly defined than our common-sense conceptual schemes. . . . [a scientific scheme] owes its clearness and simplicity to the fact, among others, that it has reference to a limited class of phenomena, or to certain aspects of phenomena, and to a limited class of problems."[20]

Finally, Henderson's constructivism is revealed in his statement of the utility criterion for concepts and theories. A constructed definition or theorem, or a systematic set of definitions and theorems, is good only if it is useful for the scientific work in hand. One of his heroes was the great Greek physician and medical writer, Hippocrates. Henderson usually refers to him as a model of several scientific virtues, especially for social science. But he was aware of some of the substantive defects of Hippocrates' medical theories. He discusses these defects and then goes on to tell why, in terms of the utility criterion, Hippocrates' theories were so important to medicine for more than a thousand years: "Nevertheless, his conceptual scheme worked and for a long time worked well. This is, in fact, the test of a conceptual scheme and the only test: it must work well enough for the purpose of the moment. A conceptual scheme survives just so long and just in so

[18] See "An Approximate Definition of Fact," p. 160 of this volume (emphasis inserted).
[19] See p. 86.
[20] See p. 87.

far as it continues to be convenient to use it for the purposes of scientific work."[21] Henderson then appeals for support to Poincaré, the philosopher of science whom he much admired, and he amplifies his own statement on changes in scientific theory and on his constructivist views:

> In a discussion of scientific hypotheses, Henri Poincaré once remarked, "These two propositions, 'the external world exists,' or 'it is more convenient to suppose that it exists,' have one and the same meaning." The proof of this assertion is that in scientific work no use can be made of the proposition, "the external world exists" that cannot be made of the statement "we assume for the present purpose that the external world exists." Moreover, all our conceptual schemes are in a state of flux. There is hardly one we now use that was used in precisely its present form 50 years ago. It is therefore dangerous to believe that a conceptual scheme is a description of some ultimate metaphysical reality. In other words, belief in the "truth" of a conceptual scheme is for scientific purposes not only irrelevant but misleading.[22]

As we shall see at other relevant points, Henderson's writing and teaching were characterized by certain pithy phrases (e.g., "an induction from my experience," "a first approximation") that neatly summed up his views and sentiments on the matter at hand. Much of his viewpoint on the constructivist character of scientific concepts and theories was expressed in the maxim, frequently and passionately repeated, "Never dispute about words." Although he stressed the importance of making abstract classifications of recurrent aspects or uniformities in events, he also continually warned against disputes over what these patterns were to be called. He felt that there was too much dispute over words, especially in social science, and that this prevented sufficient search for the uniformities in events. Here is a good statement of Henderson's feelings; he is referring to some writings by Thucydides on revolutions:

> Do we not find here plain statements of uniformities in events, or if you object to this use of the word "uniformity," do we not find

21   See p. 76.
22   See p. 76.

plain statements of recurrent aspects of phenomena—peculiarities of the actions and of the utterances of men in times of civil strife? . . . resolving once for all not to engage in disputes about words may we not leave the further discussion of this question to the philosophers? Let others call them what they will, or what they feel they must, we shall seek out and study the recurrent aspects of phenomena. Others may dispute about the name, we shall study the thing.[23]

Henderson, who admired Pareto for many reasons, gives him the credit for this bit of wisdom about not fighting over definitions. He says:

Throughout the Treatise Pareto takes pains to avoid in his own discussions the ambiguities and other difficulties that result from the use of words . . . and one of his most important and constantly repeated precepts is: *Never dispute about words*. To these ends, he makes frequent use of letters instead of words as symbols for carefully formulated definitions, and he also employs letters as a test for verbal derivations.[24]

Although Henderson knew well the essential functions of theory in science, he abhorred what he sometimes called "grand" theory. He much preferred theory that was, in his characteristic and reiterated phrase, a "walking-stick to help along the way." Henderson's aversion to "grand" theory was stirred by the highly generalized and oversimplified theory in social science that was common in his day—a theory too far removed from the corrective of empirical observation. In the lectures he speaks against the "pretentious systematization of knowledge that lacked solid objective foundation."[25] It was this lack of "solid objective foundation" in the social science theories of his time that he found repugnant; but he was not opposed in principle to highly generalized, systematic, and comprehensive theory. Thus, it should be no surprise that Pareto's theory of the social system, which *is* highly generalized, systematic, and comprehensive, was very attractive to him. He felt it was based on a "solid objective foundation," al-

23   See p. 105.
24   See p. 133.
25   See p. 69.

though his successors in social science have not agreed with him. Since Henderson's death, Pareto is seldom spoken of by social scientists, and when he is, it is only for pieces of his thought, such as the theory of the circulation of elites, not for his generalized theory of the social system. Except for Pareto, however, Henderson felt that "the social sciences today suffer from defects that are not unlike the defects of medicine to which Hippocrates was opposed. . . . a great part of the social science of today consists of elaborate systematization on a very insufficient foundation of fact."[26] The following description of Hippocrates was really a prescription for the social science of his day: "Hippocrates endeavored to avoid myths and traditional rules, the grand search for philosophical truth, the authority of philosophical beliefs, the concealment of ignorance with a show of systematic knowledge."[27]

It was also typical of Henderson that, although he was himself most insightful in these matters, he warned social scientists about oversophistication in the methodology and philosophy of science. Henderson liked to be rational about what he was doing, and insisted that others be rational; but he had a strong bias for the practical, especially when he felt it was being submerged by excessive rationality. He warned against some of the stultifying methodological concern of the social science of his time:

[It is] useful to warn against anxiety about or anxious striving for high systematization and rigor. It is the fashion among many social scientists and psychologists to devote much attention to what is called "methodology." . . . such discussions are ordinarily a mere nuisance to those whose aim is to get on with scientific work. The position adopted . . . is that we may well judge from experience what procedures are likely to be effective in scientific work. . . . elaborate discussion of methods and of logic and the search for rigor are to be noted only in philosophical writings, in the pseudo-sciences, and in the sciences that have reached a high development. . . . It is ordinarily far more useful to get to work on the phenomena and so

26   See pp. 69–70.
27   See p. 70.

acquire familiarity with things than to spend time talking about "methodology."[28]

If Henderson seems to be overstating matters here, if there seems to be some inconsistency with his own ardent and knowledgeable concern for the methodology of science, it is because of the conflict between two values that he held strongly: The value of rigor and precision in science and the value of doing the practical thing everywhere in human affairs; not least in science itself.

Henderson seems not to have seen the point that the social sciences, as what we may call latecomers to the development of science (by analogy with the economists' discussion of latecomers in the economic development process), may have advantages over the sciences that reached maturity first. As latecomers, the social sciences may be able to develop faster using the methodological sophistication worked out by their predecessors. But there is no reason to believe that the social sciences will proceed through exactly the same steps as the other sciences did on their way to the common goal. Indeed, it is very likely that this developmental process will be different, and somewhat syncopated; and this is what some, though not all by any means, of the methodological discussion in the social sciences is really about.

THE ROLE OF OBSERVATION AND EXPERIMENT   For all his emphasis on the importance of theory in science, Henderson knew well the complementary and reciprocal functions of theory and observation, or, as he often chose to refer to it more generally, "experience." He was himself distinguished as an experimentalist as well as a theorist in biochemistry. A phrase he often used when making an empirical generalization about human behavior was "it is an induction from experience that. . . ."

For the social sciences, Henderson said little about experiment as highly controlled observation of events. He lived at a time when there was even less social science experimentation than the little that occurs today. As a practical man in science, he devoted himself to what he thought was immediately possible, and he seemed

[28]   See pp. 85–86.

to feel that only forms of observation less controlled than experimentation were then available to social science. Although he felt that the way social scientists obtained their data could be considerably improved, he never suggested that this could result from experiment. Instead he recommended, in what are two of his characteristic phrases, "close observation" of things and "intuitive familiarity with things."

Henderson often compared medicine and the social sciences, both as branches of science and as practicing arts. He esteemed in medicine the knowledge and useful practice that had been accumulated as a result of long centuries of "close observation" and "intuitive familiarity with things." When he preached to the social sciences about observation, therefore, he often spoke of medicine, especially of Hippocrates. In his writing and teaching he presented some of the cases of Hippocrates as models of the usefulness of this methodology in making scientific discoveries and empirical generalizations.[29] What Henderson says of Hippocrates he would have liked to say of all competent social scientists: "This is one sign among many that Hippocrates was no casual and no ordinary observer. On the contrary, he was a constant observer with whom observation was a great part of the business of life, a skillful observer whose skill depended upon both native capacity and long practice."[30]

Note here how Henderson suggests the intimate and necessary relation between "long practice" and the valued arts of "close observation" and "intuitive familiarity with things." Henderson felt that these were lacking in many social scientists because of their closeted studies and remote observations of social behavior.

Henderson greatly admired what he called men of affairs because he felt that their position of responsibility required them to have "long practice" in successful diagnosis of, and decisions about, human events. He expresses his regard in the following statement: "Hippocrates resembles Richelieu, or Lyautey, or

---

[29]   E.g., see pp. 71 ff. of this volume, for a long presentation and exposition of the significance of one of Hippocrates' cases.
[30]   See p. 72.

Robert Walpole, or Bismarck, or Cavour more than he does Hobbes, Hegel, Mill, or Marx."[31] The choice of these specific examples reveals Henderson's prejudices, since he presents no "solid objective foundation" that the former were less often in error about human affairs than the latter; nor is there any a priori reason to believe this. But Henderson was certainly right in stressing that "practice" often has a beneficial effect on theory, just as the reverse is often true. The benefit is mutual and reciprocal.

Henderson saw this because he most admired the men who were outstanding both in theory and in practice. He appreciated Hippocrates for both qualities. Hippocrates' notion of *vis medicatrix naturae* is a theoretical generalization of considerable abstractness. One might add that Richelieu and Bismarck never produced anything like it.

Distinction in both theory and practice was probably also why Henderson so esteemed Chester I. Barnard, who as president of the New Jersey Bell Telephone Company was a very successful man of affairs, but who as the author of *The Functions of the Executive*[32] was a distinguished social science theorist.[33]

This admiration of theory plus practice made Henderson critical of the social scientists of his time. He expressed his contempt in the following statement:

The psychologists and sociologists are the professional custodians of what little scientific knowledge we possess that is conversant with personal relations. But from them we have, as yet, little to learn, for they are in general little aware of the problem of practicing what they know in the affairs of everyday life. Indeed, skill in managing one's relations with others is probably less common among professional psychologists and sociologists than among the ablest men of affairs or the wisest physicians.[34]

31   See p. 71.
32   Cambridge, Mass.: Harvard University Press, 1938.
33   On Barnard's work, see the biography by F. J. Roethlisberger in *International Encyclopedia of the Social Sciences* (New York: Macmillan and Free Press, 1968).
34   See "Physician and Patient as a Social System," pp. 202–3 of this volume.

Because of Henderson's strong conviction that "close observation" rather than experiment was all that was possible for the social sciences in his time, and because of his abhorrence of all "grand" theory other than that of Pareto, he recommended that the social sciences be like natural history, not abstractly theoretical like physical or biological science. Again, his model was Hippocrates and his natural-history approach to disease. He says:

> Throughout a great part of his work Hippocrates is thus moving step by step toward the widest generalizations within his reach. In great part he is seeking a natural history of acute disease. . . . His success was great, and the whole history of science goes far to support the view that such a methodical procedure is a necessary step in the development of a science that deals with similarly complex and various phenomena.[35]

Henderson is right when he says that the history of science shows that relatively more empirical, natural history formulations provide a useful approach to the "complex and various phenomena" that physical, biological, and social data all appear to be before being mastered and simplified by the constructions of more generalized, systematic, and comprehensive theory. But empirical formulations are not exclusively useful: as the history and sociology of science demonstrate, there is more than one approach to building a better science. Generalized and systematic theory-building is no less useful in the social sciences than in the physical and biological sciences. The social scientists may be able to profit from their predecessors' experience with the virtues and defects of "grand" theory and therefore employ it more successfully than has been done in the past. At this point in their development, the social sciences will probably profit from a variety of approaches. Mathematical models probably have some use at the present time, although it is usually hard to order any empirical data to them. There is a functional division of labor in all the sciences, partly built around different approaches. Although this division of labor has its costs, it also produces net advantages, both

[35]   See p. 73.

from the specialization it makes possible and from its integrating and coordinating functions.

Because theory and observation have reciprocal effects, the methodologist or philosopher of science who is as knowledgeable about both as Henderson was is bound to have some doubt about their relative primacy. Henderson certainly was ambivalent, sometimes coming out in favor of theory, other times favoring the primacy of observation or experiment. For example, appealing to an "induction from experience," he says, "The whole long history of science clearly shows that observation and experiment are in one respect the primary features of scientific investigation, because when they give rise to well-established and thoroughly confirmed data and when these data are incompatible with theory, . . . then the theory and the previous conclusions yield and suffer modification or destruction, as the case may be."[36] This does, of course, happen, apparently more frequently in what Kuhn has called "normal science"—science in which the basic system of theory, or "paradigm," does not need to be changed.[37] But there is "resistance" in science as well as acceptance, and sometimes established theories do not yield to recurrent anomalous facts.[38] Sometimes what Kuhn has described as "scientific revolutions" are necessary, in which the basic system of theory, or "paradigm," is actively reconstructed by some scientist. In sum, either theory or observation may be primary in science, and the task of both the sociology and the philosophy of science is to specify the conditions under which the primacy of each (or the coexistence of both) is likely to occur. The ambivalence that Henderson experienced can never be eliminated, but it can probably be reduced as the sociology and philosophy of science further specify the relations between theory and observation.

THE ROLE OF THE TRIVIAL, THE OBVIOUS, AND THE VULGAR IN

[36] See p. 78.
[37] See Thomas S. Kuhn, *The Structure of Scientific Revolutions* (Chicago: University of Chicago Press, 1962).
[38] On the nature of "resistance" and on some of its social and cultural sources, see Bernard Barber, "Resistance by Scientists to Scientific Discovery," *Science* 134 (1961) :596–602.

SCIENTIFIC RESEARCH   As we have seen, Henderson disliked "the pretentious" in theory, as indeed in all things. He felt that pretentiousness and other sentiments make social scientists define some things as trivial, dirty, obvious, or vulgar when they are not intrinsically so. He felt that the history of science shows that almost anything may be important to the development of good science, and so he warned against excluding things because of irrelevant feelings or prejudice. One of his favorite phrases was "nothing is trivial but thinking or feeling makes it so."

Henderson repeats this theme many times. At the very beginning of the Sociology 23 lectures he says:

> This illustration has been chosen because, among other reasons, it is a simple case that is likely to seem trivial. Note well, however, that nothing is trivial, but thinking (or feeling) makes it so, and that we must ever guard against coloring facts with our prejudices. There was a time not so very long ago when electromagnetic interactions, mosquitoes, and micro-organisms seemed trivial. It is when we study the social sciences that the risk of mixing our own prejudices and passions with the facts, and thus spoiling our analysis, is most likely to prevail.[39]

Henderson also felt that people are too quick to dismiss matters as obvious. Here is one of his statements about the importance of making the obvious quite explicit:

> Some readers will think these theorems obvious, and feel them accordingly unimportant. Well, the experience of all highly developed sciences shows that the clear, explicit formulation of "the obvious" and its incorporation in the systematic treatment of a subject is both necessary and very convenient. We are all liable to neglect, or overlook, or forget such things, especially when we wish to, and above all when we so wish unconsciously. One definition of the obvious is: An important proposition that we wish to disregard.[40]

In this matter, as in so many others, Henderson had the medical analogy in mind. He knew how much attention medicine had to pay to the trivial, the obvious, the dirty, and the vulgar, and he

[39]   See p. 60.
[40]   See p. 62.

wanted the social sciences to learn from his much-esteemed doctors. Henderson speaks with strong feeling in the following statement and makes one of his frequent references to medicine:

> For the doctor the excretory organs and functions are in general neither more nor less important than the "organ of thought" and thought itself. Either may be important or unimportant as the case may be. . . .
> Now the study of those features of the interactions between persons that occur very widely or generally in human affairs must evidently be concerned with very common or vulgar phenomena. It must also involve the methodical consideration of much that to many persons seems trivial because it is not considered high or noble. Further, it must require the constant or repetitive use of familiar, obvious propositions in a manner that must sometimes seem overmeticulous and pedantic. But obvious things are important, familiarity is a cause for overlooking things, nothing as I have said, is trivial but feeling (note the residue) makes it so, common things are often the uniformities, and in order to make a successful analysis or synthesis it is necessary to take account of the necessary factors and to do so in the necessary way. For deciding whether something is scientifically necessary, experience shows that observation, experiment, logic, or perhaps most often trial and error are the tests. The fact that somebody thinks it vulgar or trivial or obvious is irrelevant, and unless he is a qualified investigator so also is his opinion that it is unimportant.[41]

Sociologists have been more willing than historians or political scientists to investigate the apparently trivial; indeed, they have sometimes been charged with making a virtue of it. Henderson would have approved of this willingness, though he might not always have admired the results of particular studies.

THE PROBABILITY CHARACTER OF SCIENTIFIC STATEMENTS In Henderson's time there was less quantification in the social sciences, except for economics, than there is today; at least quantification that orders measures of things to some abstract and systematic set of concepts. Henderson probably would have mixed feelings about the greatly increased quantification that now exists in the social sciences. On the one hand, he approved very strongly

[41]   See p. 109.

in principle of quantification; on the other hand, he might feel that some mathematical models of social systems and processes are "pretentious" and immature.

Henderson expressed his general approval of quantification in the social sciences in a statement that might well serve as the battle pennant of today's quantifiers and mathematizers. It is, he said,

a very important fact, which should never be forgotten in studying social phenomena, that nearly all supposedly qualitative questions turn out on examination to be quantitative. . . .

Consider such political issues as centralization of authority, labor, the tariff, and relief, or indeed any proposal for the restriction of the individual. A moment's reflection will show that the problems involved are quantitative and that each includes many factors. Yet in public discussion the issues can hardly ever be treated quantitatively.[42]

Given his favorable view of quantification for the social sciences, it is not surprising that Henderson thought of all statements in those sciences (and in the others as well) as probability statements. Very early in the Sociology 23 lectures he says, speaking of science in general, "In observational and experimental science *we are concerned with probability, never with certainty, with approximation never with absolute precision.*"[43] A favorite expression preceding or appended to many of his generalizations was "to a first approximation." In a paper ironically entitled "An Approximate Definition of Fact" he said, "My statements are to be regarded as *approximate* not exact, as *probable* not certain. . . . The only certainty about statements of experience . . . is that they are *not* certain and *not* precise. . . ."[44] And in counseling his students on how to use a conceptual scheme of the generalized social system that he was offering them he said, "Fix once for all in your mind that you are seeking *rough* approximations and *sufficient* probabilities, cheering yourself with the assurance that all the results of all the experimental sciences are but approximations and probabilities." If Henderson's tone in delivering this precept was passionate and

42   See p. 142.
43   Author's emphasis. See p. 62 of this volume.
44   See p. 160.

even dogmatic, his probabilistic and approximational counsel about generalizations was effectively communicated to his students.

THE SOCIAL PROCESS OF SCIENTIFIC DISCOVERY   Henderson, we have seen, was widely read in the history and philosophy of science. Homans and Bailey report that he gave the first course in the history of science at Harvard College, about 1910.[45] Many physicians have been interested in the history of medicine and science; Henderson was probably enough of a physician to have developed early and always maintained this "natural" medical interest.

Since he was a close observer of what he and others around him did, Henderson's interest in the history and philosophy of science inevitably slid over into a protosociology of science. For example, when Henderson is discussing the "delusion" of some scientists that they are discovering some part of "ultimate reality," he goes on to point out, in true sociology of science fashion, that this delusion has the social function of providing strong incentives for scientists to continue their hard work.[46] Thus, he recognizes that a single belief may be analyzed both in terms of its functions as an ideology and in terms of its substantive scientific validity.

But most important of all, Henderson saw that public scientific behavior, what scientists write in their scientific papers or say in their speeches and even their autobiographies, does not accurately portray what they actually do—the social process of scientific discovery. In his introduction to Claude Bernard's *Introduction to the Study of Experimental Medicine*, he says:

The discoverer of natural knowledge stands apart in the modern world, an obscure and slightly mysterious figure. By the abstract character of his researches, his individuality is obliterated; by the rational form of his conclusions, his method is concealed. . . . the unfortunate effects are enhanced by convention which today prescribes a formal, rigorous and impersonal style in the composition of scientific literature. . . . [we] often seek in vain the personality and

[45]   *The Society of Fellows.*
[46]   See p. 77.

the behavior of the person behind the modern scientific printed page. Yet whoever fails to understand the great investigator can never know what science really is.

Such knowledge is not taught in the schools. Even more than scientific memoir, the treatise and lecture are formal, logical, systematic. As much as possible science is made to resemble the world which it describes, in that all vestiges of its fallible and imaginative human origin are removed. Since the publication of Euclid's immortal textbook this has been the universal and approved usage. . . .

[What we lack] is understanding of the art of research and of the inevitable conditions and limitations of scientific discovery, and understanding, in short, of the behavior of the man of genius, not a rationalized discussion of scientific method.[47]

Some fifteen years after writing this, Henderson put the matter more succinctly. "Discussions of scientific method," he said, "are often more concerned with the publications of men of science—with their finished product—than with the habits, attitudes, and characteristic behavior of such men while they are at work and especially before they write their papers or books."[48] Fortunately, in the twenty-five years since Henderson's death there has been a flourishing of the history and sociology of scientific discovery that Henderson so early saw was lacking. He would have enjoyed the results.[49]

A Critique of Positivism and Excessive Rationality

Our times do not find it hard to accept the importance of the emotions, of values, and of irrationality as generic and fundamental aspects of human behavior. But Henderson was the child of a positivistic, rationalistic age, when both the social sciences and much common sense held that reason was predominant in human

[47]   See, "The Process of Scientific Discovery," pp. 149–50 of this volume.

[48]   See p. 68.

[49]   For a history of science example, see especially Kuhn, *Scientific Revolutions*. For a sampling of the sociology of science work, see "The Social Process of Scientific Discovery," in *The Sociology of Science*, ed. Bernard Barber and Walter Hirsch (Glencoe, Ill., The Free Press of Glencoe, 1962).

affairs and that the emotions and sentiments were mere relics of an earlier stage of human history. This positivism and excessive rationality were especially strong during the early and middle years of Henderson's life. Toward its end, Freudian ideas about the emotions and anthropological ideas about culture began to weaken the strength of positivism. And historical events themselves, especially Nazism, undermined men's faith in all-triumphant reason.

Henderson passionately opposed the positivistic view of human behavior.[50] He fought against this "error" endlessly in both his teaching and his writing. Perhaps he fought too violently, as we all tend to do when we are struggling against what has been deeply inculcated in us by our times and our training. No doubt he felt himself a voice crying in the wilderness, shouting all the louder because of the indifference and hostility he felt all around him.

It is often remarked, in the analysis of the social sources of social theory, that one good way to understand a social theorist's ideas is to see what he was fighting against. Henderson's counteractive, polemical stance against the prevalent positivism of his time is evident at several points in his work. His critique of positivism and excessive rationality cannot be understood without a close familiarity with this prevailing spirit.

So we find Henderson reiterating ideas about the emotions and sentiments that we take completely for granted now, only twenty-five years later. In the Sociology 23 lectures, his exhortation to remember that all is not logic and rationality is one of the most frequent themes, appearing first in his preface. Here is one characteristic statement:

Very often it is not the meaning of the uttered words that is important, but the attitudes and sentiments that they reveal. I repeat; many things—in many circumstances, most things—that men say are neither true nor false; they are expressions of hopes and fears, of anxieties and obsessions, of likes and dislikes, of aspirations and encouragements.[51]

[50] For a contemporaneous, scientific, theoretically based critique of positivism, see Talcott Parsons's classic study of the development of social theory, *The Structure of Social Action* (New York: McGraw-Hill, 1937).
[51] See pp. 81–82.

Another appeals to "experience" as well as to psychology and biology, but not to the social sciences, which he felt were hopelessly wrong on this point:

It is a well-established induction from experience, thoroughly confirmed by general psychological, physiological and biological considerations, that men are more often moved by passions and prejudices, wishes and strong sentiments, hopes and fears, than by reason. . . . [and this point] will be illustrated over and over again.[52]

One reason for Henderson's great interest in Pareto was that he especially liked Pareto's concepts of *residues* (sentiments or values) and *derivations* (beliefs functioning as ideologies, or value-preference-justifications). These concepts showed that Pareto shared his own convictions about the importance of values and emotions in social interaction. As we shall see, when Henderson laid out a model for a generalized social system, two fundamental conceptual components were the residues and the derivations, along with economic interests, science, logic, and other rational elements in behavior. Here is a statement of how Henderson viewed the residues:

The exhibition of the residues, no less than eating, drinking, or breathing, may be recognized as a major function of the human organism. It is therefore necessary to take note that the role of the residues (or of the sentiments that they manifest) is at least as important as the role of the logical activities of men. Indeed, nearly everything that is accounted noblest and best, and also worst, in the actions of men depends upon (i.e. is a function of) residues. . . . they are of the first importance in the social system, and . . . their importance is in no way diminished, but rather increased, by their independence of logic.[53]

At one point in speaking of Pareto, Henderson is speaking for himself as well. Pareto, he says, felt he had dealt sufficiently with science, logic, and economic interests in his writings on economics. These are important elements in the social system, no doubt. But Pareto, and Henderson himself, we feel, is "anxious to emphasize

52   See p. 84.
53   See p. 98.

the overwhelming importance, relatively, of what he calls non-logical actions, as contrasted with logical actions, in nearly all human affairs except those that are economic, and a few others like the work of applied scientists. This conclusion of Pareto's is *contrary to the traditional, intellectual interpretation of history and human affairs.*"[54] And, Henderson continues, "our upbringing and our education predispose us to overestimate their [science and logic] importance in most things."[55] We see his polemical stance at another point, in an exhortation to his students. "You should give particular attention," he tells them, "to residues and derivations. These are the elements with which you are probably least familiar and they are as often as not those that call for the greatest attention."[56]

Henderson's attack on positivism led him into very harsh judgments about "intellectuals," who, he thought, ignored the importance of sentiments and values. In a paper written in the late 1930s, when the New Deal was the political order of the day, he said:

All human relations involve the sentiments. One of the commonest and worst errors of "intellectuals" is to ignore this larger generalization. For this reason, especially, their rational Utopias, from Plato's to the New Deal, are not only impossible in fact, but inhuman. If they were possible, they would still be intolerable.[57]

No wonder even his sympathetic friends Homans and Bailey note that "his politics were vigorously conservative."[58] It should be added, perhaps, that he felt some other social types were equally bad: "As for what is harmful to the community, I cannot be explicit, but this I know, that I fear the 'intellectuals,' the sentimentalists, and the uplifters—to me they are all one—even as I do the politicians and the profiteers."[59]

[54] Emphasis added. See p. 100.
[55] See p. 100.
[56] See p. 112.
[57] See "Aphorisms on the Advertising of Alkalies," p. 242 of this volume.
[58] *The Society of Fellows.*
[59] See p. 245.

THE CONCEPT OF SYSTEM AND SOCIAL SYSTEM

An essential key to understanding the sociological thought and influence of Henderson is to remember that he came to the study of the social sciences after he had long and successfully used the concept of the system both in his biochemical research and in his philosophical writings. Early in his career, Henderson had been much impressed by the concept of the physicochemical system in the work of Josiah Willard Gibbs, probably the greatest of American scientists until quite recent times.[60] As Russett put it,

> Gibbs' physico-chemical system, Henderson felt, validated the concept of system as a genuine abstraction, useful despite the fact that it was a creation of the imagination. Systems imposed boundaries and mapped out relationships: within them, facts made sense. They were ordered and interrelated. They became amenable to logical consideration. . . . [Henderson wrote] "Just as Newton first conclusively showed that this is a world of masses, so Willard Gibbs first revealed it as a world of systems."[61]

For the concept of system, and more specifically for his biochemical research, Henderson also owed a large intellectual debt to the great French physiologist Claude Bernard.[62] Bernard had established modern physiology on a theory of system and equilibrium, the chief concept of which was the notion of the *milieu intérieur*, the relatively stable and self-equilibrating internal system of the organism. Both Henderson and his long-time colleague at Harvard, W. B. Cannon, who originated the concept of "homeostasis," developed and made more precise these notions of Bernard's, largely through applying the new research techniques of modern physics and chemistry.[63]

[60] In what follows, I am much indebted to the excellent general history and analysis, including a whole chapter on Henderson as a central figure, in Russett, *Concept of Equilibrium*.

[61] Ibid., p. 112.

[62] He acknowledged his debt by writing an introduction to the translation of Bernard's classic work, *An Introduction to the Study of Experimental Medicine*. See pp. 149–58 of this volume.

[63] One of Cannon's books which has been read by many social scientists is *The Wisdom of the Body* (New York: W. W. Norton, 1932). His

Henderson's interest in medicine also confirmed his belief in the usefulness of the concept of system for theory and action. One of the oldest principles in medical science and practice is the principle of *vis medicatrix naturae,* the healing power of nature. This principle has to do both with the human organism as a system that restores itself from "illness," or disequilibrium, to "health," or equilibrium, and with the processes by which this restoration is achieved, Henderson often referred to the principle of *vis medicatrix naturae* and traced it back in Greek medicine to Alcmaeon and Hippocrates:

Before Hippocrates, about 500 B.C., Alcmaeon of Croton had expressed the opinion that health is an isonomy or harmony (we may say equilibrium) between opposites, sickness a state of monarchy or disequilibrium. Now the widest of all generalizations in the work of Hippocrates is this, that as a rule sick people recover without treatment.[64]

Henderson then goes on to give his own definition of equilibrium in a system, a definition borrowed, in his own translation, from Pareto: "A state such that if a small modification different from that which will otherwise occur is impressed upon a system, a reaction will at once appear tending toward the conditions that would have existed if the modification had not been impressed."[65] Or, "Equilibrium is an equilibrium of forces, more or less like the equilibrium, for instance, in a box spring; that a small modification leaves the forces substantially intact; and that the forces tend to reestablish the state that would have existed if no modification had occurred."[66]

In any use of the concept of system, whether generalized to all phenomena or applied only to "action" phenomena, one of the main problems is the nature of the relationship between the sev-

---

autobiography is also of great interest to social scientists, especially for its contributions to the sociology of science: *The Way of an Investigator* (New York: W. W. Norton, 1945).

[64]   See p. 73.

[65]   Ibid.

[66]   Ibid.

eral conceptual components of the system. In short, there is the problem of "causality." Henderson felt that the concept of system provided a better approach to the problem of causality than did simplistic cause-and-effect notions. He preferred ideas of mutual dependence, indirect effects, disequilibrating effects, equilibrating effects, and the like. In applying these to social systems, he says:

> Because every factor interacts in a social system, because everything, every property, every relation is therefore in a state of mutual dependence with everything else, ordinary cause-and-effect analysis of events is rarely possible. In fact, it is nearly always grossly misleading; so much so that it must be regarded as one of the two great sources of error in sociological work.[67]

At another point, Henderson amplifies his analysis:

> In a social system, and, as a rule, elsewhere, an action initiated in a certain thing leads to modifications everywhere in the system, and these modifications to further modifications which involve the very thing in which the process originated. So it is both "cause" and "effect." . . . Thus, reasoning from cause to effect in the study of concrete phenomena is often even more misleading than more general reasoning of the same kind.[68]

Henderson was pointing to the value of analyzing systems in terms of the mutual dependence of their components in a state of equilibrium; to the processes that have since widely come to be called "feedback" processes; to the existence of unintended, undesirable, and unpredictable effects in system processes; and to the fact that often no single alteration in a system is sufficient to produce a specified desired effect.

A common response to the notion of the mutual dependence of factors in systems (or "multiple causation" as it is sometimes loosely called) is that it does not make possible decisions and practical policy. "If everything is related to everything else, why do anything?" is the way this might be expressed. Henderson was aware of this difficulty and of the need for a practical guide to

[67] See p. 139. The other source of error is "the intrusion of a person's own sentiment."
[68] See p. 143.

action in the face of complex system processes. After warning about the complexity of reality as it shapes itself in systems, therefore, he was willing to be practical and approximate; indeed, he most admired those "men of affairs" and doctors who were willing to be so. "Experience shows," he says, "that a single factor may sometimes be usefully regarded, in a rough approximation, as a sole determinant of events."[69] But he still despised analysis or action that proceeded on simplistic models not based on "realistic" notions about complex systems.

Henderson felt that the concepts of system and equilibrium were applicable to every kind of phenomenon. After giving his version of Pareto's definition he says:

> This definition applies to many phenomena and processes, both static and dynamic. It applies not only in the fields of pathology and sociology, but very generally in the description of almost all kinds of phenomena and processes. It is indeed a statement of one of the most general aspects of our experience, a recognition of one of the commonest aspects of things and events.[70]

Henderson's statement may be taken as an early prediction of the widespread use of systems analysis in nearly every branch of present-day learning.

Believing as he did in the universal scope and great power of the concept of system, Henderson naturally found Pareto's use of it in social science analysis enormously attractive. He compared Pareto to Gibbs: "Pareto's social system is in some respects analogous in its usefulness to Gibbs's physicochemical system. This system of Pareto's disregards physical, chemical, and physiological phenomena, but makes possible in some measure the consideration of all interactions between persons. Like Gibbs's system, it is clear and simple."[71] Pareto's generalized social system is "the most convenient conceptual scheme now available," he added, thus indicating his conviction of its superiority to all other social science.[72]

[69]   See p. 147.
[70]   See p. 73.
[71]   See p. 88.
[72]   See p. 88.

Henderson felt that Pareto's concept of the generalized social system applied to concrete social systems of all kinds and sizes. "A social system," he said, "may consist of two or more persons. . . . For many purposes a family may be considered as a social system, for others a town, for others a state; and it is not impossible to make some progress with the consideration of the whole world as a single social system."[73]

It is clear that Henderson meant the concept of the social system to apply to all of what are now sometimes called the "action sciences"—that is, all disciplines that study the meanings communicated in interactions between two or more persons acting in roles or role-sets.[74] For example, when Henderson was classifying the many subjects taught at modern universities, he included in one of his two classes "history, literature, economics, sociology, law, politics, theology, education, etc."[75] A little further on he says:

> The social system thus defined and characterized is clearly an instrument that may be employed in studying all the above mentioned subjects of the first class; for, like history, literature, law, and theology, all are conversant with the interactions of individuals in their manifold relations, with their sayings and doings; while none can dispense with consideration of the mutual dependence of many factors.[76]

"The concept of equilibrium" (and its related concept of system), says Russett, "was present in social science from the latter's very inception with Comte and Spencer in the second half of the nineteenth century."[77] As social science has developed, these con-

---

[73]   See p. 89. The only concrete social system that Henderson himself intensively considered in writing was a two-person system, a dyad, in "Physician and Patient as Social System."

[74]   It should be noted that present-day social science analysis has become more analytical than Henderson's. It does not usually refer to individual "persons" in social systems, but rather to the roles or role-sets or collectivities or idea-systems or cultural patterns in which they act or which they express.

[75]   See "Pareto's Science of Sociology," p. 182 of this volume.

[76]   See p. 185.

[77]   Russett, *The Concept of Equilibrium*.

cepts have continually been refined and improved. No small part in this development, Russett suggests, was played by Henderson and the social scientists he influenced. The refinement and improvement consisted in seeing the connection among such ideas as system, equilibrium, process, mutual dependence, group, the difference between physical and biological notions of system and equilibrium, and the difference between equilibrium and system as theoretical concepts and empirical generalizations.[78]

In the 1950s and 1960s, the use of the concept of system has become widespread in the social sciences. But, says Russett, although "the idea that society, or a particular aspect of society such as political life, can be analyzed as a system of interdependent parts is by now a commonplace of social research . . . it has come to be so only rather recently. In the early 1930's the idea (outside economics) was present, if at all, only intuitively. . . . it was reserved for Henderson, a man of science, to fix the idea in the vocabulary of social thought."[79]

The Usefulness of Pareto's Work

Because of the interpenetration of the several major themes we have been discussing, we have already said much about Henderson's view of Pareto's work.[80] In his paper "An Approximate Definition of Fact," Henderson says "It is impossible for me to specify my indebtedness to this work. Perhaps most of the present paper is in substance, and especially in method, partly attributable to Pareto."[81] Perhaps the most important reason for this influence was

[78]   Ibid., esp. pp. 117–21.
[79]   Ibid., p. 118.
[80]   On the substance of Pareto's sociology, see pp. 181–90 of this volume, where there is an extended exposition and discussion by Henderson; or L. J. Henderson, *Pareto's General Sociology: A Physiologists's Interpretation* (Cambridge, Mass.: Harvard University Press, 1937) ; or the book by two "students" in Henderson's Pareto seminar, George C. Homans and Charles P. Curtis, Jr., *An Introduction to Pareto: His Sociology* (New York: Alfred A. Knopf, 1934) ; or Vilfredo Pareto, *The Mind and Society*, 4 vols., edited by Arthur Livingston (New York: Harcourt, Brace, 1935).
[81]   See p. 178, n. 19.

Henderson's delight in Pareto's ideas about system, equilibrium, and the generalized social system as a conceptual scheme for the analysis of all human interaction, which we have already discussed.

We should note one qualification. A man often finds in a work more than other people do, mostly because he himself brings something, often a good deal, to it. This was probably true of Henderson's reading of Pareto. As Russett has put it:

> Henderson did more than merely transmit a view of social equilibrium previously conceived by Pareto—he shaped the idea as well. It cannot really be said that Pareto added anything to Henderson's understanding of scientific method. Rather, Pareto's work was simply proof to Henderson that the analytical tools and concepts with which he had long been familiar were more widely applicable than he had realized. *Henderson read Pareto, as it were, from memory.*[82]

Henderson probably read not quite "from memory," but certainly he found a great deal to underline and amplify in Pareto because of his own intellectual history and scientific research. He was at least somewhat aware that he was adding something of substance or emphasis. At one point in his book on Pareto, which, as Russett says, "reveals as much about Henderson as it does about Pareto," he raises a significant question: "It is an interesting and probably unanswerable question how far Pareto was clearly aware of the position of the social system in his book."[83] If "Pareto spoke Henderson's language," as Russett says, it was still left for Henderson to master the grammar of this language and to teach it effectively to social scientists.[84]

Pareto also appealed to him for a number of lesser reasons. He shared with Pareto a strong critique of positivism, excessive rationality, and "the intellectuals," who were especially infected with these vices. In his review of Pareto's work in the *Saturday Review of Literature*, Henderson quotes Pareto's view: "Like Chinese Mandarins, European 'intellectuals' are the worst of rulers."[85] In

[82]   Russett, *The Concept of Equilibrium*. Emphasis inserted.
[83]   Russett, *The Concept of Equilibrium*, p. 115; Henderson, *Pareto's General Sociology*, p. 96.
[84]   Russett, *The Concept of Equilibrium*, p. 114.
[85]   See p. 189 of this volume.

the same place, Henderson speaks of Pareto as "a man of the world and a scholar."[86] Except for some early work as an engineer Pareto was hardly the "man of affairs" so admired by Henderson; it is likely that Henderson was letting the wish be father to the thought.[87] Certainly Pareto gave the impression of the "tough-mindedness" often associated with men of affairs, and this was basically what Henderson approved of.

Finally, Pareto appealed to Henderson because of his wide learning and scientific character. In his *Saturday Review of Literature* article, Henderson has this to say of *The Mind and Society* (the translation of Pareto's *Traité Générale*): "Industry, skill, method, encyclopedic knowledge, initiative, originality, stubborn consecutive continuous thought are terms that describe it. It is a scientific treatise."[88] For Henderson there was probably no higher encomium to award anyone. If Pareto had truly joined the social sciences to the natural sciences, an achievement Henderson very much wanted to see, it is only to be expected that he would put Pareto in the great company of Gibbs, Bernard, and even Newton.

Medical Sociology

For Henderson, the necessary and desirable relations between medicine and the social sciences were two way, each influencing the other. As he says explicitly at one point: "The practice, teaching, and science of medicine have never been isolated from the other affairs of men, but have modified them and been modified by them."[89] Henderson thought sociology could learn from medicine the technique of "close observation" of cases and the resultant formulation of wider and wider generalizations. This was because he knew little of the experimental and survey research techniques

---

[86]   Ibid.

[87]   For brief notes on Pareto's life, with larger attention to his economic and sociological theory, see the biographies by Maurice Allais and Talcott Parsons, *International Encyclopedia of the Social Sciences* (New York: Macmillan and Free Press, 1968).

[88]   See p. 189 of this volume.

[89]   See "The Relation of Medicine to the Fundamental Sciences," p. 191 of this volume.

that were just emerging in the social sciences. We have also seen that Henderson felt the social sciences could profit from being, like medicine, applied as well as basic sciences. He wanted solid, objective knowledge of social interactions and social systems to be available to men who needed to apply them, the "men who practice the professions or engage in business."[90]

But Henderson also thought the social sciences should have fundamental influences on medicine. He felt that medicine as an art was badly in need of an infusion of sociology. Here is his description of the backward condition of medicine's understanding of its social aspects:

Medicine is today in part an applied science. Mathematics, physics, chemistry and many departments of biology find application in this hospital and in the practice of all skillful physicians. Meanwhile, the personal relations between physician and patient remain nearly what they have always been. To these relations, as yet, science has been little applied.[91]

Indeed, Henderson felt that in his time medicine was worse in this respect than it had been before. He felt that the Hippocratic view, which had prevailed well into modern times, had had a "general view of the patient living in an environment that is social as well as physical."[92] But the recent development of "scientific medicine," to which Henderson had himself contributed, had been made at a cost. He felt that in this development the "laboratory men" had defeated the "clinical men" in medicine and that the older, Hippocratic view of patients as social beings had been lost. The patient, he said, is now often "a mere *case*"; "his personality and his relations with other persons [are] not even thought of."[93] As a result, "There is a need to fix and clarify the ideas of physicians concerning the half-forgotten sociological aspects of medical

90   See p. 63.
91   See "Physician and Patient as a Social System," p. 202 of this volume.
92   "The Practice of Medicine as Applied Sociology," *Transactions of the Association of American Physicians* 51 (1936), p. 1.
93   Ibid., p. 2.

practice and to give appropriate instruction to medical students."[94]

In his discussion of the social aspects of medicine, Henderson tended to focus on the social interactions in the two-person, physician-patient social system, because he felt that this system was relatively more simple than others and because he felt it made a good didactic case to expound his general view that all kinds of medical problems should be seen as parts of social systems and analyzed accordingly. He certainly was aware of the larger social systems in which physician and patient were involved, directly and indirectly:

> If physician and patient constitute a social system, it is almost a trivial one compared with the larger social system of which the patient is a permanent member and in which he lives. . . . I suggest that it is impossible to understand any man as a person without knowledge of this environment and especially of what he thinks and feels about it; which may be a very different thing.
>
> . . . it is the business of the physician never to forget these social factors; to acquire skill in the diagnosis of social conditions and in the recognition of the social elements in the etiology of disease.[95]

Henderson was not, of course, only pointing to a deficiency in medical practice; he had a remedy to recommend to the doctors he was addressing. First he told them that they could expect very little from the great majority of contemporary social scientists. Their deficiency,

> for which nobody is to blame, might perhaps be modified if it were possible to apply to practice a science of human relations. But such a science is barely growing into the stage where applications are possible.
>
> The psychologists and sociologists are the professional custodians of what little scientific knowledge we possess that is conversant with personal relations. But from them we have, as yet, little to learn. . . . So the personal relations of the physician with his patients and their families are still understood, when they are understood, at the empirical level, as they were in the days of Hippocrates.[96]

94   Ibid., p. 3.
95   Ibid., p. 13.
96   See p. 202 of this volume.

His remedy for the deficiency was, as we might expect, found in Pareto, in the conceptual scheme of the generalized social system. This scheme is valuable because it uses the concept of system and because one of its essential components is the residues, or sentiments, which Henderson thinks are particularly neglected in the practice of medicine. There are many who think that his charge still holds and that the physician in practice could still learn essential things from the good, if limited, diagnosis of and advice about physician-patient relationships that Henderson gives in "The Physician and Patient as a Social System" and "The Practice of Medicine as Applied Sociology." Even Henderson was not sure his diagnosis and advice were adequate, but he said, "I think Pareto's system the best we have."[97]

Since Henderson's time, the sociology of medicine has flourished in scope, in quantity of workers and research, and probably in quality.[98] Neither Pareto nor Henderson has had much direct effect on this new work, to judge from the lack of citations to them, but Henderson probably had considerable indirect effect through Talcott Parsons's work in this field, which is cited frequently.

Henderson's Influence

If L. J. Henderson's influence on contemporary social science has been fairly large, it is not because his own writings and teachings reached a large number of individuals but because the few whom he did directly affect have themselves had a large influence. A count of scientific citations will demonstrate this.[99]

Henderson's first mode of influence was informal contact with scholarly peers and juniors. Most of these, as we have indicated, were his Harvard colleagues and students. Among the most notable

---

[97] "The Practice of Medicine as Applied Sociology," p. 15.
[98] For one representative sample of recent work in this field, see Howard E. Freeman, Sol Levine, and Leo G. Reeder, eds., *Handbook of Medical Sociology* (Englewood Cliffs, N.J.: Prentice-Hall, 1963).
[99] After considering Henderson's indirect influence and his influence through informal contact and teaching rather than writings, let citation-counters beware!

were those in the Harvard Business School group who produced the Western Electric studies—men like Elton Mayo, T. North Whitehead, and Fritz J. Roethlisberger.[100] Another notable example was Chester I. Barnard, businessman and social scientist, and author of *The Functions of the Executive,* which has had a considerable influence on social science studies of leadership and interaction in organizations. And there was a diverse group of Harvard professorial colleagues, scattered through the several professional schools and the arts and sciences faculties, with whom Henderson interacted informally. Henderson invited many of these men to lecture to his Sociology 23 class, and we shall list them when we discuss Henderson's teaching.

Henderson's second channel of influence was the Harvard Society of Fellows: he was a founder, and first chairman of the Senior Fellows, who selected the Junior Fellows. Since the only social scientist who was a Senior Fellow was Crane Brinton, Henderson's activities in the Society of Fellows provided relatively little scope for affecting his peers, though his influence on Brinton was important for a brief time. But it offered large scope, through selection decisions and subsequent meetings of the society, for affecting his juniors. The most notable examples are the sociologists George Homans and William F. Whyte and the anthropologist Conrad M. Arensberg.

His third mode of influence was his writing, both journal articles and a small book, *Pareto's General Sociology.* As this collection of Henderson's social science writings shows, the number of his journal articles was not large, and not one was published in a regular social science journal. No wonder he was not known to social scientists beyond Harvard, except those who had once been at Harvard and their students. In addition, the most complete statement of Henderson's social science views, his Sociology 23 lectures, has never been published before, although in mimeographed form the lectures did have some circulation among those outside the course. Finally, Henderson's book, *Pareto's General Sociology,*

100   Mayo, *Social Problems;* Mayo, *Human Problems;* Whitehead, *The Industrial Worker;* Roethlisberger and Dickson, *Management and the Worker.*

though it had two small printings in the 1930s when more people read Pareto, soon went out of print and has come back only recently through a small firm which specializes in reprinting books for which there is a small demand.[101]

Henderson's final mode of influence was his teaching, to which he attached great importance. Indeed, in his work in social science Henderson clearly thought of himself as entirely a teacher, not as a discoverer. His central purpose was made explicit in his Sociology 23 lectures (and in the manuscript based on them which he had hoped, just before his death, to see published):

The purpose of this book is professional formation, not discovery. Speaking a little more precisely, the purpose is to contribute to that part of the professional formation of historians, of political and social scientists, of practitioners of the professions, and of men of affairs that is or may be common to the professional formation of all such persons, because the medium in which they all work is, speaking very generally, a common medium. For, as we have noted, they are all concerned with interactions between persons.[102]

Henderson believed that "we already possess the beginnings of a science of general sociology. . . . that this science is in a very early, not to say primitive state, that its generalizations are few and that they consist, in large part, of very rough approximations. . . . [but] that such as it is, this science is useful."[103] Never thinking that he himself was an original discoverer in social science, Henderson wanted only to teach the usefulness of what already existed.

Henderson's teaching influence exerted itself through his "Pareto Seminar" and through his Sociology 23 course, Concrete Sociology—a title which indicated the importance he attached to the use of concrete cases for making sociological analyses. Henderson started the Seminar on the Sociology of Pareto, as Homans and Curtis call it, in the fall of 1932 and it continued for seven or eight years.[104] The seminar members were chiefly Henderson's col-

---

[101]   New York: Russell & Russell, 1967.
[102]   See p. 106 of this volume.
[103]   Ibid.
[104]   Unfortunately, it is hard to get precise information about the seminar, since no notes or minutes have been published. A full-scale bi-

leagues on the Harvard faculty, men like Schumpeter, Parsons, and Brinton, though they included some outsiders from the Boston intellectual community. Some advanced graduate students also attended the seminar. One was Robert K. Merton. Apart from Henderson's own work, writings inspired by the seminar consist chiefly of the Homans and Curtis book expounding Pareto and some articles by the American critic and journalist, Bernard DeVoto, in the "class" magazines that helped to bring Pareto to the attention of the general American intellectual community.

Henderson's Sociology 23 was first offered in the spring of 1938. It was primarily for undergraduates, but some graduate students and even senior faculty attended sporadically. He continued to give this course until his death in 1942. For the first years, his teaching assistant in the course was George Homans. At first Henderson explicitly labeled the course "experimental." Its purpose, as we have seen, was to teach students how to understand and decide about social interaction in any kind of social system. It sought to accomplish this by presenting an outline of the generalized social system and by showing, through concrete cases, how this generalized social system could be applied in a wide variety of actual social systems.

Henderson spent a few hours at the beginning of each semester commenting upon the latest version of the three "lectures" that he had written out, and a copy of them, mimeographed and bound in paper, was given to each student. After these few hours of comment, often passionate in tone, the rest of the course was taken up by invited guest lecturers, each of whom was supposed to apply the conceptual scheme of the generalized social system to some concrete case material which he knew thoroughly, with "intuitive familiarity," from his own experience. During the first year, although almost every guest lecture had much to offer in some way, as often as not it was hard to see any close connection between the generalized social system and the account being given.

---

ography of Henderson, or any complete history of social science in America should include such information on this very important intellectual venture.

But Henderson would often interject comments during the guest lectures that somewhat increased their relevance.

To give some sense of the enormous range of specialties and materials students heard about in Sociology 23 during its first run, here are the twenty-five lecturers and their topics, in the order of appearance: Crane Brinton on changes in illegitimacy legislation in the French Revolution; George Homans on rural England in the thirteenth century; Elton Mayo on the organization of work in a Pennsylvania factory; Conrad Arensberg on the structure of Irish peasant life; T. N. Whitehead on the Hawthorne-Western Electric research; Arthur Darby Nock, historian of religion, on some topics in the sociology of religion; Talcott Parsons on social aspects of medical practice; President-Emeritus A. Lawrence Lowell on the development of the English parliamentary system; Fritz J. Roethlisberger on the Hawthorne research; Melvin Copeland of the Harvard Business School on executive authority in a manufacturing plant; Dean Wallace B. Donham, also of the Business School, on the unionization of street railway workers in 1917; the anthropologist Eliot D. Chapple on social interaction in Yankee City; the political scientist Pendleton Herring on the politics of national budget balancing; a psychiatrist, Dr. Monsell, on a case of neurosis in a young man; Dr. David Dill of the Fatigue Laboratory on physiological and social research on men working at high temperatures; Dr. Ross McFarland on the assimilation of Italian immigrants into American society; Dr. Roger Lee on social and psychological aspects of illness; Dr. Arlie V. Bock, clinician and director of the Harvard Health Service, on the training of young physicians; Professor Bullock of the Business School on the politics of revaluation of taxable properties; the anthropologist Clyde Kluckhohn on the Navaho; Nathan Isaacs of the Business School on agricultural legislation in the 1930s; Chester I. Barnard on a riot among the unemployed in New Jersey in the 1930s, when Barnard was the head of a council to manage unemployment relief; Dr. Reynolds on social determinants of illness; Dean Fox from the Business School on social and psychological aspects of students' behavior; and E. B. Wilson on his activities as a science statesman on the National Resources Committee.

As to Henderson's influence on particular social scientists who came into contact with him through one or more of these modes, we are in the favorable position, not always present for essays in intellectual history, of having considerable written, fairly specific, acknowledgement of this influence by those who were subject to it. We do not have to say that a man "must have been" or "probably was" influenced by Henderson, as is so often heard in intellectual history; we can say flatly that he was, because the explicit and proud avowal of debt is in the writings of those who were influenced. Even so, we must observe some caution in making such attributions. Even when forthrightly acknowledged, influence is not a simple thing.

First, even written assertion of intellectual exchanges does not prove that debts exist, or at least proves nothing beyond minimal obligations. For example, in the preface to the Sociology 23 lectures manuscript intended for publication, Henderson acknowledges the "kind advice and assistance" of only half a dozen persons, including the anthropologist Clyde Kluckhohn. We have seen that Kluckhohn lectured in the Sociology 23 course on his specialty, the Navaho. It would be easy to conclude that Henderson had probably influenced Kluckhohn. Yet when we examine Kluckhohn's work, nowhere do we find such influence. There is no reference to the notion of a generalized social system. Even in *Mirror for Man: The Relation of Anthropology to Modern Life*, his most comprehensive book on the nature of anthropology, Kluckhohn does not refer to the generalized social system. Indeed, in this book, presented as a kind of *summa* of Kluckhohn's work, there is mention in the acknowledgement of about a hundred different people, about sixty of whom are acknowledged for intellectual obligations; but Henderson is nowhere named. In his conversation, Kluckhohn often used Henderson's phrases "to a first approximation" and "an induction from my experience." Beyond that, apparently, and despite Henderson's mention of him, Henderson's influence on him was minimal.

A second important caution in attributing influence, even when it is acknowledged, is that intellectual products often have multiple and diverse sources, not single and exclusive ones. When

Talcott Parsons acknowledges the influence of Henderson and Pareto on his concept of social system, he does not mean to exclude other influences, such as those of W. B. Cannon, the classical economists, and the functional anthropologists.[105] Sometimes not all the multiple sources of a certain scientific concept or proposition are mentioned. Just as Henderson has sometimes been mentioned and others left out, so probably sometimes Henderson has not been mentioned when others are explicitly acknowledged.[106]

Finally, a third caution about attributions of influence requires the intellectual historian to distinguish between debts for substantive intellectual matters and debts for social and moral (value) support. These may occur quite separately or in various combinations of amounts. Where they occur together, there will probably be the strongest disposition to make explicit and precise acknowledgment of both kinds of debt. But where there is intellectual debt without social and moral support, the debtor may be less willing to acknowledge intellectual influence. It seems that those to whom Henderson gave social and moral support as well as intellectual stimulation were most ready to acknowledge him. Those who were put off by his social and personal stance, even though intellectually influenced, were less likely to feel indebted.

Now to our discussion of some social scientists whom Henderson affected and who have themselves had considerable influence on others.[107]

GEORGE C. HOMANS Both debts we have mentioned, for intellectual substance and for social and moral support, are owed to Henderson by the social scientist he probably influenced the most —George C. Homans, professor of sociology at Harvard. Very

[105] See Talcott Parsons, *Essays in Sociological Theory* (Glencoe, Ill.: The Free Press, 1949).
[106] I myself am one who, in discussing social systems, would be likely to refer to Parsons and not to Henderson, although I learned much from Henderson about systems. I would refer to Parsons because of the social and moral support I got from him as my teacher. I did not continue in interaction with Henderson beyond the Sociology 23 course.
[107] These brief discussions are intended only to show the influence of Henderson and are not intended to be a comprehensive or intensive discussion of the work of these social scientists.

early in his intellectual career Homans, when only twenty-two and just out of Harvard College, came under the direct and continuing influence of Henderson. He was invited to join the Pareto Seminar in 1932 and was a member of the first group of Junior Fellows in the Society of Fellows. In 1934, with Charles P. Curtis, to whom he later dedicated his book *Social Behavior: Its Elementary Forms*, as "friend and teacher," he published *An Introduction to Pareto*.[108] The *Pareto* introduction is dedicated "To the Only Begetter of This Ensuing Book, Lawrence Joseph Henderson."

The *Pareto* book was only an excursion for Homans, who seems always to have been an easy as well as an excellent writer. His major scholarly work during the 1930s was his classic contribution to sociological history, *English Villagers of the Thirteenth Century*.[109] In the preface, acknowledging the help of the Senior Fellows of the Society of Fellows (this work was done while he was a Junior Fellow), Homans gives his "warmest thanks" to Henderson (along with the economic historians N. S. B. Gras and Edwin F. Gay), "who read and criticized the manuscript in detail." In the first twenty-four chapters of this book it would be hard to find any explicit indication of the influence of either Henderson or Pareto. However, in the very last chapter, "The Anatomy of Society," Homans indicates that he has, up to that point, described the life of English villagers of the thirteenth century "in the usual literary manner and in the language of common sense."[110] In the last chapter he intends to translate his description into "another and more abstract language," the language of a conceptual scheme that has guided him throughout his study. In twelve pages he then lays out a concise account of a model of the "anatomy of society"—an anatomy of any society, not just that of thirteenth-century England. It is clear that this is Homans's version of the generalized social system. It builds heavily upon Pareto and Henderson, both substantively and methodologically, but it adds some new elements —particularly the concept of function, borrowed from the social

[108]   *Social Behavior* (New York: Harcourt, Brace & World, 1961); *An Introduction to Pareto* (New York: Alfred A. Knopf, 1934).
[109]   Cambridge, Mass.: Harvard University Press, 1941.
[110]   Ibid., p. 402.

anthropologists; the concept of leadership, taken from Chester I. Barnard; and the concept of social classes, taken from Lloyd Warner.

Homans makes one explicit reference to Henderson's *Pareto*, and at several points he employs Henderson's phrases. Consider the opening paragraph of the chapter, where there is no reference to Henderson:

> In many sciences the men who have to deal with the facts in detail are also the men who *construct the theories* about the facts. This circumstance is probably useful: no theory is likely to endure which does not arise directly out of long-continued, *intuitive familiarity* with the welter of facts which it attempts to order. Useful or not, it is a fact of sociology and social anthropology—to take one science—that after a man has been studying a particular human society, he often tries to construct a *conceptual scheme* which he hopes can be used to describe not only that society but many other societies besides. He tries to make *statements of uniformities* in the organization of *social systems* in general.[111]

This quest for the discovery of a useful conceptual scheme for the analysis of social systems in general was the focus of Homans's next book, *The Human Group*, which many social scientists consider his magnum opus despite the great productivity that has followed it.[112] In the preface, Homans again explicitly acknowledges Henderson: "In this book as elsewhere, my chief intellectual debt is to three great men, Lawrence Joseph Henderson, Elton Mayo, and Alfred North Whitehead, under whose influence I was lucky enough to come rather early in life." But his debt to Henderson is also obvious in his central purpose: to construct a highly abstract, highly systematic, and highly comprehensive model for the analysis of social systems. If, in contrast to the last chapter of the *English Villagers*, his concentration is on "the human group" rather than "society," it is probably because he wishes to get at smaller-scale social systems that are somehow empirically manageable, or at least more so than whole societies. We may note here Hender-

---

111   Ibid. Emphasis inserted.
112   New York: Harcourt, Brace, 1950.

son's influence on Homans's ardent desire to be as close as possible to "the facts." Henderson had taught Homans the importance not only of conceptual schemes but also of "experience" and "intuitive familiarity with things."

Many of the older concepts of Henderson are used by Homans in *The Human Group*—interaction, sentiments, equilibrium, and mutual dependence. But, as in the last chapter of *English Villagers*, he adds other ideas, such as norms, and external and internal systems. As he says, he also gives up or transforms some of the components of Henderson's generalized social system. The overall result is not greater complexity of the conceptual scheme; he is the student of Henderson in striving for simplicity—for a theoretical model with a small number of variables, the better somehow to abstract at least some significant aspects of the phenomena of social systems.

In his later work, notably in *Social Behavior: Its Elementary Forms*,[113] Homans continues to pursue Henderson's goals of generalization and simplicity for a conceptual scheme applicable to all human behavior.[114]

TALCOTT PARSONS Henderson also has had an important influence on Homans's colleague, Talcott Parsons, who has been for over thirty years the leading figure in sociological theory. Henderson and Parsons first came together at Harvard through their common interest in Pareto.[115] In his first and classic work, *The Structure of Social Action: A Study in Social Theory with Special Reference to a Group of Recent European Writers*, Parsons speaks in the preface of four debts "of outstanding significance."[116] One of these is to Henderson. "Professor Lawrence J. Henderson," Parsons says, "has subjected the manuscript to a most unusually thorough critical examination, which led to important revision at

113   New York: Harcourt, Brace & World, 1961.
114   For Homans's own view of his work, see his article "A Life of Synthesis," *American Behavioral Scientist* 12 (1968) : 2–8.
115   See a first article on Pareto by Parsons in *Encyclopedia of the Social Sciences* (New York: Macmillan, 1933), and a second in the *International Encyclopedia of the Social Sciences* (New York: Macmillan and The Free Press, 1968).
116   New York: McGraw-Hill, 1937, pp. vi–vii.

many points, particularly in relation to general scientific methodology and to the interpretation of Pareto's work." Part of what Parsons has in mind by his reference to "general scientific methodology" is clear from several references to Henderson in the section on Pareto and from such remarks as this: "In other words, in Professor Henderson's phrase, all empirical observation is 'in terms of a conceptual scheme.' "[117]

But an even more important methodological influence came in connection with the concept of social system. Parsons has always been eager to point out how grateful he was for what Henderson, and Pareto, taught him about the importance of the concept of the social system.[118] As early as the introduction to his first set of collected essays, Parsons speaks of this debt,[119] but perhaps his fullest statement comes in the preface to *The Social System*, in which he first laid out his conceptual scheme for the analysis of social systems:

> The title, *The Social System*, goes back, more than to any other source, to the insistence of the late Professor L. J. Henderson on the extreme importance of the concept of system in scientific theory, and his clear realization that the attempt to delineate the social system as a system was the most important contribution of Pareto's great work. This book therefore is an attempt to carry out Pareto's intention, using an approach, the "structural-functional" level of analysis, which is quite different from that of Pareto, and, of course, taking advantage of the very considerable advances in our knowledge at many points, which have accumulated in the generation since Pareto wrote.[120]

Parsons did not accept the particular approach to the concept of system of Pareto and of Henderson. He was careful to point out in the introduction to his first collection of essays that he also had

---

[117]   Ibid., p. 28; and see a longer statement on this same point about relations between "fact" and "conceptual scheme," with credit to Henderson, at pp. 41–42.

[118]   In his several acknowledgments of debt on this score, Parsons always couples the names of Henderson and Pareto.

[119]   See *Essays in Sociological Theory, Pure and Applied* (Glencoe, Ill.: The Free Press, 1949).

[120]   Glencoe, Ill.: The Free Press, 1951, p. vii.

been very much influenced by W. B. Cannon's version of systematic biological theory.[121] He felt that Cannon's biological model was more readily adaptable to social science than was that of Pareto, which was constructed on the model of the science of mechanics. Out of preference for the biological model, Parsons formulated the generalized social system as what he called a "structural-functional" system, that is, certain components were taken as structural elements and treated as relatively stable points of reference for functional and dynamic analysis. He rejected the system-model of mechanics not on principle but because the data of social behavior were not yet sufficiently quantifiable to be easily ordered to the fully dynamic analysis possible with the system-model of mechanics. The "structural-functional" model was chosen because it was *presently* the most possible and most helpful one.

Parsons has sought to be fully explicit on one other difficult point about the use of the concept of system about which some critics have felt that Pareto and Henderson were obscure. The concept of system, says Parsons, and the conceptual scheme for a generalized social system are conceptual abstractions, tools for the analysis of empirical phenomena, and not empirical phenomena themselves. The empirical applicability and helpfulness of his conceptual scheme for a generalized social system are left completely open to empirical testing and subsequent revision based on such testing. They have no absolute and final claim to empirical status in themselves.[122]

In addition to his influence in the area of general scientific methodology, Henderson influenced Parsons in one substantive area—medical sociology. In *The Social System*, chapter 10, "Social Structure and Dynamic Process: The Case of Modern Medical Practice," Parsons seeks to demonstrate how a concrete subsystem of the social system, such as medical practice, can be the subject of his conceptual scheme. As he says, "This field [medical practice] has been a subject of long-standing interest" to him, and

[121] Ibid. p. viii.

[122] Parsons's most explicit statement on this whole point is in *Essays in Sociological Theory*, rev. ed. (Glencoe, Ill.: The Free Press, 1954), p. 71 n.

Henderson's ideas had a powerful influence.[123] He acknowledges his debt in the first footnote in the chapter: "For general comparison with this chapter, the reader may be referred to L. J. Henderson, 'Physician and Patient as a Social System.' " It is likely that this particular influence on Parsons has spread to much of the current field of medical sociology.

WILLIAM F. WHYTE   Henderson's influence on Whyte was predominantly social and moral support rather than a substantive theoretical or methodological contribution.

The most direct and concrete account of Henderson's influence on a contemporary social scientist can be found in the methodological appendix to William F. Whyte's monograph *Street Corner Society: The Social Structure of an Italian Slum.*[124]

Whyte was chosen a Junior Fellow by Henderson and his colleagues in 1936 and was eventually given four completely free years to carry out his research. Like most novices, he originally constructed a grandiose plan of research in the Italian "slum" in the North End of Boston that has since come to be known to sociologists everywhere as Street Corner Society. With his overambitious project statement in hand, he approached Henderson for advice. Here is what happened:

> We spent an hour together, and I came away with my plans very much in a state of flux. As I wrote to a friend at this time: "Henderson poured cold water on the mammoth beginning, told me that I should not cast such grandiose plans when I had done hardly any work in the field myself. It would be much sounder to get in the field and try to build up a staff slowly as I went along. If I should get a ten-man project going by fall, the responsibility for the direction and coordination of it would inevitably fall upon me, since I would have started it. How could I direct ten people in a field that was unfamiliar to me? Henderson said that, if I did manage to get a ten-man project going, it would be the ruination of me, he thought. Now, the way he put all this it sounded quite sensible and reasonable."[125]

123   Parsons, *The Social System*, p. 428.

124   This appendix is in the enlarged edition (Chicago: University of Chicago Press, 1955). The original edition, without the appendix, was published in 1943. Whyte's only major work, this book has been widely used in undergraduate sociology teaching.

125   Ibid., p. 284.

On the theoretical side, Whyte did not find Henderson's favorite, Pareto, very helpful. He got much more help from social anthropology. Another Junior Fellow at this time was Conrad M. Arensberg, the social anthropologist who was about to publish his work on the Irish countryman, based on two years of field research supported by the Society of Fellows.[126] Arensberg, says Whyte, "worked with me on field research methods, emphasizing the importance of observing people in action and getting down a detailed report of actual behavior completely divorced from moral judgments."[127] Whyte also learned from reading the social anthropologists:

I spent my first summer following the launching of the study in reading some of the writings of Durkheim and Pareto's *The Mind and Society* (for a seminar with L. J. Henderson, which I was to take in the fall of 1937). I had a feeling that these writings were helpful but still only in a general way. Then I began reading in the social anthropological literature, beginning with Malinowski, and this seemed closer to what I wanted to do even though the researchers were studying primitive tribes and I was in the middle of a great city district.[128]

But Whyte says he was most influenced intellectually by the new conceptual scheme for the study of social interaction worked out by Arensberg and Eliot Chapple, another social anthropologist. "They felt," says Whyte, "that whatever else might be subjective in social research, one could establish objectively the pattern of interaction among people: how often A contacts B, how long they spend together, who originates action when A, B, and C are together, and so on."[129] Whyte eventually used this theory to great advantage in *Street Corner Society*.

But Henderson, though he did not successfully communicate the basic concept of social system to Whyte, still exercised "pervasive" influence on him, especially informally in the Society of

---

[126]   See Conrad M. Arensberg and Solon T. Kimball, *Family and Community in Ireland* (Cambridge, Mass.: Harvard University Press, 1940).

[127]   Whyte, *Street Corner Society*, p. 287.

[128]   Ibid., p. 286.

[129]   Ibid., p. 287. Published accounts of this work by Arensberg and

Fellows meetings. Here is Whyte's vivid picture of how Henderson behaved:

> L. J. Henderson provided a less specific but nevertheless pervasive influence in the development of my methods and theories. As chairman of the Society of Fellows, he presided over our Monday-night dinners like a patriarch in his own household. Even though the group included A. Lawrence Lowell, Alfred North Whitehead, John Livingston Lowes, Samuel Eliot Morison, and Arthur Darby Nock, it was Henderson who was easily the most imposing figure for the junior fellows. He seemed particularly to enjoy baiting the young social scientists. He took me on at my first Monday-night dinner and undertook to show me that all my ideas about society were based upon softheaded sentimentality. While I often resented Henderson's sharp criticisms, I was all the more determined to make my field research stand up against anything he could say.[130]

Many people fled from this kind of criticism, others avoided it more subtly; but those who could stand their ground with Henderson or return to the field of action were almost always benefited.

CRANE BRINTON   Our final example is Crane Brinton, Henderson's long-time colleague at Harvard, a member of the History Department and eventually one of the Senior Fellows of the Society of Fellows. In the 1930s, when he was already a mature and distinguished historian and the author of several notable works in British intellectual history and the history of the French Revolution, Brinton came under the influence of Henderson and, through him, of Pareto.

Henderson's influence is shown most in Brinton's renowned book *The Anatomy of Revolution*.[131] In addition to his general intellectual debt to Henderson, Brinton acknowledged a very specific one in the foreword of this book: "I wish also to thank those

---

Chapple can be found in Eliot D. Chapple, "Measuring Human Relations: An Introduction to the Study of Interaction of Individuals," in Genetic Psychology Monographs 22 (1940): 3–147; and Chapple, "The Interaction Chronograph: Its Evolution and Present Application," *Personnel* 25 (1949): 295–307.
[130]   Ibid., p. 288.
[131]   New York: W. W. Norton, 1938; rev. ed., New York: Prentice-Hall, 1952.

of my friends and colleagues with whom I have discussed the subject of this book for the last two years, and especially Professor L. J. Henderson, the effects of whose care, taste and judgment ought to be evident everywhere in a work he has gone over with great thoroughness." Although Brinton only once refers to his general intellectual debt, it is evident to anyone familiar with Henderson's work. Note the following passages:

Our aim in the following study is the modest one of attempting to establish, as the scientist might, certain first approximations of uniformities to be noted in the course of four successive revolutions in modern states.[132]

Their firmest laws or uniformities are to be regarded as tentative. They may be upset at any time by further work.[133]

But the only important reasons why we should prefer our electric discharge to Jupiter or Thor as a conceptual scheme (to account for thunder and lightning) is that it is more useful, and that we can by using it get on better also with other conceptual schemes we use for similar purposes.[134]

. . . a fact in the natural sciences we define with Professor L. J. Henderson as "an empirically verifiable statement about phenomena in terms of a conceptual scheme."[135]

He is interested less in beauty and neatness of definition than in having his definitions fit not his sentiments and aspirations, but the facts. Above all, he does not dispute over words.[136]

And Brinton's general intellectual debt is also evident in the conceptual scheme he finally adopted for the analysis of his selected revolutions. He would have liked, he says, to have adopted "the conceptual scheme of a social system in equilibrium, as best developed in Pareto's *The Mind and Society*. . . . Its use in the study of revolution is in principle clear."[137] But Brinton was

[132]   Ibid., p. 14.
[133]   Ibid., p. 16.
[134]   Ibid., p. 18.
[135]   Ibid., p. 19.
[136]   Ibid., p. 20.
[137]   Ibid., p. 24.

shrewd enough to recognize the difficulties of actually using what might be possible in principle. He felt he had to settle for something less:

> This conceptual scheme of the social equilibrium is probably in the long run the most useful for the sociologist of revolution. It is for our purposes, however, a bit too ambitious. It needs for full success a more accurate grasp of more numerous variables than we can at present manage. Though it need not necessarily be formulated in precise mathematical terms, it ought to be formulated in terms more close to those of mathematics than we can honestly employ. In other words, it is better suited to a complete sociology of revolutions, or a "dynamics of revolution," than to our modest study of the anatomy of four specific revolutions. We are here attempting merely a preliminary analysis, attempting to classify and systematize at a relatively low level of complexity.[138]

The something less that Brinton decided to settle for was what he alternately referred to as a "conceptual scheme" and a "metaphor" borrowed from the science of pathology. This scheme or metaphor of "a kind of fever" he defined as including the following elements: prodromal signs, mounting fever, crisis frequently accompanied by delirium, convalescence, and, finally, restoration to health, a state in which system conditions are only somewhat different from those existing before the fever, so that the system is considerably like it was before the prodromal signs began to appear.[139] Using this scheme and these conceptual elements, Brinton was able to discern several apparent uniformities in the four "popular" revolutions he selected, though he was careful to point out that there were other types of revolutions which his scheme could not satisfactorily handle. Whatever its limitations, his analysis has not been made obsolete by later work.[140] Through Brinton, Henderson's influence on contemporary historical sociology continues to operate.

[138]   Ibid., p. 25.
[139]   Ibid., pp. 25–26.
[140]   For a recent survey of work on revolutions, see the article on this subject by Walter Laqueur, *International Encyclopedia of the Social Sciences* (New York: Macmillan and Free Press, 1968).

L. J. Henderson's
Social Science Writings

1

SOCIOLOGY 23 LECTURES

1941–42

Editorial note: This is the 1941–42 edition, previously unpublished. It is published here by permission of Lawrence J. Henderson, Jr. Because they are the most mature, comprehensive, and systematic statement of Henderson's sociological views, his Sociology 23 lectures are printed first, out of chronological order. Comparison of this edition with the 1938 version indicates that there was no basic change in Henderson's views over this short time period; but amplification of various minor points and provision of additional examples resulted in an expansion from about sixty to about seventy-five manuscript pages.

The preface and page 1 of the lectures refer to the "present volume" and "this book," and reveal that Henderson was on the verge of publishing a book containing three parts—the lectures themselves, excerpts from writings on social science and from other authors he was fond of quoting, and a few selected lectures by his guests in the Sociology 23 course. Because of his death in 1942 and because of the absence of his close associates on World War II duties, the book was never published. Only the lectures are published here.

Preface

THE PRESENT VOLUME is the outgrowth of a Harvard course called "Concrete Sociology," in which during a period of four years nearly thirty persons have collaborated. Among these collaborators are scholars, scientists, physicians and men of affairs. The book has three parts. The first part is founded upon the introductory lectures of the course, which have been revised as experience has suggested and amplified to meet the needs of readers rather than hearers. This part of the book although written by me bears at many points the marks of the kind advice and assistance of many of the collaborators in the course, especially of President A. Lawrence Lowell, Mr. Chester I. Barnard, Professors Elton Mayo, Crane Brinton, Arthur D. Nock and C. K. M. Kluckhohn, and Mr. George C. Homans. It hardly needs to be said that while many of the merits of the work are derived from these collaborators the author is alone responsible for defects because he has made the final decisions about the content of the book, the form of presentation and the conclusions. In such circumstances responsibility is indivisible. The second part of the book, comprising brief excerpts taken chiefly from the writings of well-known authors, has been newly put together. The third part consists of some of the cases that have been presented by the persons who have collaborated in the work of the course.

It is the purpose here as it has been in the course to analyze and describe some of the more important elements, factors and aspects of the interactions of men. This makes necessary naming and classifying many things, some of which are vulgar enough, while others include what we all feel to be noblest and best in human life. Experience shows that there are those to whom this procedure is painful and repulsive, much as to others, though for very different reasons, the study of insanity is. Perhaps most readers who for such reasons may find the introductory lectures very distasteful will do well to go no farther.

Cynics also may be warned that this book can hardly serve their purposes, unless indeed it should first modify them. For one result of this study seems to be that such things as personal integrity, the bonds of family, discipline, decorum, loyalty, friendship, religious devotion, and, in general, all the simple virtues are far more important in the social process than other things which have often been the chief concern of intellectuals. The simple virtues are great things, but they are somewhat different things from what many persons take them to be, and it seems desirable that some persons, at least, should try to study them as they are.

The description of what such things are and of what most of

the other elements and factors and processes of the social system are is still in a preliminary stage of rough approximation. The present book aims at this only: to teach thoroughly and to exemplify a few of these rough descriptions and approximations.

In Part I numerous references are made to Part II. The reader is urged to make use of the excerpts thus designated as illustrations of the text of Part I. For careful study such use is all but indispensable. It has not been possible to arrange the excerpts according to a rational system of classification and they are accordingly placed in alphabetical order and invariably referred to by title only. However, the great number of references to excerpts adjoined to the classification of residues in Chapter III of Part I (pp. 53–56) will serve as a not too incomplete analysis of one aspect of Part II.

Chapter 1: Procedure in a Science

The subject of this book is "concrete sociology." "Sociology" will be here defined as the science that is conversant with a certain class of phenomena. This class of phenomena includes all events and processes in which interactions between two or more persons occur. In general, we shall limit our study to phenomena in which such interactions between persons seem to be important, or not conveniently negligible.

An example may help to fix our ideas and to illustrate the meaning of the above statement: A and B, two men previously inexperienced, had been engaged for about a month in sawing logs with a crosscut saw. One day B was replaced by C, an experienced sawer and more powerful man. A, working with his new partner C, found his day's work more fatiguing and judged it less effective than his work with B. He said, "The boss is riding me."

The following comments are to the point and should be carefully noted: (1) By abstraction the physical aspects only of the day's work may be considered, for instance the efficiency, in the thermodynamical sense, of the work of A and C. Such a study is physical and physiological, not sociological. (2) By another abstraction the cost of the labor of A and C may be separated out for study. Such a study is economic (in the narrow sense of the term), not sociological. (3) Accordingly, for certain purposes the interactions between A and B, and those between A and C, may be disregarded. But for other purposes they cannot be conveniently disregarded. Thus, it may be desirable to know how far A's belief that his efficiency had diminished is due to an actual lack of physiological (neuro-muscular) coordination between A and C, that is, to inadequate physiological interaction between the two individuals, and how far it is due to A's resentment at the change of partners, which may be a psychological interaction between A and X, Y or Z, say the boss, B's wife or B himself. This is a sociological problem. (4) It may then be well to know how far A is correct in thinking his work less effective. Then (1), (2) and (3) may all be involved. This is also a sociological problem. Accordingly, sociological studies may, and in general do, involve physical, physiological, psychological and (even in the strict sense) economic factors. But in any event, comformably to our definition, they involve at least interactions between persons.

A's remark is the expression of an attitude. It may or may not be a true or partly true assertion.

This illustration has been chosen because, among other reasons, it is a simple case that is likely to seem trivial. Note well, however, that nothing is trivial, but thinking (or feeling) makes it so, and that we must ever guard against coloring facts with our prejudices. There was a time not so very long ago when electromagnetic interactions, mosquitoes, and micro-organisms seemed trivial. It is when we study the social sciences that the risk of mixing our own prejudices and passions with the facts, and thus spoiling our analysis, is most likely to prevail.

For our present purposes all this is most important and the considerations involved in the analysis of this simple case are the better grasped because the case is simple. Moreover, the very simplicity and familiarity of the case have helped to draw our attention to three general aspects of interaction between persons: first, such interaction often takes the form of mutual adaptation and skill in "teamwork"; secondly, it often involves strong sentiments; thirdly, words are often an expression of attitudes or sentiments.

In such cases they often have no other "meaning" and may there-fore be regarded as neither true nor false.[1] Everyone knows these facts, though many are prone to forget them if it is convenient to do so, but for our present purpose they must be fixed in the mind and *invariably* applied when relevant. They have a deep physi-ological foundation in the establishment of conditioned reflexes.[2]

So we have already a definition and three theorems (or laws):

Definition: Sociology, *as we choose to say*, is conversant with the interactions between persons.

Theorems: *As experience shows*, (1) interactions between persons often take the form of mutual adaptation and skill, (2) they often involve strong sentiments, (3) words often express sentiments or attitudes and sometimes approximately nothing else.

Note well that definitions are, within limits, arbitrary; but theorems or laws are not, because they depend upon inductions from experience and upon deductive reasoning.[3] The test of a defi-nition is its convenience; the test of a theorem is its accord with experience, i.e., observation and experiment.

If I say "infanticide is a crime," I may well be confusing a defi-nition and a theorem. The confusion is resolved by stating a defini-tion such as: a crime is what is so recognized by a court. Then a theorem may follow to the effect that in many communities known to us all forms of infanticide are crimes. In doubtful cases a defini-tion of "infanticide" may be also necessary, e.g., the sacrifice of an infant at birth in order to save the mother's life may or may not be included in the definition of the term.

In general, a definition is convenient when clear, univocal, and frequently relevant. In general, a theorem is the more trustworthy the more widely it has been tested by observation and experiment. It should be relied on only within the limits of experience. Form-

---

[1]   See d'Épinay, Poincaré, Pollock, Antivivisection.

[2]   It is still an open question whether the term "conditioned reflex" is a convenient one, because, as Sherington suggests, the differences be-tween reflexes and conditioned reflexes may be more important than the resemblances, for the purposes of physiological research. Throughout this book the term is used because it is today the usual label for a certain class of phenomena, and without any other implications.

[3]   See Durkheim, Reinach.

erly no swans were black and no chemical elements could be disintegrated. In observational and experimental science *we are concerned with probability never with certainty, with approximation never with absolute precision*,[4] and I repeat: Scientific generalizations should be regarded as valid only within the limits of our experience of time, place, temperature, pressure, social structure, etc.

Some readers will think these theorems obvious, and feel them accordingly unimportant. Well, the experience of all highly developed sciences shows that the clear, explicit formulation of "the obvious" and its incorporation in the systematic treatment of a subject is both necessary and very convenient. We are all liable to neglect, or overlook, or forget such things, especially when we wish to, and above all when we so wish unconsciously. One definition of the obvious is: An important proposition that we wish to disregard. Voltaire has a phrase, "le superflu, chose très necessaire"; he might well have added, "l'évident, chose indispensable."[5]

In order to fix this idea it may be useful to consider two examples: (1) In medical practice there are many considerations leading to the rule that when you do not know what to do you should in general, do nothing, or as little as possible beyond the immediate care of the patient.[6] Under pressure to "do something" these considerations are sometimes disregarded, or not thought of, even by physicians who are familiar with them. This would probably happen more rarely if the rules of expectant treatment were today more clearly formulated and more systematically presented to medical students and young physicians by their teachers and masters. (2) Many liberals express contempt and disgust at the behavior of the masses in response to advertising and propaganda. The same persons often express unqualified confidence in the referendum as a means of reaching sound decisions about complex political and social problems.[7] Now it is an induction from experience that people are more often than not emotional, irra-

4   See Henderson.
5   See Maine (II).
6   See Falkland.
7   See Maine (III).

tional, or at least nonlogical in making decisions. If such liberals were as familiar with this as they are with the multiplication table, some of them might form less absolute conclusions.

The subject of this book is *concrete* sociology. We shall be chiefly occupied with the study of cases, that is with concrete things and events. The cases are of two kinds: those of Part II, comprising excerpts from literature chosen as a means of illustrating the text of Part I; and those of Part III, a selection of cases that have been presented in the Harvard College course of which this book is an outgrowth, which are offered as problems in analysis. The excerpts are chosen from all sorts of writings, ancient, medieval and modern; they include fact and fiction, prose and poetry, wise and unwise judgments and opinions; they present many kinds of occurrences from private life, from public life and from business; and they include descriptions of many kinds of experiences. This choice conforms to the definition of sociology that we have adopted. It is determined by the purpose to elucidate some of the most general uniformities in the interactions between persons. This purpose arises from the conviction that it is now possible to give a scientific treatment of certain uniformities of this kind, and the expectation that these uniformities are sufficiently extensive to serve not only the needs of sociologists, but also those of historians and political scientists, as well as of men who practice the professions or engage in business.

METHODS AND PROCEDURES

For the moment, we are concerned with a brief introduction to the study of the excerpts. This introduction should fix certain ideas, delimit our work, and provide a provisional scheme of analysis and procedure.

Near the end of the *Nicomachean Ethics*,[8] Aristotle prepares the way for his transition to the study of politics with the following remarks:

Must we not admit that the Political Science plainly does not stand

[8]   Everyman's Edition, Book X, pp. 260–61.

on a similar footing to that of other sciences and faculties? I mean, that while in all other cases those who impart the faculties and themselves exert them are identical (physicians and painters for instance) matters of Statesmanship the Sophists profess to teach, but not one of them practises it, that being left to those actually engaged in it: and these might really very well be thought to do it by some singular knack and by mere practice rather than by any intellectual process: for they neither write nor speak on these matters (though it might be more to their credit than composing speeches for the courts or the assembly), nor again have they made Statesmen of their own sons or their friends.

One can hardly suppose but that they would have done so if they could, seeing that they could have bequeathed no more precious legacy to their communities, nor would they have preferred, for themselves or their dearest friends, the possession of any faculty rather than this.

Practice, however, seems to contribute no little to its acquisition; merely breathing the atmosphere of politics would never have made Statesmen of them, and therefore we may conclude that they who would acquire a knowledge of Statesmanship must have in addition practice.

But of the Sophists they who profess to teach it are plainly a long way off from doing so: in fact, they have no knowledge at all of its nature and objects; if they had, they would never have put it on the same footing with Rhetoric or even on a lower: neither would they have conceived it to be "an easy matter to legislate by simply collecting such laws as are famous because of course one could select the best," as though the selection were not a matter of skill, and the judging aright a very great matter, as in Music: for they alone, who have practical knowledge of a thing, can judge the performances rightly or understand with what means and in what way they are accomplished, and what harmonises with what: the unlearned must be content with being able to discover whether the result is good or bad, as in painting.

Now laws may be called the performances or tangible results of Political Science; how then can a man acquire from these the faculty of Legislation, or choose the best? we do not see men made physicians by compilations; and yet in these treatises men endeavour to give not only the cases but also how they may be cured, and the proper treatment in each case, dividing the various bodily habits. Well, these are thought to be useful to professional men, but to the unprofessional useless. In like manner it may be that collections of laws and Constitutions would be exceedingly useful to such as are able to speculate on them, and judge what is well, and what ill, and what kind of things fit in with what others: but they who without this qualification should go through such matters cannot have right judgment, unless they have it by instinct, though they may become more intelligent in such matters.

Elsewhere Aristotle says,[9] ". . . people who have spent their lives observing nature are best qualified to make hypotheses as to the principles that bring great numbers of facts together."

The substance of what Aristotle said so long ago has been many times repeated. For example, Sainte-Beuve once wrote:[10] "Commynes completely justifies for me the phrase of Vauvenargues: 'The real politicians know men better than those whose trade is philosophy: I mean that they are more truly philosophers.' "[11] In another place Sainte-Beuve reports a similar judgment of Chesterfield's on Cardinal de Retz, and only the other day Monsieur de Saint Aulaire, a former French ambassador to London, remarked of Richelieu:[12] "One recognizes in him as in Lyautey a technician of general ideas." During the French Revolution, Gouverneur Morris remarked,[13] ". . . none know how to govern but those who have been used to it and such Men have rarely either Time or Inclination to write about it. The Books, therefore, which are to be met with, contain mere Utopian Ideas." Hazlitt expressed much the same opinion when he said,[14] "The most sensible people to be met with in society are men of business and of the world, who argue from what they see and know, instead of spinning cobweb distinctions of what things ought to be."[15]

Some years ago a young Oxford don came to the conclusion that men who have missed the highest academic prizes and gone out into the world seem, thirty years after when they come back

9   *De generatione et corruptione*, 1, 2, 10.

10   "Philippe de Commynes," last p. Causerie of 7 May 1850.

11   "Memoirs de Cardinal de Retz," last p. Causerie of 20 Oct. 1851.

12   *Richelieu*, Dunod, Paris, 1932, p. 40.

13   *Diary*, 9 Nov., 1790.

14   *Table-Talk. Essays on Men and Manners*, Humphrey Milford, p. 101.

15   See La Bruyère, Bagehot (IV).

to Oxford, better men than their successful competitors who have stayed on to lead the academic life. He was so much struck by this contrast that he resigned his fellowship and left Oxford. An English scholar who has become an administrator of public affairs, and therefore knows both the academic life and the life of affairs, told this tale. In reply, it was suggested that it is not merely experience of the world which changes and develops men in this way, but still more the practice of deciding and acting under the burden of responsibility for the consequences. This suggestion was unhesitatingly accepted. Indeed, observation and experience clearly indicate that nothing contributes more to the difference that Aristotle recognized between men of action and theorists than practice or lack of practice in deciding and acting under the burden of responsibility.

The man who has the habit of action under responsibility is deeply modified and differently oriented because of this experience.[16] It is not too much to say that his whole organism is in a different state from that of a person who has not the habit of action under responsibility. This is not conceived, and can only with difficulty be imagined, by young, inexperienced students, or even in many cases by theorists who without practical experience have devoted much study to a subject. But unless a man, young or old, is aware of the importance of this psycho-physiological adaptation, that is, of the nature and effect of certain kinds of conditioned reflexes and of the way in which both action and understanding are thereby modified, he can hardly understand many aspects of the interactions between men.

Accordingly, Aristotle's criticism may still be made, more than two thousand years after, of much of our current political science *and, in general, medicine only excepted, of the branches of science that are conversant with experiences and affairs of daily life,* that is to say, with events in which interactions between persons are important.[17] Meanwhile, medicine has progressed. Why?

Aristotle's explanation may still be given. In the complex busi-

16   See Caesar, Elizabeth.
17   See Bagehot (I), Cochin.

ness of living as in medicine *both* theory and practice are necessary conditions of understanding, and the method of Hippocrates is the only method that has ever succeeded widely and generally. The first element of that method is hard, persistent, intelligent, responsible, unremitting labor in the sick room, not in the library: the all-round adaptation of the doctor to his task, an adaptation that is far from being merely intellectual.[18] The second element of that method is accurate observation of things and events, selection, guided by judgment born of familiarity and experience, of the salient and the recurrent phenomena, and their classification and methodical exploitation. The third element of that method is the judicious construction of a theory—not a philosophical theory, nor a grand effort of the imagination, nor a quasi-religious dogma, but a modest pedestrian affair or perhaps I had better say, a useful walking-stick to help on the way—and the use thereof. All this may be summed up in a word: The physician must have, first, intimate, habitual, intuitive familiarity with things; secondly, systematic knowledge of things; and thirdly, an effective way of thinking about things. His intuitive familiarity must embrace his systematic knowledge and his way of thinking as well as the things he studies.

[18]   Cf. Galileo, *Dialogues Concerning Two New Sciences*, Macmillan, New York, 1914, p. 1. "Indeed, I myself, being curious by nature, frequently visit [the arsenal of Venice] . . . for the mere pleasure of observing the work of those who, on account of their superiority over other artisans, we call 'first rank men.' Conference with them has often helped me in the investigation of certain effects including not only those which are striking, but also those which are recondite and almost incredible."

Consider also the famous fifth postulate of Euclid: "If a straight line meet two straight lines, so as to make the interior angles on the same side of it taken together less than two right angles, these straight lines, being continually produced, will at length meet on that side on which are the angles which are less than two right angles." Few things in the whole range of science have been more discussed than this and many attempts have been made to find a more convenient postulate. In general, few among those suggested as substitutes permit a successive development of theorems as simple as Euclid's and, while others may be simpler in form, it is doubtful if they appeal so strongly to visual and kinesthetic intuition. Accordingly, one may at least conjecture that the special form of Euclid's postulate was as much determined by intuition as by reason.

Without these three qualifications no man[19] can be trusted to think scientifically. It is one of the broadest of inductions that competent men of science are no more logico-experimental than other men when they step outside the field in which they have acquired intuitive familiarity with things.

Discussions of scientific method are often more concerned with the publications of men of science—with their finished product—than with the habits, attitudes and characteristic behavior of such men while they are at work and especially before they write their papers or books. It is partly for this reason that the importance of intuitive familiarity with things is often little appreciated. Note well that this intuitive familiarity includes not only intuitive familiarity with the objects of an investigation but also with the systematic knowledge and with the effective way of thinking. Such all-round intuitive familiarity is almost indispensable—indeed, it may be fairly said to be quite indispensable—for effective scientific work of every kind. One conspicuous result of it is the intuitive avoidance of pitfalls.

At each stage of his work before the final formulation and exposition, a skillful investigator is more often than not hardly aware of what he is doing, and much of his thinking is of the nature of revery and free association. In early stages especially, his speculation is likely to be curiously untrammeled. There is an old tale of Faraday, the source of which I have been unable to recover, about a conversation of his with a colleague. After a time Faraday became silent and his friend then asked him what he was thinking about. He replied—as I remember the story—"If I were to tell you what I am thinking about, you would think me insane." Few have thought as successfully as Faraday, but many thousands of men of science could probably have given a similar answer on a similar occasion.

Your reveries run on what you are interested in. For effective scientific work it is necessary that your reveries should in large measure run on your work, for you must be interested in it, or rather, perhaps, you must be interested in order that your reveries

[19]   See Harvey, Garden, Pavlov.

may run on your work. But it is also necessary that these reveries should run—one cannot say skillfully—in a way the result of which is equivalent to the result of skill in work. Now for this, intuitive familiarity is necessary.

Experience shows that this is the way to success. It has long been followed in studying sickness, but hardly at all in studying the other experiences of everyday life. The method of this course depends upon the conviction that there is much to be gained by cautiously following the procedure of Hippocrates in the study of the interactions between persons. Let us, therefore, consider more carefully what Hippocrates did and what he did not do.

Hippocrates was in reaction chiefly against three things: first, against the ancient, traditional myths and superstitions which still prevailed among the physicians of his day; secondly, against the recent intrusion of philosophy into medical doctrine; thirdly, against the extravagant system of diagnosis of the Cnidian School, a body of contemporary physicians who seem to have suffered from a familiar form of professional pedantry. Here Hippocrates was opposing a pretentious systematization of knowledge that lacked solid objective foundation; the concealment of ignorance, probably more or less unconsciously, with a show of knowledge. Note well that such concealment is rarely altogether dishonest and that it may be performed in thorough good faith.[20]

The social sciences today suffer from defects that are not unlike the defects of medicine to which Hippocrates was opposed. First, social and political myths are everywhere current, and if they involve forms of superstition that are less apparent to us than the medical superstitions of long ago, that may well be because we recognize the latter class of superstitions for what they are while still accepting or half-accepting the former class. For instance, "the dictatorship of the proletariat" as used by Lenin, "race" as used by Hitler, "communism" as used by Stalin, and "majority rule" as used by Roosevelt[21] are myths.[22] How many of us recognize all four for what they are? Secondly, there is at least as much phi-

20   See Durkheim.
21   Cf. Kent, *The Great Game of Politics*, New York.
22   See Maine (III).

losophy mingled with our current social sciences as there was at any time in the medical doctrines of the Greeks. Thirdly, a great part of the social science of today consists of elaborate systematization on a very insufficient foundation of fact.

Hippocrates endeavored to avoid myths and traditional rules, the grand search for philosophical truth, the authority of philosophical beliefs, the concealment of ignorance with a show of systematic knowledge. He was concerned first of all not to conceal his own ignorance from himself. When he thought abstractly, or in general terms, his thought was limited and constrained because he had wide intuitive knowledge based on the habit of responsible action in concrete situations. There is a test for this kind of thinking: the question, "for example?" Those who generalize from experience almost always pass this test; others do not. Indeed the test is frequently destructive of unfounded generalization and is likely to lead to painful embarrassment. For this reason its use is often inexpedient.

Experience shows that there are two kinds of human behavior which it is ordinarily convenient and often essential to distinguish:

1) Thinking, talking, and writing, by those who are so familiar with relevant concrete experiences that they cannot ordinarily forget the facts, about two kinds of subjects. These are: (*a*) concrete observations and experiences which are representable by means of sharply defined or otherwise unambiguous words; and (*b*) more general considerations, clearly and logically related to such concrete observations and experiences.

2) Thinking, talking, and writing about vague or general ideas or "concepts" which do not clearly relate to concrete observations and experiences and which are not designated by sharply defined words.[23] On the whole, the works of Plato belong to this second class, the Hippocratic writings to the first class.

It is surprisingly easy even after twenty-three hundred years to imagine Hippocrates going about his work and to discern his methodical procedure. First of all, he was a practicing doctor. His life was spent in the treatment of patients. That was the milieu in

23   See Plato, Goethe (II), Calvin, Hegel.

which he lived and thought. It is more than possible that Aristotle had Hippocrates in mind when he wrote the lines above cited, and it seems safe to say that Hippocrates resembles Richelieu, or Lyautey, or Robert Walpole, or Bismarck, or Cavour more than he does Hobbes, Hegel, Mill, or Marx.

The so-called genuine works of Hippocrates[24] reveal a method in the exploitation of everyday experience with the lives and deaths of men that can never be too carefully studied. But we must confine ourselves to a few important aspects of the Hippocratic method.

In the beginning are the cases. The very first of these is as follows:[25]

Case I

Philiscus lived by the wall. He took to his bed with acute fever on the first day and sweating; night uncomfortable.

Second day. General exacerbation, later a small clyster moved the bowels well. A restful night.

Third day. Early and until mid-day he appeared to have lost the fever; but towards evening acute fever with sweating; thirst; dry tongue; black urine. An uncomfortable night, without sleep; completely out of his mind.

Fourth day. All symptoms exacerbated; black urine; a more comfortable night, and urine of a better colour.

Fifth day. About mid-day slight epistaxis [nosebleed] of unmixed blood. Urine varied, with scattered, round particles suspended in it, resembling semen; they did not settle. On the application of a suppository the patient passed, with flatulence, scanty excreta. A distressing night, snatches of sleep, irrational talk; extremities everywhere cold, and would not get warm again; black urine; snatches of sleep towards dawn; speechless; cold sweat; extremities livid. About mid-day on the sixth day the patient died. The breathing throughout, as though he were recollecting to do it, was rare and large. Spleen

24   In speaking of Hippocrates, I mean the author or authors of these works, and wish to express no opinion about the man of that name, whose life is little known. We need here feel no concern for the question whether this man wrote these works.
25   *Hippocrates*, Loeb Classical Library, G. P. Putnam, New York, 1923, Vol. I, p. 187.

raised in a round swelling. Cold sweats all the time. The exacerbations on even days.

This case is fairly typical of the collection. The following points are important and should be carefully noted: (1) It consists of bare observations of bare facts, uncolored by theory or presupposition and condensed to the very limit of possible condensation. These are the practicing physician's data, freed so far as possible from everything that is not a datum. (2) The data are of two kinds. The first kind, contained in the first part, are single observations. The second kind, contained in the second part, are uniformities observed throughout this particular illness of this particular person. (3) The curious form of breathing referred to is the first mention now known of what is called Cheyne-Stokes breathing. Apart from one other reference to the phenomenon in another Hippocratic case, it is the only known reference before the eighteenth century of our era. This is one sign among many that Hippocrates was no casual and no ordinary observer. On the contrary, he was a constant observer with whom observation was a great part of the business of life, a skillful observer whose skill depended upon both native capacity and long practice. Such at least is the interpretation that all current medical experience forces upon us.

The next step after the recognition of uniformities in a particular case, is the recognition of a wider kind of uniformity: the recurrence again and again in different cases, often otherwise very various, of single events or of the uniformity observed within a single case, for example: regularities in the duration of certain fevers, the frequent discharge of fluid through the nose in what we now call diphtheria, and in general the prognostic importance of a wide range of symptoms. The most famous of all the descriptions of such uniformities is that of the so-called facies Hippocratica, the appearance of the face at the point of death in many acute diseases: "Nose sharp, eyes hollow, temples sunken, ears cold and contracted with their lobes turned outwards, the skin about the face hard and tense and parched, the colour of the face as a whole being yellow or black."

Throughout a great part of his work Hippocrates is thus moving step by step toward the widest generalizations within his reach. In great part he is seeking a natural history of acute disease or at least of those acute diseases that were prevalent among his patients. His success was great, and the whole history of science goes far to support the view that such a methodical procedure is a necessary step in the development of a science that deals with similarly complex and various phenomena.

Beyond this stage there is one even wider generalization that plays an important part in the writings and thought of Hippocrates. This is the principle that came to be known, and is still remembered, as the *vis medicatrix naturae*. For the purposes of sociological study, it is an important principle and we must now examine one or two aspects of it precisely.

Before Hippocrates, about 500 B.C., Alcmaeon of Croton had expressed the opinion that health is an isonomy or harmony (we may say equilibrium) between opposites, sickness a state of monarchy or disequilibrium. Now the widest of all generalizations in the work of Hippocrates is this, that as a rule sick people recover without treatment. The conclusion of Hippocrates was that the state of health is similar to that state defined by Pareto in his Treatise on General Sociology, *The Mind and Society*,[26] as equilibrium: "a state such that if a small modification different from that which will otherwise occur is impressed upon a system, a reaction will at once appear tending toward the conditions that would have existed if the modification had not been impressed."[27]

This definition applies to many phenomena and processes, both static and dynamic. It applies not only in the fields of pathology and sociology but very generally in the description of almost all kinds of phenomena and processes. It is indeed a statement of one of the most general aspects of our experience, a recognition of one of the commonest aspects of things and events. For example: (1) A ball which is in a cup, and which is struck a blow that is not too hard, will return to its original position; (2) a candle flame

[26]   New York, Harcourt, Brace, 1935, pp. 1435–1442. But I quote my own translation.
[27]   See Bentley, San Francisco.

which is deflected by a draft that is not too strong will resume its original form; (3) a trout brook that is "fished out" will, if carefully protected, regain its former population of fish; and (4) to take a Hippocratic instance, an infant after a disease that is not too severe will gain in weight until that weight is reached which is approximately what would have been reached if there had been no sickness. In statics this definition is applicable only to what is there called stable equilibrium, and there are, of course, other kinds of phenomena which resemble those of unstable or neutral equilibrium in statics, to which the definition does not apply, but since they have little "survival value" they are probably not very common.

Pareto's definition bears the marks of centuries of further work in science and logic. But the Hippocratic analysis comes to much the same thing as Pareto's definition. In both cases there is the underlying theory that equilibrium is an equilibrium of forces, more or less like the equilibrium, for instance, in a box spring; that a small modification leaves the forces substantially intact; and that the forces tend to reestablish the state that would have existed if no modification had occurred, just as a box spring which has been depressed when one lies down on it resumes its original form when one gets up. So in February 1937 the people of Louisville, driven away by a flood, returned to their homes when the flood receded; and a few weeks later life was going on with little change. So within a decade the traces of the earthquake and fire in San Francisco could hardly be seen, or the devastation of the war of 1914–18 along the battlefront in northern France. In such cases the "forces" that tend to produce "the conditions that would have existed if the modification had not been impressed" are what we describe as habits, sentiments, and economic interests.

It should now be evident that Hippocrates, perhaps under the influence of Alcmaeon, made use of his broadest generalization, that sick people usually recover without treatment, in order to construct a conceptual scheme or theory of the nature of sickness. It is herein that he differs from men like Richlieu, Lyautey, Robert Walpole, Bismarck, and Cavour. He differs from them in that he was both a practitioner and a theorist, while, so far as we know, they were practitioners who made use of no general all-embracing theory or conceptual scheme.

In order to construct a useful conceptual scheme, Hippocrates proceeded to analyze the phenomenon, as he abstractly conceived it, into elements. This analysis and the resulting elaboration of the theory need not detain us. To them we owe the survival of such words as "crisis" and "coction." But the theory, having served its purpose, is obsolete, like Ptolemy's astronomy.

We must, however, note carefully that this obsolete theory, like so many others, once served its purpose well. In particular it was the firm support of the Hippocratic principle of expectant treatment and of the precept "Do no harm," a principle and a precept which still preserve their utility in the practice of medicine and even in government and the affairs of everyday life, and which are too often disregarded by physicians, surgeons and politicians.[28]

Bagehot clearly recognized the importance of this principle and often pointed it out, for example, in the following passage:[29] "One may incline to hope that the balance of good over evil is in favor of benevolence; one can hardly bear to think that it is not so: but anyhow it is certain that there is a most heavy debit of evil, and that this burden might almost all have been spared us if philanthropists as well as others had not inherited from their barbarous forefathers a wild passion for instant action."

The Hippocratic conceptual scheme suffers from one particular defect that should be carefully noted: it presents a view of the physiological system in a state of equilibrium, without giving a satisfactory picture of the constituent parts of the system or of the

[28]   See Disraeli, Guizot, Oliver (I).
[29]   *The Works of Walter Bagehot*, Vol. IV, p. 566, Hartford, Conn., 1889. This quotation is from "Physics and Politics," a work in some respects unfortunately influenced by early "Darwinism," by the writings of Herbert Spencer and of contemporary anthropologists, to all of which Bagehot ascribed too much weight or intellectual authority. But, after errors of judgment and fact have been deleted, "Physics and Politics" remains an important and original work. Possibly Bagehot's bad health while writing this book may explain the defects, for Bagehot had been of all the Victorians one of the freest from the influences of intellectual authority.

forces that operate between these parts. We now know that it is convenient and reasonably satisfactory to think of the constituent parts as chemical substances, fluids, cells, tissues, and organs; and of the forces as the forces with which theoretical physics and theoretical chemistry are concerned. Such a conception was not available to Hippocrates. Nevertheless, his conceptual scheme worked and for a long time worked well. This is, in fact, the test of a conceptual scheme and the only test: it must work well enough for the purpose of the moment. A conceptual scheme survives just so long and just in so far as it continues to be convenient to use it for the purpose of scientific work.

In a discussion of scientific hypotheses, Henri Poincaré once remarked:[30] "These two propositions, 'the external world exists,' or 'it is more convenient to suppose that it exists,' have one and the same meaning." The proof of this assertion is that in scientific work no use can be made of the proposition "the external world exists" that cannot be made of the statement "we assume for the present purpose that the external world exists." Moreover, all our conceptual schemes are in a state of flux. There is hardly one we now use that was used in precisely its present form 50 years ago. It is therefore dangerous to believe that a conceptual scheme is a description of some ultimate metaphysical reality. In other words, belief in the "truth" of a conceptual scheme is for scientific purposes not only irrelevant but misleading. This confusion may or may not be important for a chemist or physiologist to bear in mind, but students of the social sciences will neglect it at their peril, for the risk of the intrusion of their own sentiments into their work is serious and ever-present.[31]

For this reason, it is convenient to distinguish scientific theories from what we often speak of as ideologies. Today, clear-headed physicists no longer 'believe' their theories; but Marxists, Freudians, Fascists, New Dealers, and disciples of 'laissez-faire' are in general believers in dogma rather than mere users of theory. Physicists use both the undulatory theory and the corpuscular theory of light in their modern forms, but it is hard to find anyone

[30]   *La valeur de la science*, Paris (no date), p. 272.
[31]   See Plato, Reinach, Ruskin, Spedding, Pollock.

who uses both the Marxian and the Fascist theories of society, and perhaps impossible to find a single person who uses both and believes neither. Of course, this is partly due to the fact that these theories are hardly suited to scientific use.

There is, however, another side to this question that may be mentioned here, because it involves an important sociological fact. Many investigators, especially when young, seem to be stimulated and encouraged by an emotional belief that they are about to solve a riddle of the universe or at least to contribute some permanent description of a bit of "ultimate reality." So long as they work in the scientific manner and keep their conviction that they are dealing with ultimate reality carefully segregated from their work, they may be helped and not hindered by this delusion.

In the preceding analysis I have tried to show how the works of Hippocrates illustrate the statement with which I began, that "The physician must have, first, intimate, habitual, intuitive familiarity with things; secondly, systematic knowledge of things; and thirdly, an effective way of thinking about things." I now ask you to consider briefly a remark of Robert Hooke's[32] which is particularly interesting because it states explicitly some of the most characteristic features of the work of a scientific investigator. In one respect, much more than Hippocrates, Hooke here himself gives us an account of his procedure.

So many are the *links,* upon which the true Philosophy depends, of which, if any one be *loose,* or *weak,* the whole *chain* is in danger of being dissolv'd; it is to *begin* with the Hands and Eyes, and to *proceed* on through the Memory, to be *continued* by the Reason; nor is it to stop there, but to *come about* to the Hands and Eyes again, and so, by a *continual passage round* from one Faculty to another, it is to be maintained in life and strength, as much as the body of man is by the *circulation* of the blood through the several parts of the body, the Arms, the Feet, the Lungs, the Heart, and the Head.

This statement sums up a part of what has just been said of the Hippocratic method and adds further considerations.

We may note, to begin with, that it is a statement of what men

[32]   *Micrographia,* 1665, preface.

do in scientific work, rather than of the product of their work or of the "method of science." It is behavioristic rather than rational. Secondly, it emphasizes the importance of continuous, persistent occupation with a subject. Thirdly, it makes quite clear the need for both observation and experiment, on the one hand, and for theory, on the other hand. Again, it implies that the activity of the man of science is all one process, like the circulation of the blood, that in a sense we do violence in analyzing it into parts, and that all these parts are united in an organic whole, the activity of the investigator. So far, then, it confirms what has been said while putting the emphasis on another aspect of the subject.

Hooke's statement, however, gives a certain primacy to the hands and eyes, to observation and experiment.[33] Here again his statement is a fair description of the Hippocratic procedure, and the whole long history of science clearly shows that observation and experiment are in one respect the primary features of scientific investigation, because when they give rise to well-established and thoroughly confirmed data and when these data are incompatible with theory or with previous conclusions, then the theory and the previous conclusions yield and suffer modification or destruction, as the case may be.

An interesting statement of Leonardo's[34] expresses the same opinion: "It seems to me that those sciences which are not born of experience, the mother of all certainty, and which do not end in known experience—that is to say, those sciences whose origin or process or end does not pass through any of the five senses—are vain and full of error."

There is one addition to Hooke's statement that we must now make. It is not enough to mention the hands and eyes. We must add the ears if we are to study the interactions of men, for in these phenomena our data come from what we hear as well as from what we see and do. Speech is our chief means of communication and therefore a primary factor in human interactions. Even this platitude has to be stated and restated.

---

[33]   See Rousseau.
[34]   *Trattato della Pittura*, 33.

There is a sect of psychologists who will have nothing to do with what men say (unless they are fellow behaviorists talking about behavior or members of another sect of psychologists quarreling with the behaviorists). I warn you against worrying about their inhibitions. There have been few psychologists in the history of the human race and many doctors, and the doctors have always found it necessary to take account of what patients tell them. If a doctor were to refuse to listen to his patients, he would cut himself off from information that experience shows to be indispensable for the skillful practice of the profession. It may be left to the reader's imagination to picture a sick and suffering behaviorist consulting a physician who refuses to listen to the report of symptoms. Let him also reflect on what Molière might have done with such a scene. Perhaps further reflection, with such a picture in mind, may suggest that certain dogmas of behaviorists are partly "rationalization."

Hippocrates says clearly[35] that among the circumstances from which he framed his judgments were "talk, manner, silence, thoughts, . . . the nature and time of dreams, . . ." Nevertheless, it is also necessary to distinguish between what you see for yourself and what you are told by another. This corresponds to the ancient distinction in medicine between signs and symptoms, signs being what the doctor himself observes, for instance, *rubor, tumor, calor* in a patient with an abcess. Symptoms are what he cannot observe but is told, for instance, *dolor* in the same case. Note, however, that if a patient says to you that he feels pain, then it is your datum, your own observation, that the patient *says* he feels pain.

One of the greatest difficulties in medical practice arises from the fact that the patient's report of pain is, like most things that people say about their bodily sensations or their private affairs, often untrustworthy[36] on two scores. In the first place, accurate description of such things is nearly, if not quite, impossible, and even moderately successful description is rare. And, in the second place, the patient may be trying to deceive you or, for any one of

---

[35]   Op. cit., Vol. I, p. 181.
[36]   See J. Jackson.

many reasons, conscious or unconscious, so phrasing his statements that there is a tendency to deceive.

The crude data of sociology may be roughly described as consisting of what men say, of what they do, and of what happens to them, in so far as these things are significantly related to their interactions.

The difficulty that hearsay, whether oral or printed, makes up a great part of the crude material out of which social science must be constructed can neither be gainsaid nor obviated. But it can be lessened, and, so far as we now know, the best way to lessen it is to follow the practice of skillful physicians.

When a skillful physician tries to appraise the meaning and significance of what he is told, his interpretation is modified by long familiarity with facts such as these: the patient may be truthful or a liar, well-balanced or hypochondriacal, courageous or fearful, calm or excited, hysterical or neurotic or stable, capable or incapable of self-analysis, and so on. He may be a person fully capable of reasoned, logical interpretations of his own experience, or he may be one in whom nearly all expression is emotional and unreasoned.[37] He may or may not have something to conceal. There may well be certain guiding principles of his thought and conduct, such as a hypochondriac's unconscious assumption that everything not perfectly safe is dangerous, or a young man's that everything not perfectly successful is a failure, which prevent him from saying things because they never occur to him, and some of these things may be very important for the doctor's information. In accordance with his judgment of such things, his interpretation of the patient's utterances will vary.

With such things in mind, or so well-known that they come to mind spontaneously at need, the physician listens, first, to what the patient wants to tell, secondly, for implications of what he doesn't want to tell and, thirdly, for implications of what he can't tell. Further, the physician avoids the intrusion of his own assumptions, beliefs, and feelings. He bewares of the expression of moral judgments and of bare statements of bare truth or bare logic. He

[37]   See d'Épinay.

avoids leading questions but encourages the patient to talk freely and discursively. He does not argue.

So by degrees an experienced, skillful physician often obtains from a patient's own statements a good understanding of what it is important for him to know.

The procedure of a skillful lawyer is often somewhat similar to that of a doctor, and the law courts or still better the lawyer's office, no less than the consultation room, afford material that will teach a wise man much about the interpretation of what men say. In his interesting book, *The Endless Adventure*,[38] F. S. Oliver has a small chapter on "The Variety of Witnesses." A few quotations from this will be useful:

> The great majority . . . were mindful of their oath to this extent— they were resolved to tell "nothing but the truth." Few, however, were willing to tell "the whole truth." There was nearly always something that a passing honest witness was anxious to keep back. . . . The transparently frank and open witness was much rarer. . . . Then there was the loquacious egotist, whose testimony was a tissue not so much of lies as of illusions. . . . There was the fly-away witness who darted zig-zag like a woodcock. . . . There was the cool and sophisticated witness, unwilling to tell a positive untruth if he could help it; but anxious at the same time to produce a general impression that was false. . . . Then there was the witness . . . whose overmastering desire was to tell the whole truth without omitting a single circumstance that had ever come under his observation, or—if the judge would let him —that he had ever heard tell of.

All this shows very clearly that the interpretation of hearsay is a difficult art, but it is a necessary part of the art of the physician and of the lawyer, and not less of the scientific student of the interactions between persons. One important feature of the skillful practice of this art is clearly illustrated and should be evident in the above quotation. Very often it is not the meaning of the uttered words that is important, but the attitudes and sentiments that they reveal. I repeat; many things—in many circumstances, most things —that men say are neither true nor false;[39] they are expressions of

38   Houghton Mifflin, Boston, 1931, pp. 20–21.
39   See Poincaré.

hopes and fears, of anxieties and obsessions, of likes and dislikes, of aspirations and discouragements.

Experience shows that, like other arts, the art of interpreting or appraising what men say cannot be learned without practice, and unfortunately that practice is not enough, for not everyone can become a good diagnostician, like the good physician, of disease and of the private troubles of men, like the skillful lawyer and competent man of affairs, of the complex situations of everyday life and of the purposes that men try to hide.[40] As Aristotle remarked, politicians rarely succeed in communicating their skill to their own sons. In like manner even some of the best medical students turn out to be mediocre internes in a hospital. But the really good hospital interne goes through a change which is perhaps the most remarkable change that can be observed anywhere in our educational system.

More often than not skillful diagnosticians reach a diagnosis before they are aware, or at any rate conscious, of the grounds that justify their decision. If asked to explain the reasons for the diagnosis, they often clearly show by their behavior that they are obliged to think them out, and that to do so is an awkward task. This is true of doctors, of lawyers, and of men of affairs. It is here cited as one mark of a kind of skill, hardly ever learned except by long practice, that is indispensable in the interpretation of what men say.

One of my colleagues is a professor of medicine who has collaborated in the course "Concrete Sociology" upon which the present book is founded. Not long after he had for the first time read this statement about "snap" diagnosis, the report of a case in his clinic was presented to him by an assistant in the presence of some medical students. He heard the report of the history of the case, of the physical examination, of the symptoms, etc. When it was then suggested that the diagnosis was pulmonary tuberculosis he at once replied: "No, it isn't, it's asthma [of neurotic origin]." Thereupon a student very properly asked: "Dr. X, why do you say that?" And Dr. X, as he later told me, was obliged to pause and

[40]   See Bagehot (I), J. F. Stephen (II).

think for what seemed to him not less than two minutes before he could give his reasons, because before he could give them he had first to find them.

The probability that a diagnosis is correct is less than the probability that a careful deduction from accurate measurements is correct. But when better ways do not avail, experience shows that the conclusions of the skilled diagnostician may be cautiously used with good results even for scientific purposes. Not less important is the fact that practice in diagnosis is a means of becoming thoroughly familiar with the material in which one works and that skill in diagnosis is an unmistakable sign of that familiarity.

One of the principal reasons why Aristotle's criticism of academic teachers of political and social science hits the mark is that those who lead the intellectual life rarely feel the need or the desire to practice the diagnosis of what men mean and wish from what they say. And few social scientists have learned that the relevant question is often not "What does this mean?" but "Why does he say it?"[41] Now what men say makes up such a large part of the crude data of the social sciences that practice in the art of this kind of interpretation is all but an essential part of the professional formation of a social scientist, as it is of a doctor, lawyer, or businessman. To be sure, there are numerous specialties in the social sciences where the importance of this kind of skill is less than it is in general throughout the field. But any social scientist neglects this part of his training at his peril. Indeed, we are here concerned with one implication, in some respects the most important one, of the rule that the social scientist must avoid the intrusion of his own sentiments and skillfully interpret the role of the sentiments of others if he is to be a good workman.

The way in which sentiments and emotions play an important role in what men say may be clearly illustrated by an analysis of language in relation to thinking. Language is the vehicle of thought, and words are chiefly motor habits or symbols which carry the meaning of experiences. A child becomes so emotionally conditioned to the words used in describing experiences that it is

41   See d'Épinay, Calvin, Reinach.

exceedingly difficult for him upon reaching maturity to extricate himself from the emotional accompaniment of his words, whether they relate to religion, politics, the social system, or matters of everyday life.[42] This adds materially to the difficulties confronting the social scientist in thinking objectively and interpreting what other men say.

This may be better understood by contrasting the function of words in everyday communication with their function in scientific writing. In science, words are arbitrary symbols and they are nothing more. Thus, for instance, few chemists remember the derivation of "oxygen," none attaches any scientific importance to it. All this was long ago clearly understood by Galileo, who said:[43]

Note by the way the nature of mathematical definitions which consist merely in the imposition of names or, if you prefer, abbreviations of speech established and introduced in order to avoid the tedious drudgery which you and I now experience simply because we have not agreed to call this surface a "circular band" and that sharp solid portion of the bowl a "round razor." Now call them by what name you please, . . .

It is a well-established induction from experience, thoroughly confirmed by general psychological, physiological and biological considerations, that men are more often moved by passions and prejudices, wishes and strong sentiments, hopes and fears, than by reason.[44] In some ways the most striking evidence that this is so may be found in the contrast between what they say and what they do. On this point, which will be illustrated over and over again in the cases soon to be presented, it is well to consult Bacon on *Idols*, Pareto on *derivations*, and (with due skepticism) the psychoanalytical description of *rationalization*.

The great need for and primary importance of the interpretation of what men say is, then, the characteristic feature of work in the social sciences, at one stage of that work. I have here tried to

[42]   See Bernhardi.
[43]   *Dialogues Concerning Two New Sciences*, Macmillan, New York, 1914, p. 28.
[44]   See Maine (III), Saint-Simon, Gregory of Tours, Richelieu.

present the necessary, if barely sufficient, outline of what one ought to bear in mind in studying cases. A word of comfort for those who are concerned with sociology rather than history may be added. General sociology has to do with uniformities; with recurrent phenomena or, speaking more precisely, with the recurrent features of concrete phenomena; with collections of phenomena, rather than with single events. For this reason the diagnostic task of the general sociologist is less difficult in one respect than that of the historian or of the practitioner of medicine, or law, or business. For example, let us consider medical charlatans. If we study the practice of a supposed individual charlatan, interview him and carefully find out all about what he says and does, we may well be at a loss after all to decide how far the man is a conscious hypocrite and how far he is a sincere crank, and whether he is in fact a charlatan. But if we study not merely one but one hundred supposed charlatans, it may be that the same amount of skill in diagnosis on our part will lead to a far more accurate estimate of the extent to which as a rule hypocrisy, deceit, or self-delusion prevail among such persons and the degree to which supposed charlatans are in fact properly so designated. It is often impossible to find out quickly by inspection whether a particular man is a hypocrite or an honest crank, or is in advance of his fellows, but it is very easy to know that there are charlatans and that both hypocrisy and honest delusions are prevalent among them. Speaking generally, the first problem corresponds to the work of the historian, the second problem to that of the sociologist.

The reader must not be misled by this long discussion of what men say. It is necessary in scientific work to observe *all* kinds of things that can be observed. Among these things are what men say and many other things. The principal features of an event are very often to be looked for among these other things. I have said less about them because methods and procedures for observing them and for interpreting the observations are well known.

Finally, it may be useful to warn against anxiety about or anxious striving for high systematization and rigor. It is the fashion among many social scientists and psychologists to devote much attention to what is called "methodology." This may be in itself a blameless occupation, but I think such discussions are ordinarily a mere nuisance to those whose aim is to get on with scientific work. The position adopted in this book is that we may well judge from experience what procedures are likely to be effective in scientific work. I believe it is an induction that they are of the kind described in this chapter and that elaborate discussions of methods and of logic and the search for rigor are to be noted only in philosophical writing, in the pseudo-sciences, and in the sciences that have reached a high development. There is a fact that should be pondered by social scientists: Before the nineteenth century the methods of the differential and integral calculus were not rigorously analyzed and the treatment of this highly developed part of mathematics was known to be not rigorous. We now have a rigorous calculus, which is in itself an advance in science; yet it has had very little effect upon other things and has but little modified the methods of the calculus. It is ordinarily far more useful to get to work on the phenomena and so acquire familiarity with things than to spend time talking about "methodology" or even to pay too much attention to the analysis of actual methods.

Chapter 2: The Social System

Without a conceptual scheme, thinking seems to be impossible.

The conceptual scheme of everyday thinking is, at least in large part, the common-sense world. Much of this is formed instinctively during infancy and early childhood. An infant playing with its toes seems to be instinctively engaged in *combining* visual sensations, tactile sensations, and bodily sensations arising from movement of the arms and legs, into a conceptual representation of the toes and of other parts of the body. These sensations recur in more or less the same form almost endlessly.

So far as we can judge, the conceptual representation of the toes is something like a *persistent aggregate* formed from these innumerable, physiologically independent but experimentally interconnected, sensations. The toe if seen can be touched, and if touched can be seen. The sensory paths of vision and touch are separate, but the experiences are correlated, and, by the time the infant has reached an age at which it is possible to inquire about his beliefs, the toe is a real object for him, with a fixed relation to the rest of his body, and a continuous existence in time. There is no reason to believe that this conceptual construction of the toe involves what we call reasoning or logic; or indeed any form of verbal or symbolic thinking. It does involve doing and seeing, the formation of many conditioned reflexes, and in the end a conceptual synthesis of these familiar experiences.

We shall presently see that other more or less similar, more or less different, combinations and persistent aggregates are such that they are involved in the interactions between persons. In general, they include not only "image concepts," as Levy-Bruhl calls those constructions that resemble the infant's conceptual construction of his toe, but also "rational concepts" which seem to be impossible without the use of words or symbols and which are often closely associated with the sentiments and the emotions, e.g., justice, truth, beauty.[1] These require careful attention in sociological study.

In general, the conceptual schemes of the sciences are simpler and more clearly defined than our common-sense conceptual schemes. Examples of scientific schemes are: the theory of the constitution of atoms in recent physics, the theory of the constitution of molecules in organic chemistry, Willard Gibbs's physicochemical system, Morgan's theory of the gene, Darwin's theory of evolution. Each of these owes its clearness and simplicity to the fact, among others, that it has reference to a limited class of phenomena, or to certain aspects of phenomena, and to a limited class of problems. Its usefulness depends, among other things, upon the extent to which such limitations permit useful work. Thus Gibbs's system represents the world as made up of physicochemical systems, but excludes from consideration the ordinary phenomena of mechanics, psychological phenomena, and the interactions between persons. Anybody using such a system always knows (or can know) what he is, and what he is not, talking about. Without

[1]   See Gourmont, Huxley.

this kind of aid, very few people know what they are *not* talking about.[2] But to know this is often one of the most important conditions for getting on with a job.

The position that we shall take in this book is that Pareto's social system is in some respect analogous in its usefulness to Gibbs's physicochemical system. This system of Pareto's disregards physical, chemical, and physiological phenomena, but makes possible in some measure the consideration of all interactions between persons. Like Gibbs's system, it is clear and simple.

There seems to be a psychological, if not a logical, advantage when conceptual schemes consist of *things* which have *properties* (or attributes) and *relations*. All the scientific conceptual schemes above mentioned are of this kind, and so is Pareto's generalized social system. We shall use this system because it has these and other more concrete qualities which together make it, in my judgment, the most convenient conceptual scheme now available. Remember that the test of a conceptual scheme is convenience and, in general, nothing else. Remember also that convenience often imposes a certain measure of oversimplification.

The things, or components, of this system are persons. They have properties and relations that vary widely from person to person. They are, in short, heterogeneous, both in their properties and in their relations. Their properties (or attributes) are (1) economic interests, (2) residues, and (3) derivations. Definitions of these terms will follow presently. There are also relations between the several properties of a person and, furthermore, between the properties of related persons.

The properties and relations of persons exist not in a changeless state, but in a state of flux. However, the instantaneous states and the changes are not chaotic or random states and changes. On the contrary, they are in general subject to connections and constraints of a kind that may be referred to, or considered as in a measure determined by, the condition of equilibrium discussed above and defined by Pareto as "a state such that if a small [not too great] modification different from that which will otherwise

2   See Hegel.

occur is impressed upon a system, a reaction will at once appear tending toward the conditions that would have existed if the modification had not been impressed." Cf. Louisville, San Francisco, northern France.

A social system may consist of two or more persons. Moreover, it is peculiarly convenient and perhaps even necessary in sociology as in chemistry to begin the study of systems with those in which the number of components is small. In other words, experience shows that it may be possible and convenient to conceive of two or any greater number of persons as constituting a social system. For example, we have already seen that two sawyers may, for certain restricted purposes, be regarded as making up a social system. So also, for certain purposes such as some cases of divorce, a husband and wife may be satisfactorily considered as the sole components of a social system. But in other cases of divorce, just three persons may make up the components of the system that must be recognized, and in still other cases of divorce it may be practically necessary to take into consideration still larger numbers of persons. For many purposes, a family may be considered as a social system, for others a town, for others a state; and it is not impossible to make some progress with the consideration of the whole world as a single social system. Changing circumstances seem to have led to a great increase in the number of persons who may be effectively thought of as members of a single social system. For Aristotle, the limiting size of the best state, and therefore of a social system in certain of its characteristics, was small. But it is one of the most familiar of observations that today there are interactions between persons extending throughout the world, and in truth few of us are unaware of them.

Accordingly, the choice of the components of a social system is in some slight degree arbitrary, but in the main determined by the nature of the problem that is being investigated and by the hard facts of observation. Similarly, the choice of the components and of the size of a physicochemical system is in some slight degree arbitrary but in most respects subject to like restrictions.

Persons are heterogeneous in their attributes and in their relations, that is to say, they differ, on the one hand, in their economic interests, in their residues, and in their derivations and, on the other hand, in their relations to other persons. The relations to other persons often give rise to a second order of things:[3] more or less durable associations such as families within towns, and labor unions, religious bodies, professional associations, industrial and commercial organizations, etc., within states. The things of the second order are composed of things of the first order (persons). They are, in general, groups of persons which, for certain purposes, may be separately considered as independent social systems, but which for other purposes cannot be so considered. Thus, in general, when a social system consists of more than two persons, it has a heterogeneous structure involving subgroups of persons, as well as the persons (i.e., the ultimate components) who may or may not be members of the subgroups. These subgroups are of such a character that they may be regarded for certain purposes as independent social systems, while for other purposes they cannot be so regarded.

It must be clearly understood that persons are in general members of many subgroups or organizations,[4] and it may be well to bear in mind a rough and in many respects incomplete physical analogy: As a molecule of water in a flask is now present in the liquid water and later in the air above the liquid, and again in the liquid, so a person is only intermittently a member in action of any group. This analogy is incomplete, especially because, while a molecule of water is in the air we can find no effect of its previous presence in the liquid, a person carries with him the effects of his past activities (hysteresis) and is influenced by the prospective return to those other activities. There is one further useful aspect of this analogy as a means of fixing our ideas (which is perhaps the only useful role of analogies in scientific thinking). The liquid water persists while molecules enter and leave it, and if the conditions are appropriate, it persists without change of mass. In like manner, some activities of some organizations such as the police patrol, the telephone exchange, and many continuous processes

3   See van Gennep.
4   See Barnard.

in industrial chemistry, metallurgy, etc., persist while the personnel changes from time to time in shifts. All this is "obvious" and is frequently forgotten.

Consideration of the groups and the organizations comprised within a social system is often of far greater importance than study of the ultimate component individuals. In like manner, study of the organs and tissues of the human body is often more important than study of the cells, or study of the cells than study of their chemical components. Note well that there is no reason to attach either more or less importance to persons because they are the ultimate components of the social system. In like manner, hemoglobin is, in general, neither more nor less "important" than the liver, but either may be negligible in a study involving the other. Such things are more or less important, as the case may be. Thus the liver may be more important in a case of cancer, hemoglobin in a case of anemia.

Note carefully that the subgroups of a social system, like the system itself, are different things than the sum of the component persons. So also hemoglobin is a different thing than the sum of its constituent atoms, the liver a different thing than the sum of its constituent molecules, and a man is a different thing than the sum of his organs, tissues, and fluids.

Again, note that, in general, subgroups and systems alike persist though their component persons change. This is obvious in the nation and in the village, it was formerly equally so in the family, but it may be noted almost everywhere: in churches, universities, industrial corporations, clubs, political parties, and innumerable other instances. In like manner, the component molecules of a living organism are constantly changing, but the organism persists. So it is, again, with the flame of a candle,—the time-honored analogy in this respect, to a living organism. Such enduring systems and subgroups have marked individual peculiarities which are often quite as striking as those of individual organisms; in short, they too are heterogeneous.

Finally, note that, speaking loosely, organizations, like all societies, modify the behavior of their constituent persons and that they do so far beyond the limits of anything that may be conceived as functional activity of the individual in his place as a member of the organization.[5] More often than not, men are greatly modified through membership in a well-established organization, so much so that one may say figuratively that they partake of its "individuality" and that their whole conduct is more or less influenced by its "ideals," "traditions," and "standards."

We need not take the trouble to define the economic interests, because it will suffice for the moment to say that the economic interests are what the science of economics, in the narrow sense of the term "economics," is concerned with. But they must on no account be forgotten.

The words "residue" and "derivation" are two technical terms invented by Pareto in order to escape the tricks that old terms can play. A residue is a manifestation of a sentiment. Nothing is implied by this term as to the nature of psychological states or processes, least of all that "a sentiment" is an elementary thing for a psychologist. From a physiological standpoint such a notion would seem absurd. A sentiment may be said to be a hypothetical state of an organism. Note well that we do not observe sentiments, just as we do not observe physical forces. What we observe are phenomena that we interpret theoretically as manifestations of sentiments or as manifestations of physical forces. The interactions between A and B, in so far as we interpret them as involving the sentiments, proceed as follows: A manifests his sentiments. B observes these manifestations. B's sentiments are activated or otherwise modified, and the resulting activations or modifications are manifested by B and perceived by A. Thus in the social system manifestations of sentiments may be conveniently regarded as determinants, just as the sentiments themselves may be conveniently regarded as determinants. For most purposes, indeed, it is nearly a matter of indifference whether we use sentiments or manifestations of sentiments in our conceptual scheme. But it is, nevertheless, of the very first importance to remember that for the scientific investigator, as for a component person in a social system, mani-

5   See Barnard, Edwards, Mommsen, Weber, Taine, Voltaire, Boyle, Paracelsus.

festations of sentiments are the observed phenomena. Finally, to speak a little more precisely, the residues are those relatively simple uniformities that are observed in a large number of phenomena and that we interpret as manifestations of sentiments. We could perhaps never find residues without the utterances of men, but in finding them we make use of the words that men utter and also of their other actions.

Sometimes the residues are not explicitly indicated by words because a person is not even aware of the sentiments. Thus many hypochondriacs act and talk *as if* everything not perfectly safe were dangerous, many young men *as if* everything not completely successful were a failure. For convenience, one may say that such persons manifest these sentiments, but one must be careful not to suppose that they are aware of them, for often they are not. In such cases the residues may be said to be descriptions of attitudes or of uniformities in attitudes.

A derivation is a nonlogical argument, explanation, assertion, appeal to authority, or association of ideas or sentiments in words.

It is useful to distinguish (A) derivations that can be put to the test of observation or experiment and (B) those that cannot be so tested.

Class A includes such derivations as these:

All planetary motion is circular motion.

The year 1908 will become memorable as marking the final revolt of humanity against that unspeakable stain upon civilization, vivisection. [Mrs. Fiske]

. . . the chaise leaning forward was an ease to the horses . . . the contrary would kill them. [Cited by Franklin]

In each prolonged misfortune of the Republic, whose story now reaches back more than a century and a half, historians have identified a definite episode which banished fear and aroused a national will to victory. [Grey]

. . . there must be a particular seat and fountain, a kind of home and hearth, where the cherisher of nature, the original of the native fire, is stored and preserved . . . [Harvey]

The bourgeois sees in his wife a mere instrument of production. [Marx and Engels]

National differences, and antagonisms between peoples, are daily more and more vanishing . . . [Marx and Engels]

. . . members of the Communist Party, who in all capitalist countries, Latin, Slavonic, Anglo-Saxon, are being imprisoned, tortured and murdered every day. [Needham]

You cannot so much as feel the difference . . . between two tendencies of line . . . but by your own dignity of character. [Ruskin]

. . . the religious "Hymn in honor of the Creator," to which Galen so gladly lent his voice, and in which the best physiologists of succeeding times have ever joined . . . [Whewell]

In one sense of the word "absurd," that employed in geometry for example, these derivations are absurd. They have been or can be disproved by observation, experiment, and strict logic. But even then it is possible to say, "Credo quia absurdum" (Because it is absurd, I believe it), or with Tertullian, "Certum est quia impossibile est" (It is certain because it is impossible),[6] and these are Class B derivations.

Class B includes such derivations as these:

Beauty is truth, truth beauty.

God made use of the Assyrians and of the Babylonians, to punish this people [the people of God] . . . [Bossuet]

The communion of the Church was not instituted to be a chain to bind us in idolatry, impiety, ignorance of God, and other kinds of evil, but rather to retain us in the fear of God and obedience of the truth. [Calvin]

Play the man, Master Ridley; we shall this day light such a candle, by God's grace, in England, as I trust shall never be put out. [Latimer]

> This royal throne of kings, this sceptred isle,
> This earth of majesty, this seat of Mars,
> This other Eden, demi-paradise,
> This fortress built by Nature for herself
> Against infection and the hand of war,
> This happy breed of men, this little world,
> This precious stone set in the silver sea,
> Which serves it in the office of a wall
> Or as a moat defensive to a house,

[6]   De Carne Christi, 5.

Against the envy of less happier lands,
This blessed plot, this earth, this realm, this England.

(Richard II, Act II, Sc. 1)

Now we understand why other peoples pursue us with their hatred. They do not understand us, but they are sensible of our enormous spiritual superiority. So the Jews were hated in antiquity because they were the representatives of God on earth. [Sombart]

These derivations are not absurd in the sense above specified; they are meaningless in the sense of "meaningless" now current in physics. They cannot be proved or disproved by observation, experiment, and strict logic, for they contain words and phrases that lead us out of the bounds of observation and experiment.

Unfortunately the words "absurd" and "meaningless," here used in a technical sense, act upon the sentiments of most people so that the above statements are likely to fail of their purpose. This is an instance of an important kind of interaction between persons. It suggests the usefulness of inventing new words for scientific purposes. Perhaps therefore the following remarks are more to the point. Class A derivations are (except by chance) untrue in the sense that they are not in accord with observation and experiment. For many persons they often express a "higher truth." Class B derivations involve something—beauty, God, a candle (in the figurative sense), this sceptred isle, enormous spiritual superiority—that at least for the present makes observation and experiment impossible. In short, something can be done, that the author of the derivation has not done, to test Class A derivations; Class B derivations cannot for the present be tested.

It should be carefully noted that Class B derivations are necessary to, that is largely constitutive of, theology, philosophy, oratory, poetry, and other forms of expression, and that scientific procedures can neither prove nor disprove them. This is a good illustration of the fact that derivations are useful and when used appropriately not only indispensable but unobjectionable in everyday life. On the other hand, Class A derivations are always liable to attack on logical and scientific grounds. Very often the mere passage of time makes their absurdity evident, as above in the case of the quotation from Mrs. Fiske and the second quotation from Marx and Engels.

Residues and derivations are found in the verbal utterances and the accompanying actions of men. They are obtained from the concrete phenomena by analysis and abstraction. We need an example. Here is one: Christians now practice baptism to efface sin. The ancients used lustral water for ceremonial purifications. Others have similarly used blood or other substances, and there are innumerable practices, with no common physical features, known to anthropologists that are believed or felt to restore the integrity of an individual when it has been injured by the violation of a taboo. In these phenomena two sentiments, among others, are manifested: the sentiment of integrity of the individual and the sentiment that actions favorable to this integrity can be performed. These manifestations are residues. They may be conceived as the residuum left after the variable features, such as the use of water, blood, and many other things, have been put aside. But the phenomena do also include the endless variety of ritual practices and the no less various explanations of them. These explanations are derivations. They may be conceived as derived from the sentiments that find expression as residues.

Another way of explaining Pareto's analysis of the residues in this example is as follows: (1) A large number of social phenomena involving baptism, the use of lustral water, various other rites, etc., are observed. (2) Certain uniformities, i.e., the residues, are distinguished from the many variable features of the phenomena. (3) It is then found that these otherwise various actions of men may be theoretically explained by the statement: In so far as these uniformities are concerned, men act *as if* they were actuated by a feeling of the integrity of the individual and by a feeling that when this integrity is injured something may be done to restore it. In like manner, Kepler discovered certain uniformities in the movements of the planets and Newton showed that these uniformities (Kepler's laws) may be theoretically explained by the statement: Planets move *as if* they were actuated by a force (gravitation) that varies directly as the masses and inversely as the square of the distance.

Theology and metaphysics and parts of law consist, in great measure, of systematic and extensive derivations from certain very important residues like those involving the words justice, duty, sanctity, and absolute.[7] Some of these residues are not only important, but very useful, and probably necessary for the survival of a society. The complexes of psychoanalysis, or strictly speaking the manifestations of the complexes, include another important group of residues. A rationalization is one kind of derivation.

The importance of residues far exceeds the importance of derivations. This is implied by the method of obtaining these abstractions, for, in general, that which is common to many phenomena is more important than that which is less frequent or more variable.

The residues change slowly,[8] the derivations rapidly. For example, the instinct of conformity involves a sentiment that is widely manifested as a residue. This is relatively constant. The endlessly varied actions that constitute following fashion and the no less varied explanations that accompany them and depend upon this and other residues (those associated with good taste, beauty, dignity, standing in the community, etc.) change rapidly. Such explanations are derivations. Note also that there are ordinarily fashions in derivations—often very marked fashions—ranging all the way from slang words and phrases to the forms of expression of the most serious matters.[9]

The derivations may be considered as determined, in general and to a first approximation, by the residues. This is illustrated by a familiar phenomenon, involving what Pareto calls the logic of the sentiments, namely, the determination of the premises by the conclusion. For instance, a boy wishes to persuade his father to buy an automobile. He presents a reason; this is refuted as invalid; then another; this is shown to be inconsistent with the father's sentiments; and so on until he succeeds, or abandons the attempt in despair or under compulsion. In like manner some conservatives find reasons—as many as they please—for opposing any change, some liberals for supporting any humanitarian pur-

[7]   See Lessing, Pollock, Nietzsche.
[8]   See Hippocrates, Gregory the Great, Cambon, Disraeli.
[9]   See Bernhardi, Molière.

pose, some radicals for promoting any enterprise that seeks to destroy existing institutions, while some intellectuals just "go on talking" about anything. This phrase[10] is from Bernard Shaw, who frequently illustrates the point by his own actions. Such conduct in one way or another is one of the commonest forms of human behavior.

The exhibition of the residues, no less than eating, drinking, or breathing, may be recognized as a major function of the human organism. It is therefore necessary to take note that the role of the residues (or of the sentiments that they manifest) is at least as important as the role of the logical activities of men. Indeed nearly everything that is accounted noblest and best, and also worst, in the actions of men depends upon (i.e., is a function of) residues. Vaguely recognized, this is no doubt one of the most widely known rules of worldly wisdom. What Pareto has done is to introduce a clear discrimination and a precise statement into a systematic treatment of the complex phenomena, to separate the residues from both logical and pseudological elaborations, to demonstrate that they are of the first importance in the social system, and, in particular, that their importance is in no way diminished, but rather increased, by their independence of logic.

Judging by the evidence, it appears that the residues have ordinarily preceded the derivations in the historical sequence.[11] The residues of religion have often preceded the derivations of theology; the residues of justice, personal integrity, the welfare of the community, etc., have sometimes preceded the formation of these abstractions or the formulation of laws and of legal concepts and fictions, and in like manner customary law, which sometimes found its first expression in rationalized precepts, in rules of conduct, or in common law, was later codified in statutes. The residues concerning responsibility to the family and the community, of justice, of morality, of kindness and fair play, preceded these abstractions and the systematic derivations of ethics; many of them, indeed, occur in the actions of animals where all verbal concepts seem to be absent.

10   "Man and Superman," Act III, the last speech.
11   See Maine (I), Bagehot (III), Homer, Senac de Meilhen, Sumner.

Not infrequently residues are expressions of sentiments that accompany fairly simple conditioned reflexes.[12] Then they may involve little symbolic thinking and sometimes, so far as we can see, almost none. In such cases the derivations are obviously, at least in part, rationalizations derived from the sentiments. Thus problems of the "unconscious" arise for the psychologists.

Note well, therefore, the truism that sentiments are not constituents of any form of symbolic thinking, verbal or otherwise. Of course, they often accompany symbolic thinking, and, as in the case of the boy above cited, determine its general character. It is names or symbols of sentiments that occur in symbolic thinking.[13] In general, such names and symbols are already derivations, and it is a characteristic of such names that they are, in general, vague and therefore unsuitable for the purposes of clear thinking. This is what led the late Justice Holmes to say: "I have said to my brethren many times that I hate justice, which means that I know if a man begins to talk about that, for one reason or another he is shirking thinking in legal terms."[14]

These peculiarities of the names of the sentiments, and of the other manifestations of the sentiments, add greatly to the difficulty of distinguishing, characterizing, and classifying the residues, as well as to the difficulties of diagnosis in the study of concrete social phenomena. So far as we can see, these difficulties are, for the present, unavoidable.

The separate abstract conceptual entities of Pareto's scheme, the social system, are, then, (1) persons; (2) heterogeneity, involving (a) differences in persons, (b) more or less permanent relations between persons, and (c) more or less permanent organizations, etc.; (3) economic interests; (4) residues; and (5) derivations. To these it seems necessary to add (6) science[15] and (7) logic.

---

12   See Reinach, Lewis.
13   See Tooke.
14   *Justice Oliver Wendell Holmes: His Book Notices and Uncollected Letters and Papers.* Edited by Harry C. Shriver, New York, 1936, p. 201.
15   See The Record of the Royal Society . . . , Mallet du Pan.

The term "science" is here used to include not only what ordinarily passes as natural science but also the relatively sound, trustworthy, objective knowledge that skilled workmen have of the things and processes of their craft and that everybody possesses, more or less, concerning some of the concrete objects that surround him and some of the processes in which these things are involved, for example, where to post a letter, or how to put on a shoe. Accordingly, "science" is to be contrasted with "residue."

The term "logic" calls for no comment; it is used in the ordinary sense of an elementary treatise. "Logic" takes its place in contrast to "derivation." Note that logic and derivations may be mixed in any proportions.

The absence of the explicit recognition of science and logic in Pareto's abstract development of the social system is due, as he says, to the belief that he has dealt sufficiently, to a first approximation, with these aspects of the social system, in writing his treatises on economics where their role is important. It is also probably dependent upon the fact that he was anxious to emphasize the overwhelming importance, relatively, of what he calls nonlogical actions, as contrasted with logical actions, in nearly all human affairs except those that are economic, and a few others like the work of applied scientists. This conclusion of Pareto's is contrary to the traditional, intellectual interpretation of history and human affairs. But, as I have already said, it is well-grounded in psychology and biology so that it seems today hardly open to question. However, if we are not to exclude the economic activities of men, we must add science and logic to the other factors with which Pareto's social system is concerned, not forgetting, however, that our upbringing and our education predispose us to overestimate their importance in most things. It may even be argued that the development of modern advertising, especially in this country, shows that Pareto himself overestimated the importance of science and logic in many of the strictly economic activities of men.

The following statement, kindly contributed by a man of affairs, should be a great aid to the understanding of this difficult question of the place of nonlogic in concrete economic matters:

I have recently been serving as chairman of a special committee at a bank to recommend the policy of the bank with reference to the purchase of automobile installment paper in large amounts from one of our clients which does a very extensive business in this kind of paper. It is of two kinds: retail paper, being notes of the individual purchaser of automobiles; and wholesale paper, being the notes of distributors secured by cars in stock. The volume of this business fluctuates considerably by seasons, especially the wholesale paper. It was our opinion that the amount of the bank's purchases of this paper from our client should be so limited that aggregates should not exceed four or five million dollars at any time, and we were asking our client to make arrangements to place the balance, amounting to several million dollars, with other banks.

In discussing the matter with him, he made it clear that it was necessary for him to have enough flexibility in his arrangements so that he could finance easily the peak requirements. His statement was as follows: "The individual dealer operates in connection with us as do bank depositors in relation to their banks—*almost exclusively on the basis of habit.* They make almost no intelligent discrimination within wide limits between the different purveyors of credit. If I am unable to take care of all their business as they offer it to me—so that they are obliged to secure some of their credit from others—the effect is to destroy the habit of doing business with me. My inability to take care of all their requirements, no matter how easy it would be for them to secure additional credit from others, would have the effect of terminating all relations with me. This is precisely the situation so often experienced in the case of depositors. They are governed not at all by what you might think to be intelligent self-interest but almost exclusively by the feeling of comfort, satisfaction, and security that comes from habitual relationships."

Yesterday I attended a meeting of the salary committee of the X Insurance Company in connection with the discussion of a proposed change of status of one of the second-line officers. The president had occasion to refer to the importance of inspirational and other supervisory effort in increasing the production of the salesmen of life insurance. In this connection he said: "It may be a matter of considerable surprise to you to know that beyond any question of doubt the earnings of these agents depend very largely upon the efficiency of the supervisory organization in stimulating their efforts notwithstanding that their compensation depends exclusively on their accomplishments, since they are paid only a commission on sales actually made. It is entirely probable that without such stimulation—emphasis upon competitive standing, inspirational work in general, and direct criticism of failures—their earnings would average at least one-third less than they now do, notwithstanding that they are fully aware that the pecuniary results of their work depend entirely upon what they produce."

This is an interesting confirmation of the view that pecuniary incentives are quite inadequate to secure what is regarded as appropriate effort in the absence of numerous other incentives of a nonpecuniary or nonmaterial character. While I have not come across any good confirmation as respects piece-rate payments to factory employees, I have no doubt that I shall get such confirmation. I have had some experience in attempting to introduce a piece-rate or bonus system of remuneration where increased emphasis upon pecuniary rewards had the result of minimizing other incentives to the extent that the increased pecuniary incentive was not even an offset.

I have little doubt that both the men quoted above, if approached directly on the question of the importance of pecuniary rewards in general, would confirm the current misunderstanding on this subject; and if then challenged by the contradiction to what they had previously said, as quoted above, would reply that the instances I have stated related to very special conditions and were not general. I think there may be a clue here to one of the difficulties of the social sciences. Practical men in their general intellectual statements are almost entirely governed, without knowing it, by the climate of opinion in economic matters which stems from the vague diffusion of the postulates of standard economic theories. They almost invariably regard the particular concrete problems which they are handling as exceptional cases quite unlikely to be experienced by other men of affairs, and are quite unaware that, except in secondary respects, they are dealing with conditions that are common and very general.

A similar conclusion arises from researches conducted in the Hawthorne plant of the Western Electric Company:[16]

The results from the different inquiries provided considerable material for the study of financial incentive. None of the results, how-

---

[16]   *Management and the Worker*, by F. J. Roethlisberger and W. J. Dickson, Harvard University Press, Cambridge, 1939, pp. 575–576.

ever, gave the slightest substantiation to the theory that the worker is primarily motivated by economic interest. The evidence indicated that the efficacy of a wage incentive is so dependent on its relation to other factors that it is impossible to separate it out as a thing in itself having an independent effect. The studies provided examples of a number of situations in which the wage incentive had either lost its power to motivate or functioned differently than is frequently assumed. . . .

In the Bank Wiring Observation Room a wage plan particularly designed to appeal to the employees' monetary interests failed to work as it should because it was not in line with the dominant social values of the situation.

Pareto's social system conforms to the classical type of a scientific conceptual scheme. Thus (1), as we have seen, it involves things, properties, and relations. (2) It is constructed with the help of several very broad inductions, such as the inductions that the actions of men are in great part nonlogical, and dependent upon residues (or the underlying sentiments), that what men say about most things is not logical, that no two persons are alike and that no two persons stand in the same relations to others, and so on. (3) It limits analysis to a sufficiently small number of classes of abstractions so that it is tolerably manageable. (4) The terms involved are at least relatively unambiguous. At all events, Pareto has made serious efforts to make them clear and precise.

Now that the system is before us, it is evident that in so far as it works it should be applicable to all instances of interactions between persons. Accordingly, it should be in like measure suitable for the purposes of this book, which is designed to exhibit some of the uniformities, present and historical, in the interactions between persons that are common to all human affairs: private life, business, the practice of the professions, politics, and government. In a measure we have already done this by describing the system.

HISTORICAL UNIFORMITIES

At this point it will be well, once for all, to dispose of, or at least to come to an understanding about, the famous question of historical uniformities. Those who say, as many historians do, that there are no such things as historical uniformities either refuse to recognize as the business of the historian the kind of uniformities with which, for instance, Hippocrates and all other physicians are concerned, or else they refuse to recognize them as uniformities. Whether these uniformities are called uniformities of experience or historical uniformities is a question of words. Let us not quarrel about words, but look at facts.

First, it is beyond dispute that such close approximation to identity as we observe in the phenomenon of, say, the recurrent phases of the moon are at least excessively rare in the events that are the business of historians. But now let us look at a passage from Thucydides cited by Brinton:[17]

And revolution brought upon the cities of Hellas many terrible calamities, such as have been and always will be while human nature remains the same. . . . When troubles had once begun in the cities, those who followed carried the revolutionary spirit further and further, and determined to outdo the report of all who had preceded them by the ingenuity of their enterprises and the atrocity of their revenges. The meaning of words had no longer the same relation to things, but was changed by them as they thought proper. Reckless daring was thought to be loyal courage; prudent delay was the excuse of a coward; moderation was the disguise of unmanly weakness; to know everything was to do nothing. Frantic energy was the true quality of a man. . . . The lover of violence was always trusted, and his opponent suspected. He who succeeded in a plot was deemed knowing, but a still greater master in craft was he who detected one. On the other hand, he who plotted from the first to have nothing to do with plots was a breaker-up of parties and a poltroon who was afraid of the enemy.

There is reason to conjecture that this and similar passages in Thucydides may be due in part to the influence of contemporary medical thought and even of Hippocrates himself.

Confirmation of this statement of Thucydides may be found in many other places and times. For instance, Cardinal de Retz,

17   Thucydides, III, 82 (Jowett's translation), in Brinton, Crane, *A Decade of Revolution*, New York, Harper and Bros., 1934, p. 302.

speaking of the Fronde,[18] refers to "the extravagance of such times, when all the stupid become fools and when the most sensible cannot speak or not wisely."

Do we not find here plain statements of uniformities in events, or if you object to this use of the word "uniformity," do we not find plain statements of recurrent aspects of phenomena—peculiarities of the actions and of the utterances of men in times of civil strife? Are not these recurrent aspects clearly enough described to be useful to some historians? Do they not resemble certain recurrent signs and symptoms of a disease like pulmonary tuberculosis in the extent of their variability and of their constancy? Is it not well that some historians should try to discover and to describe, as Thucydides did, such recurrent aspects of phenomena? And, resolving once for all not to engage in disputes about words, may we not leave the further discussion of this question to the philosophers? Let others call them what they will, or what they feel they must, we shall seek out and study the recurrent aspects of phenomena. Others may dispute about the name, meanwhile we shall study the thing.

I think there is room for one further observation, because it may be helpful. Look at certain comedies of Molière, for example, *Le Bourgeois Gentilhomme, L'Avare, Tartuffe, Le Misanthrope.* Are not the title roles almost devoid of personality? However unlike the abstractions of a philosopher they may be, are they not in a measure abstractions, in other words, the embodiment of uniformities that Molière has observed or divined (i.e., diagnosed) in living men? Are not some of these uniformities just residues, neither more nor less?

Now consider the scenes of these plays. In a sense, are they not sometimes, even frequently, abstract rather than concrete? Are they not rather the representation of certain uniformities observed and still observable in the lives of men than the presentation of imaginary personal experiences of the characters?

Molière, like Thucydides, was a great diagnostician. Diagnosis is impossible without knowledge and familiarity of and with the

[18]   Quoted in Sainte-Beuve, Causeries du Lundi, V, p. 193.

uniformities in events. Where Thucydides differs from Molière is that he was a conscious diagnostician. This is shown by his explicit statement:[19]

> The lack of legend in what I write will perhaps appear rather un-attractive; but I shall be content if it is judged useful by all who shall wish to see the precise shape of things which happened and of things which in accordance with human nature will happen again in such or in a similar form.

THE PURPOSE OF THE BOOK

One more step toward defining the business of this book may now be taken. We are to study concrete cases with the help of a conceptual scheme—the social system—and we are to search the cases for uniformities, present and past, social and historical, using the conceptual scheme for this purpose. Let no one suppose, how-ever, that our success will be measured by the number of uni-formities we shall find. We are to be engaged not in research, but in practice. The purpose of the book is professional formation, not discovery. Speaking a little more precisely, the purpose is to con-tribute to that part of the professional formation of historians, of political and social scientists, of practitioners of the professions, and of men of affairs that is or may be common to the professional formation of all such persons, because the medium in which they all work is, speaking very generally, a common medium. For, as we have noted, they are all concerned with interactions between persons.

This book is what it is because certain persons among those who have been interested in its preparation have reached a com-mon accord. They agree that we already possess the beginnings of a science of general sociology, in other words, of a science of the more general aspects of the interactions between persons. They agree that this science is in a very early, not to say primitive state, that its generalizations are few and that they consist, in large part, of very rough approximations. They also agree that the conceptual scheme is far from complete. They believe, nevertheless, that such

[19]   Thucydides Op. cit., 22.

as it is, this science is useful. They believe this because they have themselves experienced its usefulness.

History shows that it is often the early advances in the development of a science which are most useful in economizing thought and effort, in fixing ideas, in orienting attention and in limiting analysis to the consideration of factors that are few enough to be manageable. (This is an instance of an historical uniformity.) Such is the principal usefulness of general sociology in its primitive stage. It enables a man who has previously been unable to think effectively about many familar experiences to begin to think about them effectively. Even the mere ability to give a class-name, belonging to a well-chosen system of classification, to an individual thing or event or to some attribute of a thing is often a great help. Consider, for instance, the utility of the diagnosis "cow" or "bull" for a man in a field, "typhoid bacillus" or "colon bacillus" for a doctor, "residue" or "derivation" for the British Foreign Office studying a speech of Mussolini's or Hitler's.

But history also shows that it is more often the highly developed sciences that can be effectively and systematically applied. However, Professor Elton Mayo makes the following comment:

As a general rule a science comes into being more or less as a product of well-developed technical skill in a given area of activity. Someone attempts to make explicit the assumptions that are implicit in the skill itself. This marks the beginning of logico-experimental method. The assumptions once made explicit can be logically developed; the development leads to experimental changes of practice and so to the beginning of a science. This is not quite the situation with respect to the study of society. Historically speaking, there have been times when a very high degree of skill in the handling of human affairs was concentrated in a few leaders. The social groups of which this was true were small by comparison with modern communities. The somewhat uneven development of science, industry, and social life generally since the end of the eighteenth century has produced a situation in which specialisms are well handled, but real leadership has fallen into abeyance. I take it that it is more or less as a consequence of this that the mere possession of a conceptual scheme for social study is at present of such immense use to its possessor. The practical benefit of developing such an attitude as that described in these three lectures is so great as to be out of all proportion to the actual difference involved. The conceptual scheme in practice takes the form of prescribing categorically the various aspects of a social situation which must be inspected before action is taken. If it were nothing else, this would be an enormous protection against prejudice, against a too easy acceptance of current descriptions of the situation. This development of method has been responsible for all the recent changes of procedure in handling people in a large industrial plant.

In its present stage general sociology otherwise admits a few applications and of hardly any systematic applications. Its classifications may sometimes be practically useful, as just noted, but we can as yet hardly imagine a time when there will be an applied sociology comparable with, say, applied mechanics. Accordingly, the professional formation that we aim at is professional formation in the knowledge and use of the pure science of sociology. In the main, the applications of pure sociology are limited to the applications of the system of classification (i.e., to the systematic use of the factors into which the social system is analyzed) and to the application of single theorems, for example, those mentioned in the first chapter. In a word, general sociology bears somewhat the same relation to the work of the historian, or of the political scientist or of the man of affairs, that chemistry bore about a century ago to the work of the physician.

Young men whose bent is intellectual often feel that the only studies worthy of their attention are those like mathematics and physics that deal with high abstractions, or those like philosophy that deal with noble sentiments, or those like politics that deal with great affairs. Such attitudes have no logico-experimental foundation and their various expressions include derivations varying widely like all derivations, but always manifesting certain sentiments such as self-esteem(integrity of the individual) or that complex of inferiority of which the psychoanalysts have made so much (again integrity of the individual), as well as the need for the development of logic or pseudo-logic which is the motive of a great part of our intellectual activity. Another residue that may be frequently observed associated with these is that of the lust for knowledge, which theologians have sometimes thought one of the worst of sins and which, for all I know, may be for the Freudians just one aspect of the all-embracing libido.

The disadvantages of harboring such sentiments are revealed by the experience of the medical profession. For the doctor the excretory organs and functions are in general neither more nor less important than the "organ of thought" and thought itself. Either may be important or unimportant as the case may be. This is because for the doctor observation, experiment and logic come first and afford no ground for the distinction between higher and lower, nobler and baser phenomena or subjects.

Now the study of those features of the interactions between persons that occur very widely or generally in human affairs must evidently be concerned with very common or vulgar phenomena. It must also involve the methodical consideration of much that to many persons seems trivial because it is not considered high or noble. Further it must require the constant or repetitive use of familiar, obvious propositions in a manner that must sometimes seem over-meticulous and pedantic. But obvious things are often important, familiarity is often a cause for overlooking things, nothing, as I have said, is trivial but feeling (note the residue) makes it so, common things are often the uniformities, and in order to make a successful analysis or synthesis it is necessary to take account of the necessary factors and to do so in the necessary way. For deciding whether something is scientifically necessary, experience shows that observation, experiment, logic, or perhaps most often trial and error are the tests. The fact that somebody thinks it vulgar or trivial or obvious is irrelevant, and unless he is a qualified investigator so also is his opinion that it is unimportant.

Some readers may feel that I have at times needlessly emphasized the obvious, and at other times overelaborated an analysis. Bearing this in mind, I now declare that the reader should accept *provisionally* what I have set forth, fix it in his mind, and judge it only at the end of the book. Everything that I have said is, in my opinion, necessary, or at least useful, for the present purposes; it is founded upon experience and has been formulated with care.

Recently Talcott Parsons has shown[21] that the elements of Pareto's social system (including science and logic) are those, neither more nor less, upon which from the time of Hobbes modern political, social, and economic thought converges as the necessary and provisionally sufficient set of variables for analytical purposes. In particular, Parsons finds, in the cases of Durkheim, Marshall, and Max Weber, that when implicit factors in the work of these men have been made explicit, when omitted factors, whose absence can be shown to involve serious insufficiency, have been added, and when metaphysical factors or procedures, whose use can be shown to be scientifically unsound, have been eliminated, the result is in every case the same: they all use a set of terms, variables or concepts (call them what you will) substantially identical except for verbal differences with the seven terms that we have adopted. This statement needs to be enlarged, in order to avoid misunderstanding, with a single qualifying remark. Within certain narrow limits the terms of Pareto's conceptual scheme may be interchanged with certain others which in Pareto's scheme are secondary, or, strictly speaking, dependent variables. For example, the term "norm," which in Pareto's scheme is the name of a secondary or dependent variable, that is to say, something that can be defined by taking account of the definitions and fundamental theorems, is in other conceptual schemes the name of a primary factor or independent variable. However, the difference thus arising is merely formal (or logical). It is a kind of difference, common in the sciences, that is well understood by logicians. It depends upon the fact that in this instance it happens to be possible, within limits, to choose those variables which shall be regarded as the independent variables. Once this choice has been made, the other variables become dependent variables. In mathematics this is generally possible. For example, $y = ax + b$ expresses y as the variable dependent upon the independent variable x, but the equation is easily transformed into $x = \dfrac{y}{a} - \dfrac{b}{a}$ in which the roles of the two

[20]   See Maine (II). (Editor's note: The Henderson manuscript has no referent for this footnote.)
[21]   *The Structure of Social Action*, New York, 1937.

variables are reversed. In other fields, arbitrary choice of the independent variables is less generally possible, or convenient; for instance it is inconvenient to regard time as a dependent variable, in spite of the fact that mathematically one can write for $v = g_t + v_o$, $t = \dfrac{v}{g} - \dfrac{v_o}{g}$. Even this is not always true. If you are traveling from Boston to New York on the three o'clock train you may be pretty safe in saying when the train leaves Providence, "It is (about) four o'clock."

Chapter 3: The Use of the Conceptual Scheme

How shall we use this conceptual scheme? First, we must bear it in mind continuously. Secondly, we must cleave to it, abandoning to the best of our ability all other conflicting habits or ways of thinking. Nevertheless, thirdly, we must try to use it only in so far as we can do so conveniently and effectively. Here is a difficulty, for it must be evident that you are as yet unprepared to make free and easy use of Pareto's generalized social system. Indeed, you are faced with an awkward dilemma, which is no less awkward because it is common in the study of almost every science. In order to do your work most effectively, mastery of the conceptual scheme is necessary. But this is impossible until you have effectively done the work or in some other way, *by practice*, learned to use, or in better phrase formed the habit of using, the conceptual scheme. In short, you need intuitive familiarity with the scheme.

Accordingly you must, in the study of excerpts and cases, use the conceptual scheme in a very simple way, thus by practice slowly acquiring easy familiarity with, if not mastery of, its principal features. Then in the end you should return to the introduction, utilizing your newly acquired familiarity with facts and with the scheme as an aid in more thoroughgoing analysis.

I hold that your method in studying events that come to your notice, the cases of Part III, or the excerpts of Part II, in so far as they represent complex phenomena, should be as follows:

First, you should look for a group or groups of persons who

can be effectively regarded, bearing in mind the nature of the case, as constituting one or more social systems.

Secondly, you should look for what seem to be the important attributes of the system under the classification: heterogeneous structure, economic interests, residues, derivations, science and logic.

Thirdly, you should look for relations between these elements. Note that some of the relations will be manifest in the heterogeneous structure of the system.

Fourthly, you should look for interactions between persons.

Fifthly, you should look for changes, in particular for changes that seem to be attributable to the state of equilibrium.

Sixthly, you should look for uniformities from case to case.

Finally, in almost every case, however simple, you should give particular attention to residues and derivations. These are the elements with which you are probably least familiar and they are as often as not those that call for the greatest attention.

In doing all this, it is well to be pretty methodical: it is not well to be overanxious, to persist too long in the face of bewilderment (you must press on as best you may), or to try to be exhaustive in your analysis. Nobody ever analyzed exhaustively the kind of case that you will study, or for that matter any concrete event. Remember that a little success, and a little more, and then greater success lead to a stage when, often quite suddenly, one feels at home in the use of a conceptual scheme. Too much effort delays the process, which is like learning to swim.

The effective use of this scheme is like swimming in that, as a rule, it is more or less unconscious. Nobody was ever master of the use of a tool, physical or mental, who constantly asked himself, "What am I doing?" or "What shall I do next?" Do you know what you are doing when you talk? Do you foresee the end of a sentence when you begin it? There are few differences in the behavior and procedure of investigators more interesting and more important than that between the half unconscious, habitual use of a clear, simple, convenient, highly generalized conceptual scheme, and any other method of work. This is, in one respect, the significant difference between the work of almost all natural scientists, on the one hand, and the work of most social scientists, on the other.

Fix once for all in your mind that you are seeking *rough* approximations and *sufficient* probabilities, cheering yourself with the assurance that all the results of all the experimental sciences are but approximations and probabilities.

Make the number of persons, of interests, of residues, etc., that you finally admit to your analysis as small as you can, conveniently and with due regard for your needs of the moment.

You should require no further advice about the choice of the component persons of your system, or of the economic interests, science and logic that you admit into it. Remember, however, the warning that you will probably tend to attribute too great importance to the science and logic of the component persons; and be on your guard.

Heterogeneity is likely to make you more trouble. Therefore, carefully consider and weigh what has been said above on this subject. Look for what may be thought of as the structural relations between persons, especially the enduring structural relations that help to bind groups together, and above all—in certain cases—those that resemble a persistent framework that remains while the individuals who momentarily constitute it change, as the telephone operator, the patrolman on the beat, the working shift in a smelter, the president of a corporation, the king of England change. Here the significant fact is implied by the familiar expression "le roi est mort, vive le roi!" Remember the rough analogy: such enduring things are to the whole social system more or less as the organs of the human body are to the whole body, and the individual persons are somewhat similar to the chemical molecules of the body. But *do not* reason from this or any other analogy.

Note further that individual traits—not merely economic interests, but above all residues and derivations—are dependent upon the nature of the groups and organizations in which the individual participates. Indeed, this dependence is often so great that one may even sometimes think (roughly and in a first approximation) of some of a person's residues and derivations as caused by what we vaguely describe as his family's tradition,[1] or by his discipline as a member of a profession or of a church or of a militant party like the Bolsheviks or the Nazis, or by the nature of an organization in which he works cooperatively with others, or by his being an "aristocrat" or a "bourgeois" or a "proletarian." But such oversimplifications are dangerous and it may be as bad analysis to exaggerate their importance (like the Marxists) as to neglect them altogether (like many classical economists). Here your task is important and delicate. You must therefore make every effort to judge directly from the facts, remembering that you are trying to make a diagnosis, not to justify a prejudice or even to test a theory.

The fact should not be overlooked that a man who is a member of several different groups or organizations—as most men are— may often find himself in a position where the sentiments that have arisen through his membership in two or more of these groups conflict so that he is seriously troubled.[2] This may lead to hesitation, anxiety, fear, and so to serious neurosis and injury to his character. Do not suppose, however, that to entertain apparently conflicting, i.e. inconsistent, sentiments is in general a source of trouble. All men entertain potentially conflicting sentiments and commonly suffer not at all for so doing. But when they are already neurotic, or when they must make decisions involving a conflict of which they are aware, there may be serious trouble.

The subject of heterogeneity calls for one further remark. It is essential to know that everywhere small groups of persons are constantly and spontaneously becoming social systems. There are many well-known classes of these systems, for example, gangs of boys. But they may also arise and play a role of the greatest importance where their presence is not even suspected, for example, in industrial plants. Everybody has heard of the management's "blue-print" organization of a plant and of the organization of the workers into labor unions. But sometimes, perhaps as a rule, the formation, the activity, and the decay of little spontaneous so-

---

[1]   See Mommsen.
[2]   See Barnard.

cial systems are overlooked.³ These systems are largely independent of the planned organization and of the labor unions. Even the component persons are, as a rule, not clearly aware of their existence, and very often nobody else has seen or at all events noticed any signs of them. Nevertheless, they give rise to important and powerful residues and may, therefore, sometimes constitute the most significant elements in the heterogeneous structure of the larger systems of which they are a part. Residues and sentiments as they manifest themselves in human relations are felt as relations with persons and groups of persons. If you look for them, you will find them in some of the cases.⁴

Note well the broad induction: men often manifest strong sentiments arising from and even with reference to things they have not consciously thought about or named. Consider the behavior of dogs and then the long phylogeny of man and the short history of language.

In studying the elements of the social system, the greatest difficulties are raised by the residues. Pareto recognizes six classes:

I. Instinct for combinations.
II. Persistence of aggregates.
III. The need of manifesting sentiments by external acts.
IV. Residues relating to sociability.
V. The integrity of the individual and of what he considers dependent upon him.
VI. The sexual residue.

When studying events and processes on a large scale, I think you will do well to give thought chiefly to the two first classes of residues and I shall accordingly speak first of them. At the beginning of the second chapter enough was said to show that combinations and persistent aggregates are deeply rooted in physiological activity, and those who are acquainted with Pavlov's work will perhaps see that there is a large ingredient of the conditioned re-

³ Roethlisberger and Dickson, op. cit.
⁴ See Oliver (II), Disraeli, Saint-Simon, Maine (I), Cambon.

flex in the persistence of aggregates of more or less independent things. For instance, "home" as distinguished from "house" is such a persistent aggregate,[5] and the sentiment for it gives rise to a residue. Other examples are the "German Rhine" as distinguished from the "Rhine," and "mare nostrum" as distinguished from the "Mediterranean." The residues above referred to that arise through membership in a group or organization are often of this nature.

Pareto says of Class I: "This class embraces the residues corresponding to the instinct for combinations, which is intensely powerful in the human species and has probably been, as it still remains, one of the important factors in civilization." It includes general or random combinations like those involved in innumerable remedies that have been used in the treatment of the sick, combinations of similars and of opposites, such as unusual things and exceptional events, those inspiring awe or terror, happiness associated with good things, unhappiness with bad, assimilation of food and drink to acquire the associated character, mysterious operations in general and the mysterious linking of names and things. All these are the concern chiefly of anthropologists. But it also includes the need for combining residues and facts or observations and the need for logical and pseudo-logical developments. These are primary factors of our modern civilization.

The instinct of combinations is manifest in the activity of an entrepreneur, of a politician, especially an unscrupulous one (scruples are often due to persistent aggregates), of a commanding general, of the philosopher who makes a system, of a scientist engaged in research, of an inventor, of a criminal lawyer.[6]

Class II (called in the English translation "group-persistences") is in many respects a counterweight to Class I. Recurrent experiences, associations, routines, habits, conditioned reflexes, rituals, etc. give rise to conceptual combinations or to such as are felt rather than conceived. Such combinations often assume, conceptually, an objective existence and persist. With them strong

[5]   See Lubbock.
[6]   See Cellini, Evelyn, Fouché, Babbage, Churchill.

sentiments are often associated. Examples of persistent aggregates are: family and kinship relations, relations with places and with social classes, between the living and the dead, between a dead person and his property (relics). In like manner abstractions and uniformities persist as metaphysical or absolute principles, and sentiments are conceptually transformed into objective realities and personified (Justice). Consider Montaigne's remark: "We say, indeed, Power, Truth, Justice: they are words that denote something great, but that something we are quite unable to see and conceive." And then consider that of Justice Holmes above cited.

The persistence of aggregates is manifest in the activity of a feudal lord, of a well-disciplined private soldier, of a devout practitioner of a cult, of a judge.[7]

Both classes of residues, however, are attributes of everybody. Persons differ in the strength, relative and absolute, of the residues of the two classes. In Sparta apparently persistent aggregates were strong and combinations weak, in Periclean Athens combinations strong and persistent aggregates, in general, either weak or quiescent. In the great days of Rome and in England during the nineteenth century both classes seem to have been strong.

Persistent aggregates are preserved and reinforced[8] by repetition of the experiences and sequences of experience (combinations) which are united in the aggregate.

Often combinations predominate among the rulers and persistent aggregates among the ruled. This is all but necessary, at least at the very top and in the very lowest ranks of an army. And if the proportions in both classes are not too extreme, it seems often to make for the stability and prosperity of a country.

Long before Pareto, Bagehot clearly saw the conflict between residues of the first class and residues of the second class, and the importance of a balance between them. In "Physics and Politics" he wrote:[9]

---

7   See Leviticus, Amiel, Burke, Disraeli.
8   See L. Stephen, Coke (I).
9   *The Works of Walter Bagehot*, op. cit., pp. 473–474.

The beginning of civilization is marked by an intense legality; that legality is the very condition of its existence, the bond [residues of Class II] which ties it together, but that legality—that tendency to impose a settled customary yoke upon all men and all actions—if it goes on, kills out the variability implanted by nature [residues of Class I], and makes different men and different ages fac-similes of other men and other ages, as we see them so often. Progress is only possible in those happy cases where the force of legality has gone far enough to bind the nation together, but not far enough to kill out all varieties and destroy nature's perpetual tendency to change."

Note by way of illustration that the rulers of Russia recognize the role of the persistent aggregates of the Christian church and seek to diminish it by propaganda (derivation appealing to other residues), saying that religion is an opiate for the people. This is not a bad pejorative figure for the role of persistent aggregates. Meanwhile, they make every effort to build up new persistent aggregates favorable to their rule. To these latter the figure is neither more nor less applicable than to the former aggregates. Note too that Mussolini and Hitler are systematically trying to form and strengthen persistent aggregates by the organization of children and by all sorts of mass activities. There is reason to believe that Mussolini is even thinking in terms of Pareto's conceptual scheme. In so doing both are manifesting the instinct of combinations. Note that many objections to the "new deal" are a result of interference with routines and therefore the expression of persistent aggregates. Some of the "new-dealers" are examples of the dominance of the instinct of combinations.

In general, persistent aggregates tend to stabilize society and to bind it together, the instinct of combinations to modify society and to originate novelty.[10] The importance of the persistent aggregates rather than of reason and combinations in stabilizing society is clearly indicated by Cournot in the following words:[11]

In any event, it is not by logical combinations, by plans worked out on paper, establishing separate and distinct powers which balance or

10   See Amiel, Mommsen, Sumner.
11   A. Cournot, *Souvenirs*, Paris, 1913, p. 126.

moderate each other, that this problem of escape from despotism can be solved. There must be a certain foundation of beliefs [i.e., residues] which imposes on each power limits that it will not dare to exceed. If governments and peoples are not dominated by such beliefs, if the case is pleaded on the texts and before the court of pure logic, it is lost.

It is worthy of note that these two groups of residues are identical with two fundamental generalizations of psychological theory. The persistence of aggregates has been studied by psychologists under the various titles of laws of association; the category of thinghood; most recently, syncretism. It is also closely related with the Freudian conception of object-cathexis. The study of attention in all psychology is the study of manifestations of the instinct of combinations. In this connection it is perhaps not irrelevant to note that what Pavlov calls the investigatory reflex interferes with the process of conditioning. Now the investigatory reflex[12] seems to be related to the "instinct of combinations" and conditioned reflexes to the "persistence of aggregates." Possibly this has something to do with the tendency of residues of the first and second classes to act in opposition.

When you study small-scale phenomena you will probably find that residues of the first and second classes are often less important than residues of personal integrity (Class V), of the need of expressing sentiments by actions (Class III), and of sociability (Class IV). Mr. Chester I. Barnard holds that such is the general rule. This raises a quantitative problem which can hardly be answered without investigation, but it is safe to say, for whatever so vague a statement is worth, that the phenomena are at least not infrequently and perhaps generally, but assuredly not always, of this nature.

A partial explanation of the difference between large-scale and small-scale phenomena may be suggested by considering the difference between climate and weather. For instance, the climate of Boston may be fairly well described in terms of latitude, position on the eastern seacoast of the continent, and the season. On the

12   See Saint-Simon.

other hand, the heavy rains of July, 1938, involve the consideration chiefly of other factors, some of which are those represented on the familiar "weather maps."

Accordingly, in studying a concrete social situation, such as a simple conversation, or meeting or other more or less unitary event, you will do well to look carefully for manifestations of self-esteem or of a feeling of inferiority, for the *active* expression of all kinds of sentiments, and for the residues related to sociability.

It goes without saying that you should often look for the sex residue also, but in this day there is little danger of forgetting it, just as there is little danger of forgetting the economic interests, for the psychoanalysts have taken care that we shall remember the one and the Marxists that we shall remember the other. Of these two factors, it may be enough to say that they are often as important as dogmatists would have us believe, that they are in general immensely important, but that on the whole the danger for scientific analysis at present is probably overemphasis rather than neglect.

The complete classification of residues is as follows:

RESIDUES

I. Instinct for Combinations

> Residues of this class in great variety are observable in certain kinds of persons. See Benvenuto Cellini, Evelyn, Fouché, Galton, Talleyrand.

I–*a*. Combinations in general

> There are combinations which *seem* to have no attribute except only that of being combinations; to make room for these Class I–*a* is designed. Many folk-remedies for sickness fall in this class, e.g., most of the sixty-nine remedies for epilepsy mentioned by Pliny, and the New England practices of carrying a horse-chestnut in the pocket to

guard against rheumatism, and dosing with sulphur and molasses in the spring.

I–β. Combinations of similars and opposites

I–β1. Likeness or oppositeness in general. See Balzac, Bernhardi, Burchard, Benvenuto Cellini, Chaucer, *Clovis*, Coke, Dante, Franklin, Frazer (II), Froissart, Gregory of Tours, Shakespeare, Swift, Willibald.

I–β2. Unusual things and exceptional occurrences. See *Plutarch*.

I–β3. Objects and occurrences inspiring awe or terror. See *Cardan*, Chaucer, Clovis, Gregory of Tours, Plutarch, Willibald.

I–β4. Felicitous state associated with good things; infelicitous state, with bad. See Guizot, *Marx*, Needham.

I–β5. Assimilation: physical consumption of substances to get effects of associable, and more rarely of opposite, character. See *Frazer* (I).

I–γ. Mysterious workings of certain things; mysterious effects of certain acts

I–γ1. Mysterious operations in general. (See *Frazer* (II), Leviticus, Willibald.

I–γ2. Mysterious linkings of names and things. Circular motion, certain numbers, were formerly called perfect. In the case of numbers this residue has issued in the mathematical term "perfect number," designating numbers like 6 and 28 which are equal to the sum of their factors (including 1 but of course not the number itself), thus $28 = 1 + 2 + 4 + 7 + 14$. In modern

> usage—at least among mathematicians—"perfect number" is accordingly a technical term and the residue is absent.

I–δ. Need for combining residues. See Bacon, Calvin, Hitler, Whewell.

I–ε. Need for logical developments. See Bacon, Bundy, Calvin, Durkheim, Harvard Crimson, Hegel, Laski.

I–ζ. Faith in the efficacy of combinations. See Boccacio, Frazer (II).

II. Group Persistences (Persistence of Aggregates)

> Residues of this class are especially noticeable in certain kinds of persons, and in certain kinds of circumstances. See Amiel, Burke, Disraeli.

II–α. Persistence of relations between a person and other persons and places. See Mommsen.

> II–α1. Relationships of family and kindred groups. See Gosse, Lubbock, Mommsen.
>
> II–α2. Relations with places. See Gregory the Great, Leviticus, Lubbock, Mommsen, Willibald.
>
> II–α3. Relationships of social class. See Coke (II), Mommsen, Saint-Simon.

II–β. Persistence of relations between the living and the dead. See Mommsen.

II–γ. Persistence of relations between a dead person and the things that belonged to him in life. See Mommsen, Pike.

II–δ. Persistence of abstractions. See Goethe (II), Lubbock, Plato.

II–ε. Persistence of uniformities. See Chaucer, Poincaré.

II–ζ. Sentiments transformed into objective realities. See Elizabeth, Hardy, Lacombe, Plato.

II–η. Personifications. See Benvenuto Cellini, Chaucer, Poincaré.

II–θ. Need of new abstractions. See Durkheim, Hitler.

III. Need of Expressing Sentiments by External Acts (Activity, Self-Expression)

III–α. Need of "doing something" expressing itself in combinations. See Cheynell, Gibbon, Gregory the Great, Gregory of Tours, Lincoln.

III–β. Religious ecstasies. See Edwards, Gibbon, Vámbéry, Wesley.

IV. Residues Connected with Sociality

IV–α. Particular societies. See Barnard, Cambon, Elizabeth, Froissart (I and II), Guizot, Mommsen, Mormons, Oliver (II), Poincaré, Polybius, de Retz, Sabatier, Scott.

IV–β. Need of uniformity. See Guizot, Hazlitt, Rabelais.

IV–β1. Voluntary conformity on the part of the individual. See Polybius.

IV–β2. Uniformity enforced upon others. See Cato, Polybius.

IV–β3. Neophobia. See Cato, Lear, Mencken.

IV–γ. Pity and cruelty.

IV–γ1. Self-pity extended to others. See D'Oberkirch, (Rousseau).

IV–γ2. Instinctive repugnance to suffering. See Antivivisection, Lincoln.

IV–γ3. Reasoned repugnance to useless sufferings. See Froissart.

IV–δ. Self-sacrifice for the good of others. See Coke (II), Guizot.

IV–δ1. Risking one's life. See Elizabeth, Froissart.

IV–δ2. Sharing one's property with others. See Sabatier.

IV–ε. Sentiments of social ranking; hierarchy. See Coke (II).

> IV–ε1. Sentiments of superiors. See Bentley, Caesar, Coke (II), Elizabeth, Froissart, d'Oberkirch, Oliver (II), Plutarch, Richelieu.
>
> IV–ε2. Sentiments of inferiors. See Caesar, Chesterfield, Elizabeth, Gregory of Tours, Homer, Lewis, Machiavelli, Molière, Oliver (I), Tacitus.
>
> IV–ε3. Need of group approbation. See Bentley, Froissart, Plutarch, Richelieu, Scott.

IV–ζ. Asceticism. See Gibbon, Hazlitt, Sabatier, Vámbéry.

V. Integrity of the Individual and his Appurtenances.

V–α. Sentiments of resistance to alterations in the social equilibrium. See Coke (II), Elizabeth, Gregory of Tours, Guizot, Harvard Crimson, Hitler, Laski, Mommsen, Mormons, Poincaré, Polybius, de Retz, Saint-Simon.

V–β. Sentiments of equality in inferiors. See Gregory of Tours, Tacitus.

V–γ. Restoration of integrity by acts pertaining to the individual whose integrity has been impaired.

> V–γ1. Real subjects. See Richelieu, Schrader, Scott.
>
> V–γ2. Imaginary or abstract subjects. See Newman, Scott, Wesley.

V–δ. Restoration of integrity by acts pertaining to the offender (vengeance, "getting even"). See d'Épinay, Indulgences.

> V–δ1. Real offender. See Gregory of Tours, Richelieu.
>
> V–δ2. Imaginary or abstract offender. See Frazer (II).

VI. The Sex Residue. See Balzac, Elizabeth, Froissart (II), Hazlitt.

Pareto's classification of residues is a first attempt which in some respects resembles Aristotle's classification of animals. Perhaps nothing is more nearly certain than that it calls for enlargement and modification and there is no reason to think that it may not be replaced by a better (i.e., more convenient) classification when the time is ripe. Meanwhile, experience shows that it is tolerably serviceable. I believe, however, that certain additions may already be made to Pareto's list of residues.

Mr. Barnard points out that, while Pareto takes account of the need to manifest sentiments by actions and of the need to do something in an emergency, the need of action in general, the need to do something in general is overlooked. In Mr. Barnard's opinion, this need is one of the principal forces determining the form of human societies. He says:

Children at all ages and especially when very young manifest this instinct. The contortionist and manipulative efforts of boys when alone and not aware of being observed are instances. The inability of most persons to remain seated; or their tendency to pace the floor, or to wander aimlessly about, or to play with watch chains, etc., are other simple cases. The avidity with which they embrace opportunities to "do something" for no purpose, and entirely alone, is often observed.

Obvious as I think all this is, its significance for social science seems to me to be missed. For example, I am convinced that a large part of purely commercial transactions arise not out of economic considerations in any accepted sense but from the necessity of "doing something." People buy things they don't want—to "do something." They sell—to "do something." They build, speculate, trade—to "do something." They cover all this sincerely enough by rationalizations. Nevertheless, I believe any one observing himself or others with this clue in mind will find ample confirmation, not only in the economic, but in every other field, probably including that of scientific investigation.

Bagehot expressed almost the same opinion:[13]

[13]   *The Works of Walter Bagehot*, op. cit., pp. 566–567.

Even in commerce, which is now the main occupation of mankind, and one in which there is a ready test of success and failure wanting in many higher pursuits, the same disposition to excessive action is very apparent to careful observers. Part of every mania is caused by the impossibility to get people to confine themselves to the amount of business for which their capital is sufficient, and in which they can engage safely. In some degree, of course, this is caused by the wish to get rich; but in a considerable degree too by the mere love of activity. There is a greater propensity to action in such men than they have the means of gratifying: operations with their own capital will only occupy four hours of the day, and they wish to be active and to be industrious for eight hours, and so they are ruined; if they could only have sat idle the other four hours, they would have been rich men.

Earlier, Bagehot cites a remark attributed to Pascal[14] "that most of the evils of life arose from 'man's being unable to sit still in a room.' "

In Mr. Barnard's view I concur, believing that it is important to include action of a type that extends far back phylogenetically in the analysis of residues. The problem of introducing this kind of residue into the classification is one of convenience. I suggest that the most promising procedure is to expand the definition of the instinct of combinations so as to include what Mr. Barnard would call the instinct for pure action.

The investigatory reflex—the "what is it" reflex—of Pavlov is at the bottom of the instinct of combinations. Its manifestations may therefore be grouped with the residue of the instinct of combinations.

There is also a primitive need of response or recognition[15] which seems to be phylogenetically ancient. This appears to be a foundation of both sociality and personal integrity sentiments.

President Lowell has suggested two concrete residues that should be added to Pareto's list. The first of these is "manifestation of the desire to rule, that is, to have one's way." He thinks that this may perhaps be classified under Pareto's impulse to manifest

14 Ibid., p. 564.
15 See Pellico.

one's sentiments by means of combinations. The second is, like Mr. Barnard's pure action, a residue deeply grounded in the animal nature of man. Mr. Lowell says: "It is that of avoiding harm, or the danger of harm; and that means when some hazard is unavoidable, reducing its extent so far as possible. We may call it a residue of limiting risk." Like Mr. Barnard's residue of pure action, it seems too primitive to be thought of as a manifestation of the instinct of combinations in the more obvious sense of that term, as expounded by Pareto and illustrated by his study of the phenomena. But if we accept the enlargement of the definition of the instinct of combinations suggested by Mr. Barnard, this too would fit into Class I. Of course it is often associated with very elaborate combinations.

Pareto's classification of the residues of personal integrity seems in some respects inadequate. This may well be due to the fact that he was chiefly concerned with large-scale phenomena. Probably it will be necessary sooner or later to add to his classification subclasses corresponding to such words as vanity, pride, arrogance, conceit, humility, modesty, shyness. We need not, however, attack this problem, for we shall be able to make shift with the use of Class V in general for our purposes.

Professor Elton Mayo comments on this part of Pareto's classification to the effect that "the first two categories, $V-\alpha$ and $V-\beta$, refer upon the whole to the normal situation and might almost be described as static. These two, I am sure, could be considerably extended and with benefit. My own special interest attaches naturally to the subclasses $V-\gamma$ and $V-\delta$. These are dynamic categories. They represent the type of action the individual may take to restore his personal integrity when he finds himself in a social situation to which he is clearly inadequate. The interest of these two is that they do represent a very considerable consensus of opinion amongst those clinically interested in the handling of such persons. Upon the whole, such persons, classified in terms of the responses they make to their social surrounding, may be described under two general headings: those who are frightened and pessimistic; those who are angry and wish to destroy their surrounding. The first group believe that the world is dangerous and that one must exercise an unremitting care over all one's actions. The second group believe that the world is hostile;[16] their desire is to attack and to destroy. The latest instance of the clinical necessity of this classification may be found in a book entitled *Personality and the Cultural Pattern*, by Dr. James S. Plant. On page 103, in a chapter entitled 'Psychiatry and Pressure of the Environment,' he describes the general reaction of ineffective or delinquent children as of two kinds: the first he names panic [the world is dangerous], and the second rebellion [the world is hostile]."

One word of caution about this class of residues may be useful. The so-called inferiority complex belongs here and is to be distinguished from residue IV–$\epsilon2$, the sentiments of inferiors (personal loyalty), which in no way necessarily conflict with strong positive feelings of personal integrity.

We need not further consider the question of the expediency of a change in the classification. The history of science shows that within pretty wide limits one is free to try any change of a classification that seems expedient, and the test of the expediency of the change is convenience arising from the use of the varied classification.

Residues are recognized by the process previously described as diagnosis. It avails little to talk about them. You must learn to recognize them by recognizing them.

Do not suppose that the presence of a residue is evidence against the presence of another residue which, from a logical standpoint, is inconsistent with it, or even flatly contradictory of it. For, as I have said, everybody is inconsistent in his sentiments. Men feel that killing is right,—and wrong. So they also feel about stealing and about lying. Residues that are thus inconsistent are the great topic of casuistry, both in its common and in its technical meaning. Casuistry deals with such problems as the proper decision and action of a truthful person who can protect an innocent person from grave injury only by telling a lie, who therefore feels that telling a particular lie is both wrong and right. But casuistry consists of derivations and there are not many persons who reach

16   See Mayo, d'Épinay.

a decision by making derivations. Action in such cases is, in general, something like the resultant of the various sentiments, the casuistical explanation of the action an *ex post facto* derivation. You will find in *Conflicts of Principle* by A. L. Lowell[17] a valuable discussion of many aspects of the conflict of residues and of the accompanying conflict of derivations.

Further, note that the concrete utterances and actions of men ordinarily yield simple residues not directly but only by analysis, which is always incomplete. Utterances and actions should be conceived as resultants not merely of the sentiments manifested by these residues but also of many other complex but unmanifested sentiments. Sentiments may be now active, now passive, and the resultant manifestations of sentiments vary widely from time to time in the same person. Thus a man may at times seem to act "conservatively," i.e., under the influence of persistent aggregates, and at other times, under circumstances that appear to be similar, he may seem to act under the influence of the instinct of combinations. In any case, you may sure that no man altogether lacks sentiments corresponding to either the first or the second class of residues, that most men have a large supply of both classes of sentiments and that their utterances, while yielding a few residues on any particular occasion, arise from a very complex interaction between a large number of sentiments some of which are not expressed, either because they are balanced by others, or because they are repressed or suppressed. Therefore do not suppose that a seemingly complete analysis of the residues in a man's utterances is in any sense a complete analysis of his sentiments, or, what is even worse, that his affective state is a mere sum of atomic or elementary sentiments.

Although no men lack large numbers of residues of Class II, and other residues associated with conditioning, it can hardly be doubted that persons who suffer from anxiety neurosis can often be relatively deficient in such residues and that this deficiency is one of the important symptoms of that malady.[18] It is manifested

17   Cambridge, Mass., 1932.
18   See James, Burke, Barnard, Amiel.

chiefly, or at least most strikingly, in many cases, by hesitation. Such persons, lacking the appropriate reflex responses to many of the situations of daily life, have too many decisions to make.

Derivations are less difficult than residues to recognize, but they are not easy to cope with. Here, however, the difficulty is almost entirely due to unfamiliarity and to habit. Some people cannot learn to be good medical diagnosticians, some cannot learn to be good diagnosticians of residues, but in the long run almost any intelligent educated person can learn to recognize derivations except perhaps his own.[19]

Nearly all speech whether in the form of conversation or of oratory or of debate, and nearly all writing, except the most careful scientific writing and colorless statements of concrete sensory experiences, are full of derivations. This theorem holds for all men, always, everywhere. It holds for you and me.

Pareto distinguished four classes of derivations:

    I. Affirmation.[20]
    II. Authority.[21]
    III. Accord with sentiments or with principles.[22]
    IV. Verbal proofs.[23]

This classification is entirely independent of the distinction between Class A and Class B derivations which has been discussed above.[24] There is no conflict between the two classifications, just as there is no conflict between the classification of mammals in species and their classification as males and females.

An example of the first class of derivations is the taboo without sanction. Another common example is the unfounded assertion introduced in the course of an argument, which benefits from the assent given to the propositions that it accompanies.

Examples of the second class are familiar to all. If we may

---

[19]   See Spedding.
[20]   See Bossuet.
[21]   See Leviticus.
[22]   See Coke (I), Hegel, Burchard.
[23]   See Kant, Thucydides.
[24]   See p. 30.

judge from the current practices of many American advertisers, the expression of an opinion by any person whose name is known to the public, on any subject, regardless of the person's competency to form an opinion on the subject, will influence the actions of many readers of the opinion. Since the decisive factor in determining the policy of advertising is variation of sales, the evidence seems fairly conclusive.

There are endless examples of higher authorities, like those of Homer for the Greeks, and of the Bible for Christians. As Pareto notes, it would be difficult to say what has not been found in the Bible. And there are the many cases of the authority of traditions, such as the traditions of American college students. Appeal to the authority of custom is also common, as the sales of books on etiquette attest. It remains to note the obvious case of the authority of a divinity or of a personification.

The existence of certain types of derivations of the third class has been widely recognized, for example, by Caesar in the remark,[25] "homines id quod volunt credunt," and by Bacon, who says,[26]

The human understanding is no dry light but receives an infusion from the will and affections; whence proceed sciences which may be called "sciences as one would." For what a man had rather were true he more readily believes. Therefore he rejects difficult things from impatience of research; sober things, because they narrow hope; the deeper things of nature, from superstition; the light of experience, from arrogance and pride, lest his mind should seem to be occupied with things mean and transitory; things not commonly believed, out of deference to the opinion of the vulgar. Numberless in short are the ways, and sometimes imperceptible, in which the affections color and infect the understanding.

Bacon's reference to the unconscious character of wishful thinking is especially notable. Indeed, this whole aphorism is a good description of the kind of derivations now extensively studied by psychoanalysts under the name of rationalizations. The ex-

25   *De Bello Gallico*, Book III, Chap. 18.
26   *Novum Organum*, Book I, Aphorism XLIX.

pression *dry light* is derived by Bacon from Heraclitus,[27] and if Bacon's quotation and interpretation of the passage are correct, Heraclitus's phrase may be the earliest explicit reference to wishful thinking that is now known.

Pareto's analysis of this class of derivations is far more detailed, systematic, and extensive than earlier discussions of the subject. It does not admit of summary treatment, but must be studied in the original.

Edgeworth has very neatly shown up one of the most famous derivations of this class, saying,[28] "That the great Bentham should have adopted as the creed of his life and watchword of his party an expression which is meant to be quantitatively precise, and yet when scientifically analysed may appear almost unmeaning, is significant of the importance to be attached to the science of quantity [and of derivations]. 'Greatest happiness of the greatest number'—is this more intelligible than 'greatest illumination with the greatest number of lamps'?"

Edgeworth published this "obvious" criticism sixty years ago in a famous essay; he was a distinguished and greatly respected scholar, for many years professor in the University of Oxford; he is believed to have widely influenced the thought of economists and others. And yet who has heard of his criticism of Bentham's slogan—and who has not heard of that slogan? An accord of powerful sentiments is in action; the derivation survives, the logic is forgotten. Nevertheless, if you are to take account of both x (happiness) and y (population, number) you need not one, but two equations; and, moreover, there is not the slightest reason to believe that x and y can be simultaneously maxima, even if it is possible to assign a definite meaning to the expression "greatest happiness."

The fourth class of derivations, verbal proofs, occupy the whole of Chapter X of the Treatise. The exposition of them is even less amenable than that of the third class to brief description, but, I think, it is an equally profitable subject matter of study. The

27   Cf. Diels, *Die Fragmente der Vorsokratiker*, Berlin, 1903, pp. 82, 118.
28   F. Y. Edgeworth, *Mathematical Psychics*, London, 1881, p. 117.

derivations of the fourth class include Bacon's *Idols of the Market Place.*

We may well pause for a simple illustration. Among innumerable derivations of the fourth class, one that was generally accepted for centuries may be put in syllagistic form as follows:

> All planetary motion is perfect motion.
> All perfect motion is circular motion.
> Therefore all planetary motion is circular motion.

Here the middle term is meaningless, both premises are themselves derivations of the third class (accord with sentiments), and the conclusion is nonsense. It probably gains in plausibility because the meaningless middle term, perfect motion, drops out of the conclusion.

Now consider the following syllogism:

> All (known) perfect numbers are even numbers.
> Twenty-eight is a perfect number.
> Therefore twenty-eight is an even number.

This is sound reasoning to a well-informed person. It is so because all the terms have precise meaning, for the term "perfect number," like the term "even number," is a technical term that is precisely defined in mathematics.

There may be found in Chapter X of Pareto's work, carefully arranged and clearly presented, verbal derivations of many of the most famous authors of works on history, philosophy, sociology, and religion. It must be an exceptional person indeed who can read this chapter understandingly without discovering the nature and the source of many of his own errors.

Throughout the Treatise Pareto takes pains to avoid in his own discussions the ambiguities and other difficulties that result from the use of words, to explain them and to warn against them, and one of his most important and constantly repeated precepts is: *Never dispute about words.* To these ends he makes frequent use of letters instead of words as symbols for carefully formulated definitions, and he also employs letters as a test for verbal derivations. Since this test is often surprisingly useful and effective, it may be illustrated by an example.[29] Jeans says:[30] "If the universe is a universe of thought, then its creation must have been an act of thought." This is an enthymeme, and therefore suspect. Substituting X for *thought*, we have: If the universe is a universe of X, then its creation must have been an act of X. This should suffice to reveal the derivation, but if it does not, some other word like *love* or *matter* may now be substituted for X. A similar result may be obtained by putting Y in place of *creation* and then, if necessary, replacing Y by another word like *evolution*.

Bacon says,[31] "The doctrine of idols is to the interpretation of nature what the doctrine of the refutation of sophisms is to common logic." A moment's reflection will show that here Bacon is both discriminating between two different classes of phenomena and also asserting the need of recognizing the nature of derivations and the small importance of understanding the fallacies of logic in the business of science and of everyday life.

In order to master the subject of derivations you will do well to study Chapters IX and X of *The Mind and Society*. You must also learn to recognize your own derivations, both in ordinary conversation and in the study of sociology. You may be sure, if you have the sentiments of a "conservative" or of a "radical," of a "stand-patter" or of a "new-dealer," of an "economic royalist" or of a "bolshevik," of a "fascist" or of a "communist," of an "egotist" or of a "humanitarian," that you are forever producing corresponding derivations: assertions, appeals to authority, expressions of accord of sentiments and "principles," and all sorts of specious word-tricks. In general, you do so, as you breathe, unconsciously. But, if you will, you may become aware of either process and in a measure control it, at least occasionally and for a short time.

Derivations are as a rule sincere expressions of sentiments[32] and in order to be effective in their action on other persons it is probably necessary in most cases that they should be so. Con-

29   See Kant.
30   J. H. Jeans, *The Mysterious Universe*, New York, 1930, p. 154.
31   *Novum Organum*, Book I, Aphoriam XL.
32   See Swift (II), Mormons.

sistent, deliberate, systematic hypocrisy is an art that few can practice successfully.

I think we need not go further into the discussion of mere relations within the social system, but interactions require certain comments: Social processes, like physical and chemical processes, have velocities that appear to be determined, in general, by the specific characteristics of the factors and conditions. When the attempt is made, say, to hasten them beyond a certain point the processes often change their character and the results may be different. In both cases phenomena that are more or less vaguely described as "explosions" (figuratively in the case of social phenomena) may ensue.

For example, it is pretty evident that the attempt to do more rapidly in this country certain things about the organization of labor which were intended to be like certain things that had been done more slowly in England or elsewhere has entailed features different from those that have been observed in England. It seems probable that these differences are in part due to differences in the velocity of the process. In somewhat the same way rapid introduction of new industrial methods often causes troubles of which the origin is not chiefly economic.

One reason for all this is that legislation or the plans of the managers of a plant and also the resulting actions of government or the resulting work in a plant can and often do change more rapidly than the residues or the underlying sentiments of those who are affected. For *residues and sentiments change slowly and it is in general impossible greatly to accelerate their change.* In particular, the orders of management may constantly interfere with and frequently destroy the little spontaneous social systems involving strong persistent aggregates and other residues that spring up among the workmen. So it often comes about that the workmen are strongly disposed to resist all change. Indeed this is sometimes the chief cause of dissatisfaction among workmen. It is ordinarily unknown, as a formulated fact, to the workmen themselves, quite unknown to the management and *a fortiori* to the politicians.

It should be added that in planning legislation or the work of an industrial plant, politicians and their advisors, on the one hand, managers and their advisors, on the other hand, often disregard all residues except their own. They tend especially to disregard the persistent aggregates of everybody, for they are recruited by a process of natural selection which at present tends to eliminate men possessing certain kinds of strong persistent aggregates and they are not often aware of the strength of these persistent aggregates in the great masses.

It is a corollary of the fact that residues and sentiments change slowly, that rulers and indeed all others do well to utilize existing sentiments rather than to seek to modify them.[33] Note, however, in this connection, that though sentiments change slowly they may often be quickly activated or inactivated,[34] for example, when war breaks out or after a great victory or defeat.

Skillful activation and utilization of the sentiments of others, deliberately and according to plan,[35] is commonly spoken of as Machiavellian behavior, though probably in those cases only where the end in view is regarded as wicked. It is in fact one of the most necessary of arts, equally indispensable in family life, in private affairs generally, in the practice of the professions and in public life. Accordingly the skillful use of residues is a conspicuous and important feature of much of the best literary work.[36] As a rule, the skill of a man like Marlborough or of even so great a writer as Shakespeare in the management of the residues is probably more or less unconscious, but it may be conjectured that for the most effective activation of sentiments both conscious and unconscious effort is ordinarily necessary.[37]

In a social system all factors (persons, interests, residues, etc.) are mutually dependent or interactive. In order to fix our ideas, let us consider a relatively simple mechanical system. It may seem that we are reasoning from analogy, but this is not so. On the contrary, we shall be reasoning logically from premises stated

[33]   See Elizabeth, Caesar.
[34]   See Laski.
[35]   See Balzac, Chesterfield, Churchill, Frederick the Great, Galton, Talleyrand.
[36]   See Goethe (II).
[37]   See Manning.

above, because the mathematical formulation necessary to describe this mechanical system would be formally identical with that necessary to describe the analogous social system.

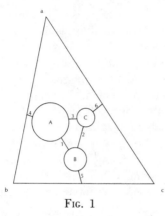

Fɪɢ. 1

In figure 1 let A, B, and C be objects connected together and to the rigid framework a, b, c by the elastic bands 1, 2, 3, 4, 5, 6. Further let each band be attached in A, B, and C to some kind of mechanism which constantly operates in some determinate manner to wind up or to unwind the elastic band, and let this action be a function of time and also of the instantaneous tensions. In other words, let each winding mechanism run on in some manner predetermined so that the winding shall in each instance vary quite definitely with time and with tension, and with nothing else directly. Further, let the masses of A, B, and C be known.

In principle such a system can be completely described mathematically if the necessary data are available, and from such a description the state of the system or of any part of the system at any instant may be deduced. For example, we may deduce the position of A one hour after the system has been set in operation. This position of A depends upon the initial state of the system, the properties of the objects A, B and C, the properties of the bands 1, 2, 3, 4, 5, and 6, and the laws of operation of the winding mechanisms.

It is evident that no single thing can be regarded as the "cause" of this position of A, but that the position of A is dependent upon the positions of B and C and upon the states of the elastic bands, and that each of these is correspondingly dependent on the position of A and also on the positions and states of the other elements of the system. In short, everything is in a condition of mutual dependence with everything else. Moreover, everything is dependent upon everything in the preceding "evolution" of the system.

Now let A, B, and C be individuals in a social system and let the configurations of the system, the bands, their tensions, and the laws of the mechanisms be replaced by the first-order properties of a social system of which A, B, and C are the sole components. Then there should be no difficulty in conceiving the nature of the state of mutual dependence among the elements of the system. Such a conception is consistent with, but of course inadequate to express exhaustively, what we know about interdependence and interaction in social systems.

Now imagine in the mechanical system a weight that is not too great placed for a time that is not too long on A, and then removed. It is evident that in general such a system will thereafter tend to return, though less precisely than a box spring, to or at least toward the state that would have existed if the system had not been interfered with from without. This is an instance of the kind of phenomenon that we have decided to designate by the term "equilibrium."

Many interactions in a social system are relatively permanent. They resemble or may be conceived as forces, connections, constraints, etc. We may also conceive them plus the factors as determining the instantaneous state and the future development of the system, in so far as the system is not disturbed from without. Accordingly, when the system is interfered with from without, they tend to restore the state that would have existed if there had been no interference. Thus, we may say that after the flood the people of Louisville were forced or constrained by their economic interests, their residues, etc. and by all sorts of relatively permanent connections to go back to their homes.

This is a convenient way of conceiving the equilibrium of the social system, just as recognizing the structure, plus the forces in a box spring is a convenient way of conceiving its relatively simple state of equilibrium. You should bear it constantly in mind. And you should bear in mind that when the system seems to be in danger of destruction or of serious injury strong residues, persistent aggregates and residues of the fourth and fifth classes are manifest. You will find them in American "public opinion" during the winter of 1932–33 and in that of the French during the first part of September, 1914, and throughout the ensuing years of war and in England today. These residues are by no means new, but they have been activated or intensified by "emergency," much as the force exerted by a spring is increased by compression. This increase of the force tends to restore the system to its "normal" state. There is no danger in thus thinking of social forces, if you never forget that you are doing so for convenience—for conceptual convenience. But experience shows that loose talk about social forces is very dangerous.

Two systems in equilibrium may respond very differently to a change of the environment. For example, there is ordinarily great difference in mountain sickness—in the onset, severity, duration and recovery—among the healthy members of a party of physiologists when they go from sea level to high altitudes to study the physiological changes which result from this change in the environment. In like manner different people respond differently to the death of a friend, to loss of employment, to a legacy, etc. So, too, different social systems respond differently to similar changes in their environment.

Because every factor interacts in a social system, because everything, every property, every relation is therefore in a state of mutual dependence with everything else, ordinary cause-and-effect analysis of events is rarely possible. In fact, it is nearly always grossly misleading; so much so that it must be regarded as one of the two great sources of error in sociological work. The other source of error, already many times referred to, is the intrusion of a person's own sentiments.[38]

[38]   See Ruskin.

Nothing is easier than to find examples of this cause-and-effect error. It may take extreme forms such as the belief that not only a person's happiness, but everything that he experiences is a reward or punishment, the result of his good or evil conduct. To this the Marxists, disregarding residues of which they, like all others, have a plentiful supply, oppose the view that human history is just economic determinism. In some measure the error pervades human thought, though it commonly assumes less extreme forms. We are all liable to it and must be always on our guard. Whitehead,[39] who describes it well, calls it the fallacy of misplaced concreteness. You will need to know some of its peculiarities.[40]

The fallacy of misplaced concreteness and the particular form that it often assumes in arguments deduced from the observation of correlations or involving "other things being equal" may be explained as follows:

Suppose the correlation between values of y and values of x is sought, either in the belief that nothing else need be considered or "other things being equal." Let the unknown relations between x, y and the other things be such that they can be expressed by the equation

$$y = \frac{x + z}{x + 2}$$

in which the value of z is a measure of the other things, say u, v, w, or in other words the value of z is a function of the values of these other things, i.e., such that z varies when u varies, when v varies, and also when w varies.

Let us now give z successively the three values 1, 2, and 3. Then

$$(1) \quad y = \frac{x + 1}{x + 2}$$

$$(2) \quad y = \frac{x + 2}{x + 2}$$

[39] Whitehead, A. N., *Science and the Modern World*, New York, Macmillan, 1926, Chap. III.
[40] See Babbage, Barnard, Guizot, Marshall, Oliver (I), J. F. Stephen (I).

$$(3) \quad y = \frac{x + 3}{x + 2}$$

And now let us compute values of y for each of the three values 1, 2, and 3 of x in each of these three cases (1), (2), and (3). This computation yields the following table of numerical values of y. The columns correspond to constant values of z (i.e., either other things are equal or their variations are compensatory). These values are successively 1, 2, and 3. The rows of the table correspond in turn to the successive values 1, 2, and 3 of x.

TABLE 1

Values of y for different values of x and z:

$$y = \frac{x + z}{x + 2}$$

	$z = 1$	$z = 2$	$z = 3$
$x = 1$	$y = 0.67$	$y = 1.00$	$y = 1.33$
$x = 2$	$y = 0.75$	$y = 1.00$	$y = 1.25$
$x = 3$	$y = 0.80$	$y = 1.00$	$y = 1.20$

A still better treatment is to find the rate of change of y as x changes, i.e., $\frac{dy}{dx}$, by differentiating the three equations (1), (2), and (3).

$$\text{For (1)} \quad \frac{dy}{dx} = \frac{1}{(x + 2)^2}$$

$$\text{for (2)} \quad \frac{dy}{dx} = 0$$

$$\text{for (3)} \quad \frac{dy}{dx} = - \frac{1}{(x + 2)^2}.$$

Evidently when $z = 1$, x and y are positively correlated, when $z = 2$ they are independent, when $z = 3$ they are negatively correlated. Accordingly, any statement about the correlation of y with x must take account of what happens when z varies or must specify the value of z, i.e., the value at which "other things are equal." But z is a function of u, v, and w, which makes for further complications. This is a simple illustration of what is ordinarily much more complex.

Imagine two men setting to work, one on January 1, the other on July 1, to measure the duration of daily sunshine. Each might well find after three or four months a high correlation between time (i.e., date) and duration of daily sunshine. But the first would observe a positive correlation, the second a negative correlation. Neither would be likely to deceive himself on this account, *because he has intuitive familiarity with the things in question and systematic knowledge thereof,* but if he were dealing with a like result from the study of unfamiliar phenomena he would probably fall into error, unless he appreciated the danger of the fallacy of misplaced concreteness.

More or less the same considerations explain the very important fact, which should never be forgotten in studying social phenomena, that nearly all supposedly qualitative questions turn out on examination to be quantitative.[41] The fact that a problem involves quantitative considerations may be overlooked, through falling into the fallacy of misplaced concreteness and supposing that but a single factor controls a situation in which many factors are in play. But it may also be overlooked because principles, prejudices, sentiments of many kinds forbid compromise. In short, either of the two great sources of error—the fallacy of misplaced concreteness or the intrusion of the sentiments—may prevent a man's seeing that a problem is not qualitative, but quantitative.

Consider such political issues as centralization of authority, labor, the tariff, and relief, or indeed any proposal for the restriction of freedom of the individual. A moment's reflection will show that the problems involved are quantitative and that each includes many factors. Yet in public discussion the issues can hardly even be treated quantitatively. Even if the advisers of our politicians knew enough to do so, which they do not, even if the politicians could be fully instructed in the intricacies of the problems, which is clearly impossible, conflicts of interests and especially conflicts of residues would remain as dominant factors. The effective polit-

[41]   See Churchill.

ical treatments of such things is qualitative and must ordinarily lead on to the fallacy of misplaced concreteness.

The simplest form of this fallacy is as follows: A correlation between two things is observed, say, values of the pressure and of the volume of a gas. A simple algebraical expression for this correlation is then found, in this instance Boyle's law, $PV = K$. One is then tempted to say that pressure is the cause that a gas has a certain volume. But reasoning from this cause, or from Boyle's law, may lead to conclusions that are misleading and altogether useless, because temperature and volume are also mutually dependent, and likewise of course temperature and pressure. The next step is to include temperature in the equation $PV = RT$. Here R is a constant. This is a much more comprehensive statement which more closely approaches concrete reality—though still a rough approximation.

In general, we exclude many factors from our consideration in observing phenomena. Thus we find simple uniformities, commonly called laws. Whenever we reason from these uniformities, in cases where the neglected factors are important, we must, as a rule, reach misleading conclusions.[42] We are, however, strongly disposed to reason in this manner because there is a strong sentiment that forms simple causal explanations of things.

But there is more than this—much more—to the difficulty. In a social system, and, as a rule, elsewhere, an action initiated in a certain thing leads to modifications everywhere in the system, and these modifications to further modifications which involve the very thing in which the process originated. So it is both "cause" and "effect." Moreover, the notion that the process originated at a certain point is, as often as not, no better than the legal fiction that it sometimes actually is in the law courts, when it becomes necessary somehow to fix responsibility for a chain of events and there is no objective test, but only a perhaps ambiguous legal convention for doing so. Thus, reasoning from cause to effect in the study of concrete phenomena is often even more misleading than more general reasoning of the same kind. This is particularly true

[42]   See Marshall.

of the interactions between men. Thus, thousands of pages have been written about the causes of the war of 1914–18. But there is no agreement about these causes, or about when or where they originated or about the chains of events that they initiated. And there can be none. Even if it were possible to eliminate the sentiments of the writers and to provide them with all the necessary trustworthy information, it would still be necessary to solve the problem of the interactions of innumerable factors throughout a considerable time. Now experience shows that this is impossible without the aid of mathematics. But there is no way of putting the facts into such form that they could be used for mathematical purposes. And even if this could be done, the merely mathematical task would be interminable. So the question is meaningless, in the technical sense of the word meaningless.

We may fix these ideas by glancing at a case of a more familiar kind. A student who has just had three or four cocktails is shaving when his roommate slams a door. He drops his razor and cuts his toe, carelessly ties up the wound and goes to the theater. His toe becomes inflamed, and he finally dies. What is the cause of his death?

The following causes, among others, may be assigned by various persons: General septicemia, by the doctor; a streptococcus infection, by the bacteriologist; there was no one to take proper care of him, by the mother; the doctor's incompetency, by the father; the slamming of the door, by the roommate; lack of discipline in the boy's upbringing, by an uncle; the boy's neglect of the wound, by a timid and also by a methodical friend; the cocktails, by a prohibitionist.

I think you will find, upon reflection, that the preceding analysis fits this case and that, unless we adopt and use some system of conventions like that required in reports of death, the question of the cause of death is, in fact, meaningless. Note that the conventional procedure is necessary even for the roughest kind of statistical work. The nearest approach to a logical statement, among those commonly made, is that death was due to bad luck. At least this implies for those who have studied what is called chance that many circumstances, all of them necessary in the determination of the event, were combined in an intricate manner and that for various reasons we find it impossible to disentangle them. One reason is that we never know them all. So it points to some among the more obvious logical difficulties that ordinarily arise in the study of mutual dependence in a social system.

The many interactions within social systems have much to do with the tendency of all sorts of social processes to undulate or pass through what are vaguely called cycles,[43] e.g., the business cycle. Search for uniformities and regularities in such cycles has ordinarily proved illusory, just as it has in the case of many meteorological phenomena and it is perhaps expedient to content ourselves with the purposely vague remark that as a rule what goes up sooner or later comes down, and what comes down goes up. Such fluctuations in general seem to have no regular periods and no regular amplitudes. But they are obviously influenced and probably on the whole determined by the interactions of many factors.

We have by no means come to an end of the difficulties that arise from the state of mutual dependence of the factors of a social system and from the condition that we define as equilibrium. For the present, however, I think we shall do well to make shift with what we have already considered, plus one more consideration.

When you notice a particular "evil" in a social system, say, chronic alcoholism, you may be tempted to think that a single change in the system, for example, a prohibition amendment, will remedy the evil and produce no other important result. Experience shows, however, that, in general, this is not the case, but that on the contrary, while the desired result may or may not be realized, many other results will certainly ensue, most of which are unpredictable.

The explanation of this is roughly as follows: Every factor of the social system is directly dependent for its continued existence upon many other factors, and these in turn upon it; that is to say, they are mutually dependent and interactive. Directly or indirectly, the existence of any factor is indeed more or less dependent upon *all* other factors and they, reciprocally, are dependent upon it. A

43   See Hazlitt, Amiel.

change in one factor is, therefore, accompanied and followed by a long series of changes involving all the factors of the system. Therefore if you would preserve a certain factor of the system you must be willing to put up with the other factors, the connections and the constraints upon which its continued existence depends. Similarly, if you would change it you must be prepared to put up with innumerable other changes—the necessary conditions of the existence of the modified factor.[44] For the present we are as a rule unable to foresee even the more important results of an experimental modification of the social system and, for reasons already sufficiently explained, there is no prospect that we shall presently be able to foresee them.

But there is a further complication. An enduring change in a social system, say, a change of the form of government or, not infrequently, an apparently less important change like the change of a law or of a technological process may involve a change from one state of equilibrium of the social system to a very different state. For experience shows that among the innumerable states of the system that can be at least vaguely imagined, very few are in fact even approximately stationary states. The changes of the system somewhat resemble the changes observed in the game of cat's-cradle. There are certain possible relatively stationary states of equilibrium and a modification leads from one of them to another, but between the two only rapid change is possible.

Millions of Americans felt that under the prohibition amendment our social system was changing rapidly toward a new state of equilibrium. They detested the trend and feared the state that they vaguely foresaw as its end. They attributed all this, no doubt oversimply but with increasing confidence, to the prohibition amendment. They repealed the amendment in order to arrest the trend and in the hope of a return to a condition more or less like the prewar equilibrium. These are assertions. Is it too much to say that they are not derivations, but that they are, on the contrary, fairly probable inductions from well-known facts?

You should carefully note the distinction between (1) the

---

[44]   See Bagehot (II).

movement toward a new state of equilibrium under the influence of an enduring influence (e.g., prohibition) and (2) the movement toward the old state of equilibrium following a temporary disturbance (e.g., the Louisville flood).

You must on no account run away with the ideas just presented. In the first place, they have been very incompletely developed, because a more complete development would be here inappropriate. In the second place, they are subject to one qualification, and it is of the greatest practical importance: Experience shows that a single factor may sometimes be usefully regarded, in a rough approximation, as a sole determinant of events. Thus many things are approximately determined by the economic interests. To this extent Marx was right. And there is nothing that you should more carefully bear in mind than this: many things are approximately determined by the residues.

We may now close these introductory remarks with three specific directions, and a final remark.

First, you should fix the content of this introduction in your mind, taking care to forget nothing and, until new habits of work are formed, to recall everything just as methodically as you can, when you study the cases.

Secondly, you should recognize as your first task, as that task which you should invariably, from the beginning, methodically perform, the diagnosis and classification of the factors of a social system as (1) component persons, (2) their structural arrangement in subgroups (quasi-independent systems), (3) economic interests, (4) residues, (5) derivations, (6) science, (7) logic. You should also invariably look for residues of the instinct of combinations and for residues of the persistence of aggregates. Do not forget, however, that your analysis will often lead you in particular cases to disregard some of these classes of factors because you find them negligible for a particular purpose and in a first approximation. There are extreme cases where it may be sufficient to consider only persons and their residues or persons and their economic interests, and so on. Some of the excerpts which follow have been chosen to make this possible.

Thirdly, you should endeavor to acquire skill spontaneously

and without too much sense of effort in the procedures which we have considered.

In the end, the result of this should be (1) that you will often, in simple instances, make a diagnosis without conscious awareness of the grounds for it and (2) that you will ordinarily use the conceptual scheme unconsciously without thinking about what you are doing. The first form of behavior is that of the skillful practicing physician or man of affairs, the second is that of the skillful natural scientist.

When such habits have been formed, you will be able to proceed more often and more effectively to your final task in the scientific study of cases. This is the clear, explicit, and logical formulation of all relevant observations, analyses, and conclusions. *In scientific work the final task must be invariably performed.* This is an induction from experience. It is a judgment from which there can be no appeal.

2

THE PROCESS OF SCIENTIFIC

DISCOVERY

1927

Editorial note: This is the introduction to Claude Bernard, *An Introduction to the Study of Experimental Medicine,* translated by H. C.
Greene, (New York: Henry Schuman, 1949), pp. v-xii. Originally
published in translation in 1927. Claude Bernard was an important
intellectual influence on Henderson and was one of, his key role-
models as a scientist. In this essay, Henderson shows his interest in
Bernard's use of the idea of system and discusses, as Bernard did, the
relation between physiology and medicine, or pure and applied science. However, Henderson is chiefly interested in the sociological aspects of the process of scientific discovery. In addition to providing
some substantive concepts and propositions about that process, he
stresses the need for further research in this area. He is expressing his
interest in what we now call the sociology of science.

Introduction

THE DISCOVERER of natural knowledge stands apart in the
modern world, an obscure and slightly mysterious figure. By the
abstract character of his researches his individuality is obliterated;
by the rational form of his conclusions his method is concealed;
and at best he can be known only through an effort of the imagination. This is perhaps inevitable. But the unfortunate effects are enhanced by convention which to-day prescribes a formal, rigorous
and impersonal style in the composition of scientific literature.
Thus while it is no more difficult to know Galileo and Harvey
than Cervantes and Milton through their writings, or to perceive
their habits and methods of works, psychological criticism will

often seek in vain the personality and the behavior of the person behind the modern scientific printed page. Yet whoever fails to understand the great investigator can never know what science really is.

Such knowledge is not taught in the schools. Even more than the scientific memoir, the treatise and the lecture are formal, logical, systematic; thus truly intelligible and living only to the initiated. As much as possible science is made to resemble the world which it describes, in that all vestiges of its fallible and imaginative human origin are removed. Since the publication of Euclid's immortal textbook this has been the universal and approved usage. Little doubt should remain that it is the best. But then the burden must fall upon the student of initiating himself into mysteries which no one will explain to him.

What he lacks is understanding of the art of research and of the inevitable conditions and limitations of scientific discovery, an understanding, in short, of the behavior of the man of genius, not a rationalized discussion of scientific method. The latter may be sought in many learned works and in the teachings of academic philosophers; a good account of the former is far to seek. It is, therefore, not the least of the merits of Claude Bernard's An Introduction to the Study of Experimental Medicine that we have here an honest and successful analysis of himself at work by one of the most intelligent of modern scientists, a man of genius and a great physiologist. This work lays bare, so far as that is possible, what others have concealed.

With due regard to such analysis and logical formulation as are indispensable for intelligibility of exposition, Claude Bernard has avoided *a posteriori* rationalization as he has *a priori* dogmatism. Thus it is possible to perceive his scientific method as the habit of the man. His life is spent in putting questions to nature. These questions are the measure of his originality. He cannot tell how they arise, but the experimental idea seems to him a presentment of the nature of things. Such ideas are, at any rate, the only fertilizing factor in research; without them scientific method is sterile, and great discoveries are those which have given rise to the most luminous ideas.

The experiment, accordingly, is always undertaken in view of a preconceived idea, but it matters not whether this idea is vague or clearly defined, for it is but the question, vague or otherwise, which he puts to nature. Now, when nature replies, he holds his peace, takes note of the answer, listens to the end and submits to the decision. In short, the experiment is always devised with the help of a working hypothesis; the resulting observation is always made without preconceived idea. Such habits are not too easily formed, for man is by nature proud and inclined to metaphysics, but the practice of experimentation will cure these faults.

Claude Bernard is at pains to point out that even so modest an abstract description of method does violence, for the sake of clearness, to the complexity of human behavior. Beyond this his method is the *art* of experimentation, an art which rests upon a perfect and habitual familiarity with the objects that he studies and with the details of his experimental procedure.

The chapters in which all this is developed are pervaded by a spirit of honesty, simplicity and modesty, the mark of a great investigator. It is not difficult while reading them to see the man at work, full of ideas, a marvelous observer, marking and taking note even of that for which he is not looking, always doubting, but serenely and without scepticism, guarding himself from his hypothesis and even from the unconfirmed observation, yet ever confident in the determinism of nature and therefore in the possibility of rational knowledge.

The subject of his investigations was physiology, in the broadest and in the most modern sense, physiology conceived as the predestined foundation of scientific medicine and as the most important part of biology. Thus his science was seen by Claude Bernard with clear but prophetic vision, for he lived almost a half century before his time. He perceived that physiology rests securely upon the physico-chemical sciences, because all that these sciences bring to light is true of organic as of inorganic phenomena. Also there is nothing but the difficulty of the task to hinder the reduction of physiological processes to physical and chemical phenomena. And yet this cannot be the last word, for physiology is more than bio-physics and biochemistry, biology more than applied physical science. He has himself, elsewhere, put the case as follows:

Admitting that vital phenomena rest upon physico-chemical activities, which is the truth, the essence of the problem is not thereby cleared up; for it is no chance encounter of physico-chemical phenomena which constructs each being according to a pre-existing plan, and produces the admirable subordination and the harmonious concert of organic activity.

There is an arrangement in the living being, a kind of regulated activity, which must never be neglected, because it is in truth the most striking characteristic of living beings. . . .

Vital phenomena possess indeed their rigorously determined physico-chemical conditions, but, at the same time, they subordinate themselves and succeed one another in a pattern and according to a law which pre-exist; they repeat themselves with order, regularity, constancy, and they harmonize in such manner as to bring about the organization and growth of the individual, animal or plant.

It is as if there existed a pre-established design of each organism and of each organ such that, though considered separately, each physiological process is dependent upon the general forces of nature, yet taken in relation with the other physiological processes, it reveals a special bond and seems directed by some invisible guide in the path which it follows and toward the position which it occupies.

The simplest reflection reveals a primary quality, a *quid proprium* of the living being, in this pre-established organic harmony.[1]

I know of no other statement of the case since Aristotle's which seems to me to present so well a biologist's philosophy.

It must not be expected, however, to find in the work of Claude Bernard a *system* of biological philosophy. He sets forth his views on the philosophy and the method of science, and they are really his views, the very convictions that he carries with him into the laboratory. But they are not a clear system of philosophy, nor a rational and logical scientific method, which neither he nor anyone else can believe in as he goes about his daily work. Hence, like everybody's real beliefs, they shade off into vague, more or

[1]   *Leçons sur les Phénomènes de la Vie Commune aux Animaux et aux Végétaux.* Paris, 1878, Vol. 1, p. 50.

less inconsistent, more or less doubtful opinions. This is reality itself.

The theory of organism is more than a philosophical generalization; it is a part of the working equipment of the physiologist, fulfilling a purpose not unlike that of the second law of thermodynamics in the physical sciences. It has been more or less clearly understood and employed from the earliest times, and Claude Bernard did but perfect it. The theory of the constancy of the internal environment, a related theory, we owe almost wholly to Claude Bernard himself. There is no better illustration of his penetrating intelligence. A few scattered observations on the composition of blood sufficed to justify, in his opinion, the assertion that the constancy of the internal environment (*milieu intérieur*) is the condition of free and independent life.[2] A large part of the physiological research of the last two decades may fairly be regarded as a verification and illustration of this theory, which as Claude Bernard perceived, serves to interpret many of the most important physiological and pathological processes. It was this theory too that led him to a clear conception of general physiology, which he regarded as the fundamental biological science.

General physiology, according to him, includes the study of the physico-chemical properties of the environment of the cell, a similar study of the cell itself, beyond this of the physico-chemical relations between cell and environment, and, generally, of the phenomena common to animals and plants. This science, of which he is the founder, was destined to remain undeveloped until long after his death. To-day, with the aid of a physical chemistry unknown to the contemporaries of Claude Bernard, it is fulfilling the promise which he alone could clearly see. He never had a more luminous presentiment of the nature of things than this vision of the future foundations of biology.

[2]   This should not be thought of as absolute constancy, and it should be understood that variations in the properties of the internal environment may be both cyclical and adaptive, that is functional, but in general may not be random and functionless. Claude Bernard's principle is the first approximation which suffices until the subject has been broadly developed.

No man is a true prophet otherwise than through the possession of such intimate knowledge of a subject that he is able to say, "Thus matters must develop." Such was Claude Bernard's prophecy of the future of his own science. His understanding of physiology had become so perfect that the future could not be wholly doubtful. He knew where the path must lead, and it is this that makes his book so amazingly modern. In other respects he is only a highly intelligent man of the third quarter of the nineteenth century. Accordingly his treatment of some subjects, such as mathematics and physics, is a little old-fashioned, especially on the logical side. In general such defects are not only slight, but also unimportant from the medical standpoint. But his discussion of statistics could hardly be written to-day. There are indeed those, though few in number, who will agree with his criticisms. But, when he wrote, the influence of Galton had not been exerted and nobody realized that statistics afford a method, at once powerful, elegant and exact, of describing a class of objects as a class.

Physiology, as defined and understood in this book, with general physiology as its foundation, is the essential medical science. Medicine has passed through the empirical, the systematic, the nosological and the morphological stages and has entered upon the experimental stage. Thus it has finally become physiological, for physiology is the larger part of experimental medicine. Such is the principal thesis of the present work, which ought not to be obscured by the consideration of incidental topics, no matter how intrinsically important they may be.

This opinion, to be sure, does not yet meet with universal approval, and yet I believe that it has been at length fully confirmed by the experience of the twentieth century. Nevertheless, the confirmation was long delayed by the emergence of the bacteriological stage in the evolution of medicine. Unforeseen by Claude Bernard, this was the result of the discoveries of his contemporary, Pasteur.

To-day, looking backward, we see how it was that bacteriological researches for a long time took the first place which Claude Bernard believed to be already assured to those of his own science. When Pasteur began the study of micro-organisms a great gap existed in our knowledge of the organic cycle and of natural history. His work and that of his successors filled this gap, completed our present theory of the cycle of life and established the natural history of infectious diseases, of fermentations and of the soil. This was perhaps the most rapid advance of descriptive knowledge in the history of science. For the moment the researches of physiologists were overshadowed and the work of the young men diverted into the new fields. In time bacteriology grew into a fully developed science, perfected its methods, exploited its domain, and then, the most pressing work well done, resigned its leadership of the medical sciences.

Meanwhile a profound influence was exerted on what Professor Whitehead has called the intellectual climate. Claude Bernard's outlook may be described as biological and philosophical, and such a point of view seems necessary for the understanding of the deeper problems of medicine. Pasteur, however, always retained the chemist's outlook, and in him the will was more important than the reflective intellect. His successors have taken a position hardly more biological and, probably of necessity, have had little interest in rational theory. Such a climate is unfavorable to the growth of experimental medicine and especially of general physiology, for both are biological and rational.

This had been vaguely understood as early as the times of Galileo, of Borelli, and of Malpighi, when the minds of men were still fresh and not yet enslaved by specialism. But even Claude Bernard, because he still lacked the aid of modern physical chemistry, hardly appreciated the possibilities, very limited but very important, of the applications of the fully developed method of rational physical science, when guided and duly restrained by the judgment of a true physiologist, in the study of the ultimate phenomena of life.

In default of the physico-chemical foundations, during a period when bacteriology was the dominant influence in medical science, and next to it, perhaps, the highly specialized science of organic chemistry, when the prevailing activity was somewhat unintellectual, physiology continued in the old paths. Not until after the turn of the century did the movement which Claude Bernard had foreseen make itself felt. To-day it is well established and should be generally recognized. The result has already been a remarkable increase of experimental investigation and of rational theorizing in the clinic. For the first time mathematics, physics, chemistry and physical chemistry, as aids to physiology, have passed into the hospitals. I believe that, for the reasons which Claude Bernard has explained, this will long remain the way of medical progress and that we have now definitely entered upon the epoch of experimental medicine.

All progress entails evils and few experimenters can understand as Claude Bernard did the phenomena of life and the philosophy of the organism. For these reasons, and for others not so good, the growth of experimental medicine gives rise to criticism, as it did a half century ago. Experienced physicians, practised in the art of medicine and rightly believing that medicine is still and must always be an art, but also uncomfortable and suspicious through ignorance of the new development, are not lacking to unite with this opposition. So far as grounds for complaint exist they are due to the absence of that high intelligence and skill of the experimenter which are necessary to understand and to solve the complex problems of physiology. Here one can only plead the palliating circumstance that all human endeavor suffers from the same weakness. On the other hand, prevailing criticism of scientific medicine itself, no less than the earlier criticism of the nineteenth century, finds conclusive answers in this book.

Medicine is but a part of human biology and the study of human inheritance, constitution, intelligence and behavior, of adaptation to new conditions of life, and of a host of other subjects, far transcends the boundaries of medicine. But everywhere throughout this vast field physiology has the same importance as in the narrower field of medicine. Thus the Introduction may serve as a guide not only for those who are beginning the study of medicine, but for many others as well.

The sciences are not equal, nor do they preserve their rank unchanged as civilization moves on. During nearly a quarter of a millennium mechanics led all the others in intellectual interest and in influence upon European civilization. It will seem to many not too bold a prophecy, for the reasons that Claude Bernard has set forth, to look forward to a century in which physiology shall take a similar place. I venture to believe that that position will be reached when the experimental method has made possible a rational science of organism.

The physiological researches of Claude Bernard have immortalized his name, but the present work and his other general writings have hardly attracted the attention which they deserve or exerted the influence of which they are capable. This is probably due both to the conflicting influence of bacteriology, organic chemistry and other sciences and, not less, to his own clearness of vision. That which he saw as the future of physiology remained for many decades hidden from others and so his writings were only half understood. Even general physiology is still hardly aware of the program which he set forth and which it has been unwittingly carrying out. There is, however, one well known instance of his influence exerted farther afield. As the idea of Balzac's *Comédie Humaine* was suggested by the biology of the early nineteenth century, so the naturalism of Zola was suggested by the works of Claude Bernard. Perhaps the result will not be thought worthy of the cause. Yet the instance is significant of the wide bearing of an interpretation of life which may be seen to be peculiarly well suited to the present conditions of the political and social as well as of the natural sciences.

Among great men, Claude Bernard should be counted fortunate in that he has not become a mythical figure. Unlike Pasteur, whose discoveries are hardly more remarkable, though their immediate influence has been immeasurably greater, and whose horizon was incontestably less broad, he remains a plain man, highly distinguished no doubt, but not obscured by the growth of a legend.

It is possible not only to see him at work, but even to discover his purposes and his feelings. The desire to relieve suffering and a sense of duty are clearly apparent, and one may read between the lines the enduring satisfaction that he felt in the society of younger men who owed to him more than they could ever repay. But weightier still are the contentment which comes from work well done, the sense of the value of science for its own sake, insatiable curiosity and, above all, the pleasure of masterly performance and of the chase. These are the effective forces which move the scientist. The first condition for the progress of science is to bring them into play.

3

AN APPROXIMATE DEFINITION

OF FACT

1932

Editorial note: Reprinted by permission of The Regents of the University of California from *University of California Publications in Philosophy* 14 (1932) : 179–99. As befits a paper published in a professional, technical journal of philosophy, this paper is itself thoroughly technical and professional in purpose and substance. It is the most complete statement of Henderson's views on the constructivist character of conceptual schemes and on the probable and approximate, rather than certain and fixed, character of such schemes in the sciences.

As in discussions of prohibition and of "war-guilt," so generally in the business of every-day life we find fact and sentiment almost inextricably commingled. If then we are to talk about fact, I suggest that we shall do well to talk about sentiment also, and try to discriminate. I think that it will be convenient to this end to talk about logic, mathematics and natural science; about poetry, religion and metaphysics; but not to forget more primitive experience, such as that of dogs, and of children.

Before setting out I wish to say as clearly as possible that I do not seek to find out what fact is. I would as willingly undertake a search for the absolute or for the unicorn, because these three undertakings, seem to me similar.[1] I prefer a different path and

---

1   If a word does not refer to something clearly recognizable without analysis, e.g., John Smith, tooth-ache, and has not received an arbitrary definition, it is, I suggest, impossible to discover what its meaning is, for it has no precise meaning and is probably employed in several different senses.

shall first set up what I hope may prove to be a convenient approximate definition of a word. I keep the word *fact* because I find that it is often used more or less in this sense. I keep it for convenience, in spite of inconveniences that are due to the frequent use of the word in other senses. I suggest that this convenience is perhaps chiefly mnemonic.

By means of this and other carefully defined words I shall try to describe certain uniformities in my experience. I am convinced by induction from experience that the most that I can thus accomplish is to find a very rough description of a few uniformities; a description that must be at best far from accurate; a description that is only one of many possible descriptions. I think this is equivalent to the statement: I shall endeavor to construct one among an infinite number of possible conceptual schemes in which a part of my experience will be contained and made available.

I give warning in advance that my statements are to be regarded as *approximate* not exact, as *probable* not certain, and that if I fail to use these words in every paragraph, my motive is solely not to fatigue you. The only certainty about statements of experience (except possibly, but only possibly, logical and mathematical experience)[2] is that they are *not* certain and *not* precise; some however are sufficiently so for every-day use, but we are often slow to find out which. I believe that even this statement is an induction from experience and that it is only probable.

A scientific fact $= F_s =$

A statement in unambiguous terms derived by logical operations from statements of experience, when the experiences stated are probably sufficiently numerous and sufficiently various in respect of observers and in respect of observations and experiments.

A common fact $= F_c =$

[2]   The probability that $2 + 2 = 4$ (assuming 3 defined as the number that follows 2, 4 as the number that follows 3 in counting) may be expressed by $1 - x$. Then the question is this: Is the value of x to be regarded as practically or absolutely zero? According to the theory of probability $x > 0$ because its value depends upon a finite number of observations. We know, however, that all mathematicians and most others feel sure that $2 + 2 = 4$. Perhaps the question is without interest except in respect of the manifestation of this sentiment.

A corroborated statement, like "here is John," that approaches very closely to a reaction to a stimulus where a gestalt is involved in the arc.

$$A \text{ fact} = F = A \text{ mixture of } F_s \text{ and } F_c.$$

In order to fix our ideas, and without further definition of the kind of mixture:

$$F = nF_s + (1 - n)F_c,$$

where $1 \geq n \geq 0$.

We have then: F_s is a member of one class of statements. F_c is a member of another class of statements. F is a member of a third class of statements, comprising mixtures, in any proportions, of members of the beforementioned two classes of statements.

Unambiguous terms include: (1) terms previously defined by an operation, e.g., arithmetical sum (adding defined), length (measuring defined), gold (analyzing defined), murder (act defined by statute), and (2) terms referring to appearances or other experiences clearly recognizable by all who are acquainted with them, e.g., the Parthenon, Signor Mussolini, Paris, Yankee Doodle, the odor of ammonia (when strong and unmixed), pain (when severe), anger (when intense).

The definition of probable is well known to present peculiar difficulties. In the case of, say, the probability that a die is true within specified limits, probability may be determined by experiment and computation. But the discussion of the probability of judgment is almost uniquely unsatisfactory in the history of mathematics.

We may note that estimates of the probability of the sufficiency of evidence to establish fact are most often verified when they are made by persons whose hopes, fears, prejudices, and other emotions are probably not involved in the estimate. It is also proved by experience that employing a large "factor of safety" is a useful precaution. This question is notoriously one of the most difficult in the whole field of science. The final appeal seems to be often to common consent, as in trial by jury. Experience shows that this is dangerous and the situation would be disconcerting were it not that we have all the natural sciences to show that the obstacle is often circumvented. I shall assume that the difficulties of logicians with the analysis of induction and the blunders of many mathematicians in the mathematical analysis of probability make it inexpedient to pursue this subject.

δ = a statement of experience, probably derived from experience by logical operations, in such terms that operations of verification can be determined by logical operations.

The presence of non-logical operations in the derivation of δ is probable in such cases as the following: Statements concerning the observed effects of prohibition made by "drys" or by "wets." Descriptions of observations of an elaborate nature made by young enthusiastic beginners in scientific work.

Experience $= \epsilon = \rho + \pi + \iota + a + \nu + \lambda + \phi$.

This is not a definition of experience, which I leave undefined.[3] It is a direction to put any experience into one or more of several classes. Hence there is involved not a question of approximation, but one of convenience in carrying out the direction.

ρ = receptor experiences, e.g., seeing.

π = proprioceptor experiences, e.g., thirsting.

ι = inceptor experiences, e.g., fearing.

a = other primitive mental experiences, e.g., attending to, remembering, associating, recognizing gestalts, forming primitive conceptual schemes, dreaming.

ν = non-logical mental operations, e.g., verbal dreaming, revery, verbally expressing sentiments and accord of sentiments.

λ = logical mental operations, e.g., verifying identity, counting, performing other mathematical operations, formulating statements.

ϕ = physical operations, e.g., turning head, moving objects, weighing, measuring.

This classification of the constituents of experience ϵ is very nearly worthless as a description of experience. It is designed to enable us to fix our attention, and is very rough for two reasons. First, psychology affords insufficient information for the purpose. Here it may be noted that ν and λ are intended to include what we

[3]   The choice to leave this, rather than some other term, undefined is made solely on grounds of expediency.

guess to be nearly absent from a dog's ϵ. Secondly, ϵ is an organic process, not a sum of parts. Therefore, subdividing it in this matter, like the subdivision of physiological activity into functions, is in a peculiar degree arbitrary, and frequently misleading unless we constantly remember that it is arbitrary.[4] Cf. "Half a sheep is mutton." In particular it may be noted that discriminations between ρ and π, π and ι, ι and α, α and ν are sometimes completely arbitrary.

In organic processes cause-and-effect analysis leads, in general, to erroneous conclusions. The only alternative known to me is mutual-dependence analysis which is, in general, impossible without the use of mathematics.

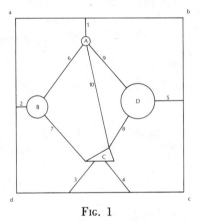

Fig. 1

Consider figure 1. The four rigid bodies A, B, C, and D are fastened to a framework a, b, c, d, by the elastic bands 1, 2, 3, 4, and 5. A, B, C, and D, are joined one to another by the elastic bands 6, 7, 8, 9, and 10. Here the conditions of statical equilibrium can be worked out mathematically, or determined empirically by introducing spring-balances into the bonds 1, 2, ... 10, and reading the balances.

---

4   For this reason it is an error to suppose that by eliminating ν and λ from ϵ we have left the equivalent of a dog's experience. At best we have a dog's experience adapted to ν and λ, which is probably a very different thing.

Now imagine the point of attachment of 5 on the frame to be moving toward b, all other points of attachment remaining unchanged. What will happen? Consider A. There will be action on A by the path 5, 9, by the path 5, 8, 10, and by the path 5, 8, 7, 6. But in each case these actions do not cease at A, just as they do not previously cease at D. The first, for example, continues along the path 10, 8 and so back to 5. If we try to think of all this as cause-and-effect we must inevitably reach a state of confusion. The analysis of such a problem, difficult at best, is possible only by means of mathematics, and leads to the view that certain variables are mutually dependent in a manner defined by expressions which are functions of these variables. Among these variables is time. In a similar, but immensely more complex way the process ϵ may be conceivable as involving the mutual dependence of an indefinitely large number of very heterogeneous variables. But nobody has hitherto succeeded even in making it thus conceivable, except as here, vaguely and by analogy.

$\gamma =$ Statement of a conclusion.

Classes of γ:

(1) $\gamma^\lambda =$ a γ derived by logical operations.
(2) $\gamma_\nu =$ a γ derived by non-logical operations.

Classes of γ_λ:

(a) $F =$ a fact.
(b) $f =$ an unverified logical conclusion.
    (Note that here λ may be approximately 0, as in "Here is John.")

Classes of γ_ν:

(a) Statements expressing accord of sentiments with things, e.g., Bourges Cathedral is beautiful.
(b) Statements expressing accord of sentiments with sentiments, e.g., Truth is beauty.
(c) Statements expressing sentiments,
    e.g., He on honey-dew hath fed and drunk the milk of Paradise.

.   .   .   .   .   .

. . . . . .

(μ) Statements that existence is real, absolute, etc.,
   e.g., This table really exists.

Let us now consider the relation $\epsilon \to \delta \to \gamma \to \mu$.

Let:

   ϵ = Seeing table *or* touching table
   δ = I see a table *or* I feel a table
   γ = This is a table
   μ = This table really exists.

Without ϵ no δ, γ or μ is possible (of course ϵ may be a decision
   to tell a lie).

With ϵ any or all (δ,γ,μ) may be possible.

I exclude μ from further detailed consideration for the following reasons. Suppose it is asserted that my dog really exists because I see, hear, touch, and smell him, did so yesterday, the day
before, etc. This assertion implies the definition of reality as some
kind of experience,[5] say ϵ_R = real (cf. cogito = sum), and con-
verts μ into γ_λ, which does not satisfy the desire for μ, with the
result that I shall presently find some other statement, about absolute reality for instance, much to be desired. If we note the usefulness, even to this day, of the geocentric conceptual scheme, we
see that what appears to be the fullest possible logical use of γ_λ may
be independent of μ. It may also be noted that most physicists seem
to have been convinced by Einstein that simultaneity involves the
relation of events to the observer. This renders very troublesome
that process so agreeable to all of us of endowing the conceptual
world with absolute qualities.

If it is nevertheless asserted that real existence can be proved,
I recall that "cogito ergo sum" and all other attempts known to

[5]   E. W. Hobson, *The Domain of Natural Science* (New York, 1923):
140–141: "The fact of experience which is regarded by Helmholtz as of
significance in relation to the theory of Geometry is that freely movable
rigid bodies exist in physical space; their dimensions remaining unaltered
during the motion. This may be stated in the more precise form that, if
a pair of particles A, B of any one such body can be brought into coincidence with a pair A^1, B^1 of another such body, then the coincidence of
congruency remains unaltered when the pair of bodies are moved in any
manner." Here existence has given place to an operation.

me are not logical operations. They are then non-logical operations. Further I note that I cannot find a single instance where μ, if assumed, can be used in any logical operation (from which $\gamma\nu$ is excluded) where $\gamma\lambda$ cannot be substituted for μ (cf. as if). *A $\gamma\lambda$ is the necessary and sufficient conclusion for a further $\gamma\lambda$.*[6] The question remains whether μ may be necessary for a ϕ, i.e., for an ι which serves as an encouragement to action. This is a psychological problem. It seems probable that many people find encouragement to certain kinds of action in the assertion of metaphysical or religious belief. At any rate it is a common experience to observe statements that skeptics have been rendered ineffectual by their doubt. The frequently expressed dislike of Montaigne's "que sais-je?" seems to be an expression of the same sentiment. But it is difficult to prove that this is the case to such an extent that upon the whole the formation of further $\gamma\lambda$'s is retarded. Perhaps the result varies with the age of the person concerned, because habits and slowly acquired sentiments are here involved.

But also I note the remarkable fact that the sentiments expressed by the simplest μ's seem to be probably the least variable of all sentiments. In particular they are very little modified by talking about them, and even those who have been trained to deny μ, retain the sentiments almost unchanged. This may be a result of the wonderful vividness and immediacy of our conceptual

---

[6]   Poincaré, H., *La valeur de la science* (Paris [no date]):272: "Mais il y a mieux; dans le même langage on dira très bien: ces deux propositions, le monde extérieur existe, ou, il est plus commode de supposer qu'il existe, ont un seul et même sens."

    Painlevé, P., *Les axiomes de la mécanique* (Paris [no date]):79: "Sous une autre forme, qui n'a de paradoxale que l'apparence, si c'est une convention de dire que la terre tourne, c'est également une convention de dire qu'elle existe, et ces deux conventions se justifient par des raisons identiques."

    Pareto, V., *Traité de Sociologie générale*, Édition française de P. Boven, Lausanne and Paris, 2 vols., 1917 and 1919, p. 986: "Mais la proposition qui affirme *l'existence* des individus ne peut appartenir à la science expérimentale; elle sort entièrement du domaine expérimental; le terme *existence*, employé de cette façon, appartenant proprement à la métaphysique. Experimentalement, dire qu'une chose existe, signifie seulement qu'elle fait partie du monde expérimental."

scheme, the common-sense world, of its absolutely indispensable uses, of its constant presence, of its rôle as the scene of all our experiences, of its consistency, and of its trustworthiness.[7] But note that the preceding sentence is in part a non-logical statement of accords of sentiments. I think the complex or aggregate of sentiments here in question may probably be one to which the term faith is generally applied. The fact is that in the long run we cannot doubt that things really exist. But at the same time we cannot make use of this belief for scientific purposes, and the meaning of the word exist is vague.

It is also necessary, in order to complete the statement, to note that a denial of real existence (e.g., Berkeley's idealism) is no less non-logical, no less a statement expressing accord of sentiments. Such assertions (μ's) are then non-logical, and neither logical nor illogical.[8]

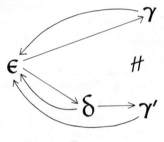

Fig. 2

We now return to the relation $\epsilon \to \delta \to \gamma$. This in full represents the uniform scientific procedure in difficult cases. Further:

[7]   Boltzmann, L., *Populäre Schriften* (Leipzig, 1905):77: "Ich bin der Meinung dass die Aufgabe der Theorie in der Konstruktion eines rein in uns existierenden Abbildes der Aussenwelt besteht, ..." and p. 80: "Wie sollte es da nicht kommen, dass man bei fortdauernder Vertiefung in die Theorie das Bild für das eigentlich Existierende hielte?" Note that these remarks, although not so intended, seem to apply to the conceptual scheme of the common-sense world.

[8]   According to Bridgman's definition of meaningless, *reality* is meaningless because no operation can be agreed upon as a definition of the word reality. See Bridgman, P. W., *The Logic of Modern Physics* (New York, 1928) chap. 1, *passim*.

I derive δ from ϵ.

I derive γ from ϵ.

Sometimes I derive γ through δ from ϵ.

I can derive γ' from δ after having derived γ from ϵ directly; then often γ' and γ disagree.

Without ϵ it is possible to derive δ from γ only in exceptional cases when the terms of γ are very precisely defined by operations, or are nearly unambiguous in their reference to a *gestalt*, e.g., the experienced hospital radiologist meets a surgeon in the hall and says: "John Smith has a fracture of the neck of the femur." Here a part of δ can be derived with fairly high probability.

δ and γ are ϵ's. Here we have organic interaction as illustrated in figure 1.

In general γ is derived from ϵ by means of λ (logical operations) and ν (non-logical operations).

Derivation of γ by means of logical operations is often facilitated by, is indeed often possible only by means of the previous derivation of δ, e.g., $\gamma =$ Diagnosis of myxedema complicated by nephritis, or formulation of Kepler's laws.

Derivation of γ by means of non-logical operations is often impeded by previous logical derivation of δ, e.g., $\gamma =$ this is a large room. If you set down carefully past experiences concerning the effect of color, lighting, arrangement of furniture upon your judgment, you will be inclined to stop at δ and say: It seems large to me. Thus γ is abandoned. But this process often arouses resentment, i.e., reacts on ι.

We may then raise the question whether δ can always be derived by λ from ϵ. Experience shows that this is often impossible, e.g., in the divorce courts.

My $\gamma\nu$, as my ϵ, can, if I am skillful enough, be stated as a δ, e.g., $\delta =$ I took great satisfaction in telling him he was a fool to do it. But this δ is very rarely derived even approximately by λ alone, in short I once more feel satisfaction in making this statement, and the organic process continues. Of course the ι will change. It may even reach the point where I shall be able to derive the γ: *I am making a fool of myself.*

In table 1, δ_4 tells nothing about γ_3. For this purpose we must

TABLE 1

	My assertion γ	My assertion δ	My experience ϵ
1	$\gamma_1 =$ **This is a room**	$\delta_1 =$ (I see a room) *or* (I recognize the gestalt) *or* (I see and recognize the gestalt) (Involves λ)	$\epsilon_1 = \rho_1 + \ldots$
2	$\gamma_2 =$ **This is a beautiful room** (Acts on A's i) (Reacts on my i)	$\delta_2 = \left\{ \delta_1 + \text{(I feel it beautiful)} \right\}$ (Involves λ and ν)	$\epsilon_2 = \rho_1 + \dot{i}_2 + \ldots$
3	$\gamma_3 =$ **This is a large room** (Acts on A's i) (Reacts on my i)	$\delta_3 = \left\{ \delta_1 + \text{(I feel it large} + \text{(I vaguely estimate it large)} \right.$ (Involves λ and ν)	$\epsilon_3 = \rho_1 + \dot{i}_3 + a_3 + \ldots$
4	$\gamma_4 =$ **This is a 6000 cu. ft. room**	$\delta_4 = \left\{ \delta_1 + \text{(I measure 10 x 20 x 30)} \text{ (I compute 10 x 20 x 30} = 6000) \right.$ (Involves λ)	$\epsilon_4 = \rho_1 + \varphi_4 + \lambda_4 + \ldots$
5	$\gamma_5 = \gamma_3 =$ **This is a large room** (Acts on A's i)	$\delta_5 = \left\{ \delta_1 + \text{(I verify: 6000} > 5000 \right.$ (Involves λ)	$\epsilon_5 = \rho_1 + \varphi_4 + \lambda_4 + \lambda_5 + \ldots$

have a definition, say: A large room is a room where $V > 5000$ cubic feet. Then the operation $6000 > 5000$ gives $\gamma_5 =$ This is a large room. This clearly illustrates the rôle of definition: $\gamma_3 = \gamma_5$ but $\delta_3 \neq \delta_5$. Note that the definition to which this result is due is arbitrary. As a result, ι has been eliminated from ϵ_5 and ν has been eliminated from δ_5 and from γ_5. Also γ_5 no longer acts on my ι. But the result of this elimination may be clearly evident in somebody's response to γ_5: "Well, it doesn't seem so to me" and then, his ι thus reinforced, he may go on to "it is a nasty little room." Sometimes his sentiment in respect of arbitrary definitions may appear in "*I call it* a nasty little room," accompanied by rejection of the arbitrary definition as not only "meaningless" but even "odious" or "immoral." Compare current political discussions about alcohol-content of intoxicating drinks.

Evidently γ_3 is more useful in expressing sentiments, ι; γ_5 in expressing observations, ρ. This is because the arbitrary definition has substituted ρ for ι in ϵ.

Room seems to be better defined than large, not so well as 6000 cubic feet. I suggest that this depends in part upon the properties of visual experiences referred to in the first paragraph of Aristotle's metaphysics.[9] For ordinary purposes mere recognition suffices. But in other cases what about closets, halls, and sleeping porches? What is a ten-room house for the buyer? What is it for the seller? Here the need of an arbitrary definition is apparent.

In table 2 the reference of γ_1 to δ_1 is ambiguous. You may

TABLE 2

(1) This is (a lump of) sugar.
(2) The square of 101 is 10201.
(3) That is disgusting (behavior).

[9]   *Aristotle's Metaphysics* (Oxford, 1928, vol. 8, Ross, Bk. A., 980 A): 20–27. "All men by nature desire to know. An indication of this is the delight we take in our senses; for even apart from their usefulness they are loved for themselves; and above all others the sense of sight. For not only with a view to action, but even when we are not going to do anything, we prefer seeing (one might say) to everything else. The reason is that this, most of all the senses, makes us know and brings to light many differences between things."

suspect that $\delta_1 = $ I recognize it, I bought it as sugar, or I have made an analysis of another piece of the same lot.

The reference of γ_2 to δ_2 is also ambiguous. You may guess $\delta_2 = $ I remember, or I perform multiplication, or, I find it in Barlow's tables.

The reference of γ_3 to δ_3 is often less ambiguous. If I am unsophisticated it is probable that $\delta_3 = $ I see behavior. I feel and notice my sentiment of disgust with respect to it. Concurrently you observe the expression of my emotions and this reacts upon your emotions.

Moreover, I may be a hypocrite, an actor, or, at the limit, I may be performing a logical operation calculated to produce a certain action upon your ι. This doubt frequently leads to one of the most difficult of all problems. For example, how far do a politician's speeches express his policy logically, how far are they to be regarded as attempts to modify the ι's of others in order to produce results entirely different from those which seem to be logically implied.[10] Occasionally a nearly pure case may be observed, e.g., Talleyrand at the Congress of Vienna, himself indifferent to all principles, choosing the principle of legitimacy on logical grounds to save French territory. Note the contrast with Woodrow Wilson at Paris, where his $\delta\nu$ can be inferred with high probability.

You deny γ_1, γ_2, γ_3. What follows?

(1) If the question is important enough, chemical analysis. Uncertainty about δ_1 is irrelevant.

(2) I say $101 = 100 + 1$. $100^2 = 10,000$; plus $2 \times 100 = 10,200$; plus $1 = 10,201$. Uncertainty about δ_2 is irrelevant.

(3) It is impossible to say. *Very rarely indeed* my statement:

[10]   Signor Mussolini attended lectures by Pareto at Lausanne. (Cf. Mussolini, B., *My Autobiography*, New York, 1928, 14). Soon after the establishment of the Fascist Government in Italy, Pareto was made a senator of the Kingdom. It is, therefore, an interesting question how far the Government of Italy during the past decade has endeavored to apply Pareto's principles to the conduct of affairs, especially in guiding opinions and modifying sentiments in the different classes of the Italian people. See Pareto, V., *op. cit.*, *passim*.

"I note our difference in sentiments." Certainty about δ_3, if it exists, is probably irrelevant. The principal feature is interaction of sentiments.

Evidently in some respects (1) and (2) are similar and (3) different.

One thing to note is that both *sugar* and *square of 101* imply a large number of operations, precisely determined and agreed upon and either wholly or in some measure mutually dependent. In the case of (2) they are mathematical operations and are considered completely mutually dependent, so that any one fully verified is as good as any other. Also they are infinite in number:

$$x = \text{any integer}$$
$$y = 101 - x$$
$$x^2 + 2xy + y^2 = 101^2$$

In the case of (1) it is known that a particular set of properties have been found associated in one case and no other. These, together with the structural formula, make up a kind of aggregate in a chemist's conceptual scheme. Each of the properties, when verified, tends to make verification of the others more and more probable, less and less necessary. The relation between some of them is almost as definite as in the case of (2) so that here the determination of one suffices for all, e.g., different methods of determining molecular weight.

In both cases, then, we have our choice of many procedures each of which is either equivalent, or nearly so, to any other. All these different procedures are clearly defined, either explicitly or implicitly.

In the case of sugar, at least, we are not concerned with precision and certainty, but only with approximation and probability. We must be content with the fact: This is probably approximately pure sugar. Nevertheless it is not difficult to make the probability entirely equivalent for practical purposes to certainty and to restrict the range of approximation within narrow limits.

In the case of disgusting behavior there is no reference to such a clearly defined aggregate of ϵ's as that called the properties of sugar. Also there is an action on the sentiments.

Disgusting behavior may be defined by legislation or fiat, like deadly sins in theology. Then verification is possible. It consists in the operation of establishing approximate identity between some properties of this behavior and some of those specified by law.

But observation shows that this is in general followed by some such response as "How ridiculous!" and the problem remains; for all men habitually make statements in accord with their sentiments, and all men seek to act upon the sentiments of others. In conversation such assertions are far more important than $\gamma\lambda$'s. So far as we know this has always been observed. There is no reason to suppose that it will cease to be. Thus even though, to assume what is absurd, all words were defined independently of the accord of sentiments, it is certain (i.e., very probable, practically certain) that some would be used independently of their definition, as *crime, libel, idiot,* now are, in order to express sentiments or to act on them.

Sentiments vary with age, sex, concentration of alcohol in the blood, from person to person, from class to class, from sect to sect, from place to place, from decade to decade. . . . The expression of sentiments with words varies very much more. It is perhaps the most variable thing in all our experience.[11]

Hence there is no reason to expect uniformity of behavior in respect of assertions like (3). In short, neither an arbitrary definition of disgusting behavior, nor a definition based upon observation of the manifestations of the sentiments of others, will work. Nobody will conform to the first, and the definition will become mere verbalism. Observations of expressions of the sentiments, unless combined with extensive observations of many other variables simultaneously, do not lead to the discovery of uniformities[12] (except in unusual cases, such as the expression of belief in the

[11]   This is one of the most important elements in the humor of Rabelais. From a very different point of view a full analysis of the subject may be found in Pareto's *Traité,* chaps. 9 and 10.

[12]   It is probable that this depends partly upon our inability to analyze our ι's as we can our ρ's and the (probably consequent) lack of clear and useful conceptual schemes for ι's.

real existences of concrete things). This is implied in Rabelais' question: "En quoi cognoissez-vous la folie anticque? En quoi cognoissez-vous la sagesse présente?"

According to Bridgman,[13] *That is disgusting behavior* is meaningless. It is meaningless because no operation can be agreed upon as a definition of *disgusting*. Here we note that the use of the word meaningless causes difficulties that illustrate the point in question, because the assertion "that is meaningless" is habitually used as an expression of accord of sentiments, and therefore acts upon them.

Suppose we try: *That is disgusting behavior* has class A meaning. *That is a lump of sugar* has class B meaning. This test shows that there is a significant distinction.

Or we might agree to say *That is disgusting behavior* has meaning, *That is a lump of sugar* is meaningless for *That is disgusting behavior* refers to our rich and significant social life, while *That is a lump of sugar* is trivial. Moreover the latter statement is no more than sticking on a label. I pause to note that this is a series of assertions of accords of sentiment. Nevertheless, I should have no objection to adopting the proposed definition of meaningless if I thought it convenient. But it would only get us into trouble with another set of people, and I have observed that brickbats have the same effects whether they are thrown by physicists or by metaphysicians.

I think we had better keep Bridgman's definition of meaningless and restrict it to the field to which it refers, namely to those operations that we call logical, observational, experimental, etc. In doing so we are but following a precept, much emphasized by Bridgman himself, that conclusions are to be recognized as applying only within the limits where the observations have been made.

I suggest that γ_3, as above shown, refers back with rather high probability to $\delta_3 = $ I see the behavior; I notice my referred sentiment of disgust; I feel satisfaction while stating γ_3. Here also appears the organic character of ϵ much more clearly than in γ_1 or γ_2. I suggest that this is related to the primitiveness of ι as compared

13   Bridgman, *loc. cit.*

with λ. Compare the series: (1) barking dog, (2) indignantly ex-postulating man, (3) man writing down conclusion of a routine habitual scientific procedure, e.g., latitude and longitude of ship at sea.

It may be convenient to say that this δ_3 is the meaning of γ_3. But note that in this sense the meaning of γ_1 is not δ_1, for here the experience of different men is uniform and $\gamma_1 > \delta_1$, because of our accumulated knowledge of the properties of sugar.

Note that γ_1 and γ_2 chiefly refer to ρ and λ; γ_3 to ι and ν. As poets and idealists also insist logic has little place in γ_3. But, like μ, γ_3 is in no sense illogical, just as

> Weave a circle round him thrice,
> And close your eyes with holy dread;
> For he on honey-dew hath fed
> And drunk the milk of Paradise.

is in no sense but a trivial one illogical. These things are non-logical. The point may perhaps be illustrated by the following tabulation:

A. Non-logical
B. Logical
   a. Correct
   b. Incorrect (illogical)

I suggest that in general logic, mathematics and natural science are logical; poetry, religion, and metaphysics non-logical.

At this point we may return to Bridgman's meaningless terms in order first to note that it is convenient to recognize three classes:

(1) Terms that are meaningless because they refer to a senti-ment, such that agreement is impossible in respect of the reference, e.g., disgusting.

(2) Terms that are meaningless because no operation for the definition is at present possible, e.g., the color of an electron.

(3) Terms that can be defined, but are not yet defined, e.g., A's function = some new mathematical function.

In respect of this classification *real* or *absolute existence* occupies a peculiar, possibly a unique, position. Here the relevant remark seems to be that no definition in terms of an operation satisfies the uniform desire of every one for proof of real existence, because such a definition is clearly arbitrary.

We now recall that it is inexpedient to retain this classification. On grounds of expediency we then remove (1) from this class and designate (1) as that class of terms that are employed in the expression of sentiments or of accord of sentiments, or in general, in non-logical conclusions.[14] In this class we place *real* or *absolute existence*.

Compare *That is John Smith* and *That is disgusting behavior*. *That is John Smith* is an F_c. It is readily corroborated by referring to other acquaintances of John Smith. *That is disgusting behavior* is a γv. It is clearly not an F_s. Neither is it an F_c, for others acquainted with disgusting behavior and a fortiori those who are acquainted with the description of the psychological process defined above as its meaning to confirm the statement. This is in general true for every $\gamma \lambda$ except a μ. Such a statement as, *That is disgusting behavior,* is neither a fact nor an error. It is, like μ, a non-fact; more specifically a statement of accord of sentiments.

I wish to state as clearly as possible the theorem: The assertion that a γv is not an F is a $\gamma \lambda$ from the definition of F.[15] As such it is independent of ι. If it acts upon your ι, that is, I suggest, because you do not accept an arbitrary definition, or feel that there is something pejorative introduced by means of it. If this is the case I suggest once more that the difficulty can be eliminated by the choice of another word in place of *fact*, in order to permit an appeal to experience to decide whether the classification we have set up is for certain purposes a useful one.

The following questions concerning the properties of F's arise: Is it in general possible to give a definition of all terms contained in F by means of uniquely defined operations? If this is possible is it expedient? Consider three F's:

[14]   See Pareto, *op. cit.*, chaps. 9 and 10, for an extensive and systematic discussion of a similar subject.
[15]   I have stated this symbolically in order to try to fix attention on the logical analysis by eliminating the action of words on sentiments.

(1) This is Paris.
(2) The square of 101 is 10201.
(3) The length of this rod is 1.000 meter.

(1) A man who knows Paris well from past experience is blindfolded in Lille, carried in a motor car to some point in Paris, unblindfolded, and released. By what operations will he verify (1)? It is evidently both impossible to say and inexpedient to suggest even very roughly a standard procedure, for this procedure is in detail quite beyond his control. Here definition of an operation that can be followed is impossible.

(2) Here an infinite number of operations are available. They are all regarded as entirely equivalent. It is possible to select one as that defining the procedure to be followed. But it is inexpedient to do so.

(3) Here Bridgman's discussion shows that in very difficult cases it is both possible and expedient, and that it may be of the very first importance in novel cases to define a unique operation. But even so we must also later refer to that aggregate of experience defined previously by *length*. We shall then have a situation which can be roughly described as follows: Common length = $length_1 + length_2 + \ldots \ldots$ Frequently the older less precise terms have to be kept for convenience as in chemistry when isomers and isotopes are discovered.

I suggest that cases similar to (1) and (2) seem to be common. In general no unique operation for identifying a known gestalt can be described. In general it is inexpedient to limit mathematical operations to those constituting a definition. In cases like (3) it is sometimes necessary, sometimes unnecessary to do so, and often also inexpedient. Here the questions of probability and of approximation are involved.

But a further consideration is perhaps more important. Except possibly in mathematics and logic we never eliminate objects merely recognized from our operations. For instance in weighing, my previously standardized set of weights is for me ordinarily such an object. So is the object weighed, if there is only one such object. Now the further you develop the precise definition of length or weight, in the manner described by Bridgman, as a very intricate set of operations, the more do you, in general, introduce such objects into the ϵ of a single experiment. Like Paris, some of these objects cannot be defined by a precise operation, or at any rate not all of them can in general be so defined. So I reach the conclusion that, when we experiment or observe, our ϵ's are always made up of ρ's involving the mere recognition of objects, plus operations of the kind described by Bridgman, and that we always employ some of these ρ's[16] with the ϵ's in deriving δ's and γ's and therefore F's.[17]

Long ago I came to the conclusion from my own work that the principal errors in thinking may be conveniently classified and described as of two kinds: First, those that depend upon the organic character of animals, of society and of experience;[18] secondly, those that depend upon failure to discriminate between fact or logical reasoning and sentiment or the expression of sentiment. I believe that Pareto, in his Traité de Sociologie Générale,[19] has gone far toward establishing this conclusion. Since my first study of his book, about four years ago, this at any rate has been my opinion, and meanwhile my own views, formerly vague, have been clarified by reflection upon the results of Pareto's powerful and extensive analysis of a wide range of phenomena.

In the present paper it has been my effort to demonstrate how difficult in the face of the mutual dependence of the factors of experience is the analysis of any part of it, but to suggest that it seems to be frequently possible, nevertheless, to discriminate between conclusions reached by approximately logical operations and others in which the expression of the sentiments cannot be

16   Even in mathematics many functions are immediately recognized by the adept, who does not ordinarily waste his time in verifying what he recognizes unmistakably.

17   There seems to be a relation between the necessity of taking something for granted in an experiment and that of taking some terms without definition in a logical enquiry. See Poincaré, op. cit., 77.

18   Compare Whitehead's prehension, Science and the Modern World (New York, 1925), passim.

19   It is impossible for me to specify my indebtedness to this work. Perhaps most of the present paper is in substance, and especially in method, partly attributable to Pareto.

conveniently neglected. To this end I have set up the definition of F and of γ_v, which resemble similar considerations of Pareto's.

It is my experience that the dichotomy thus established is a useful one. After the preceding analysis some of its features may be summed up in table 3. What I venture to assert as the conclusion of this paper is that I have found the systematic use of the two compartments of table 3, when associated with awareness of the peculiarities of the operations defined by their names (or labels), a help in thinking about many things. I have reason to believe, however, that it would have been much less so, had

TABLE 3

F	γ_v
This is John.	
$$f = \frac{m \times m'}{d^2}$$	Duty is the voice of God. The "unknowable," the "absolute," really exist. Only ideas really exist.
The sentiments of duty and affection of parents toward children are important social forces.	Parents should love and care for their children.
Everybody believes that the external world really exists.	The external world really exists.
Some physicists have believed that force really exists.	Matter does not really exist.
This is a 6000 cu. ft. room.	This is a large room.
This is a case of alcoholic intoxication.	This is disgusting behavior.
I see it and feel disgust.	This is disgusting behavior.
Acceptance of the "principle of legitimacy" will probably produce the results that I desire (Talleyrand) (because monarchs have certain sentiments).	Acceptance of the "principle of self-determination" must produce certain results that I desire (Woodrow Wilson) (because it is just).
The murder of X will probably have disadvantageous results (because there is nobody capable of governing to succeed him).	The murder of X must be committed (because it is a patriotic duty).

it not been accompanied by a conviction that whatever I might at any moment be thinking about, a great many relevant things were probably being left out of consideration because organisms are what they are.

Perhaps the most effective way of making use of the conclusion of this paper is to note and to make use of the following theorem: A logical operation performed upon a non-logical statement does not, in general, lead to a fact. For instance, this theorem suggests a rough distinction between metaphysics, esthetics, ethics, and theology on the one hand, and poetry and religon on the other.

Finally, I call your attention to a logical conclusion from the definition set forth in this paper. Of the two following assertions:

> Facts are better than metaphysical assertions,
> Metaphysical assertions are better than facts,

neither is a fact. Both are non-logical assertions and, according to Bridgman's definition, meaningless.

What we know is that facts lead toward science, metaphysical assertions toward metaphysics, toward religion, or toward poetry. We also know that disregard of the experiences behind certain facts may lead to sudden death, while either disregard of certain sentiments or action in accord with others may lead almost as speedily to social disaster.

Except in poetry or religion my sentiments favor facts. For instance, I dislike Jeans's statement: "If the universe is a universe of thought, then its creation must have been an act of thought."[20] It is for this reason that I have endeavored to make this paper exclusively empirical and logical. I hope that the result has not been a disaster, but I believe that my hope lacks one kind of meaning.

---

[20]   *The Mysterious Universe* (New York, 1930):154. This statement is obviously non-logical. It may be instructive to apply to it Pareto's test of substituting a letter for a word. This gives us: If the Universe is a universe of x, then its creation must have been an act of x, which, so to speak, unveils the non-logical character of the assertion.

4

PARETO'S SCIENCE

OF SOCIETY

1935

Editorial note: This appeared in *Saturday Review of Literature*, 25 May 1935, pp. 3–4, 10. It is excerpted by permission of the publishers from Lawrence J. Henderson's *Pareto's General Sociology: A Psysiologist's Interpretation*, copyright 1935 by the President and Fellows of Harvard College, 1963 by Lawrence J. Henderson.

Henderson took advantage of this review to offer an excellent brief statement of Pareto's sociology. It is clear how much Henderson admires Pareto; he implies that Pareto is a modern Galileo for the social sciences. Note Henderson's statement that the concept of social system is "the central feature of Pareto's sociology." Although it is a very short piece, this essay shows the great clarity and force that were characteristic of all of Henderson's writings.

THE ANCIENT RELIGION "was one of the chief causes of the prosperity of Rome; for this religion gave rise to well regulated conduct, and such conduct brings good fortune, and from good fortune results the happy success of undertakings." So four centuries ago wrote a modern thinker, setting down in judicious phrases the influence of the sentiments upon the actions of men, and consequently upon the fate of principalities and republics. Time has dealt variously with Machiavelli and with his writings. The character and motives of the man have been little praised and greatly blamed by those numerous persons who could not or would not confine themselves to relevant criticism of his work; but this work which was scientific before the birth of modern science, has on the whole withstood criticism. Long ago Bacon declared, "We

181

are much beholden to Machiavel and others that write what men do and not what they ought to do."

This work stands, but has engendered little of like quality or substance, and until the publication in 1916 of the "Trattato di Sociologia Generale," by Vilfredo Pareto,[1] there had been very little further advance in scientific description and logical analysis of the influence of the sentiments upon human affairs.

Three hundred years ago Galileo was writing his "Dialogues Concerning Two New Sciences," one of the few books that bear, like Machiavelli's, the mark of the highest originality. Unlike Machiavelli, Galileo helped to set in motion an activity that has become one of the most important and influential in the world today. The fruits of Machiavelli's labors are few and uncertain, those of Galileo's are countless and unmistakable. Why? Partly, we may be sure, because the two great Florentines studied different subjects.

It will be well, for this reason, to glance at all knowledge.

The endless catalogue of words that designate the subjects taught in our universities seems to defy rational classification. Nevertheless, I think that many of these subjects may be reasonably divided into two classes: first: history, literature, economics, sociology, law, politics, theology, education, etc.; and second: logic, mathematics, physics, biology and other natural sciences, grammar, harmony, etc. The importance of some such dichotomy is indeed widely felt, and gives rise to much discussion and to heated controversies.

Let us look at the facts dispassionately. When the adepts of subjects of the second class disagree, it is a peculiarity of their behavior that they do so most often at the frontiers of knowledge, where growth is taking place; and in the long run a debated question is ordinarily settled by observation, experiment, or some other method that all accept. This is by no means true in many, and hardly true in any, of the subjects of the first class. (Of course it

---

[1] The Mind and Society, (Trattato di Sociologia Generale). By Vilfredo Pareto. Edited by Arthur Livingston. Translated by Andrew Bongiorno and Arthur Livingston with the advice and active cooperation of James Harvey Rogers. New York: Harcourt Brace & Co. 1935. 4 vols. $20.

is true in parts of these subjects.) Now this remarkable difference between the behavior of students of the two classes of subjects is probably related to a difference in subject matter. For all the subjects of the first class do involve, and none of the subjects of the second class does involve, the study of the interrelations of two or more persons.

We are now in a position to consider the central feature of Pareto's Sociology.

An important characteristic of many of the natural sciences is the concept of a system, for example, the solar system. In order to fix our ideas we may consider Willard Gibbs's generalized description of a physico-chemical system, which is the basis of the most famous American contribution to science. A physico-chemical system is an isolated material aggregate. It consists of components, which are individual substances, like water or sugar. These substances are found singly or together in phases which are physically homogeneous solid, liquid, or gaseous parts of the system, like ice, sugar solution, or air. The system is further characterized by the concentrations of the components in the phases, by its temperature, and by its pressure.

Here is plainly a fiction, for no real system can be isolated. Nevertheless a close approach to isolation, as in a thermos bottle, is possible. So results are obtained, and then extended, even to systems that are far from isolated. Also the enumeration of the factors is incomplete. But it is ordinarily necessary to consider at least those enumerated above; when desirable, the consideration of others, like those involved in capillary and electrical phenomena, can be taken up later. Finally, the concept is often irrelevant; for instance, the consideration of a watch as a physico-chemical system would be merely a waste of time.

It need hardly be said that such apparent defects are in truth consequences of very real advantages. They are but signs of the well chosen simplifications and abstractions that make possible a systematic treatment of complex phenomena. This instrument that Gibbs has put in the chemists' service has immeasurably advanced the science of chemistry; it has clarified, directed, and economized the thought of all chemists. It enables us to understand, for example, refrigeration, the manufacture of steel, the respiratory function of the blood.

The central feature of Pareto's "General Sociology" (as "The Mind and Society" is called in the Italian original) is the construction of a similar conceptual scheme; the social system. This system contains individuals; they are analogous to Gibbs's components. It is heterogeneous (*cf.* Gibbs's phases) for the individuals are of different families, trades, and professions; of different economic and social classes. As Gibbs considers temperature, pressure, and concentrations, so Pareto considers sentiments, or, strictly speaking, the manifestations of sentiments in words and deeds, verbal elaborations, and the economic interests. Like Gibbs, Pareto excludes many factors that are important in special cases, but he, too, has demonstrated that he can do much within the limitations that he has chosen, and that such limitations are necessary.

At this point I owe it to the reader to warn him that the analogies that I have pointed out are accidental. There is not the slightest reason to believe that Pareto was led to his theory by a consideration of the properties of a physico-chemical system, and his work is in no sense an application of natural science to social science. But it is an application of the logical method that has been found useful in all physical sciences when complex situations involving many variables in a state of mutual dependence are described. From long experience Pareto was intimately acquainted with the difficulties and constraints that arise in such an undertaking. And I think he was the first person thus equipped to attack the problem of sociology.

The parts and forces of the social system, like those of all analogous systems, are conceived as in a state of mutual dependence. This arises from the fact that it is, in general, impossible to explain the phenomena in terms of cause and effect, and such an explanation gives place to the type of description previously found necessary for dynamical, thermodynamical, physiological, and economic systems. So it comes about that the central feature of Pareto's use of his theory is the analysis of mutually dependent variations of his variables. In this difficult task he has been aided not only by complete mastery, resulting from his knowledge of mathematics, of the logical principles that are involved, but also by exceptional skill in diagnosis, and by very great learning.

The social system thus defined and characterized is clearly an instrument that may be employed in studying all the above mentioned subjects of the first class; for, like history, literature, law, and theology, all are conversant with the interactions of individuals in their manifold relations, with their sentiments and interests, with their sayings and doings; while none can dispense with considerations of the mutual dependence of many factors. Pareto's Sociology, in so far as it will bear the test of experience, is thus seen to be applicable to all subjects of the first class. This is the ground for his choice of the Italian title: A Treatise on *General* Sociology.

The social system makes its appearance on page 1306 of Pareto's book. It has been preceded by a painstaking choice, discrimination, description, and classification of its elements. The first quarter of the book, a study of the non-logical actions of men, leads up to the demonstration that no other elements of the social system are more important than the sentiments. From this it is inferred that the sentiments must always be methodically considered in the study of any social system whatever. The task, however is beset with difficulties, for we observe only manifestations of the sentiments, not the sentiments themselves. Indeed, the existence of the sentiments in a social system, like the existence of the forces in a dynamical system, is an assumption, a theory, or, in Henri Poincaré's phrase, a convention. Next the sentiments often manifest themselves indistinctly; they are commonly enshrouded in words and in non-logical reasoning; their manifestations occur not singly but in aggregates. Again, our own sentiments interfere with an unprejudiced analysis of the manifestations of the sentiments of others. In particular, students of the social sciences are commonly moved by their own sentiments, "whence proceed," as Bacon said, "sciences as one would." And last, no sentiment is more troublesome than that which leads ideologists, the intelligentsia or intellectuals, and in fact all of us, to mistake as rational what is non-rational in human behavior. This is perhaps the most important of the numerous reasons why Pareto was the first to make a taxonomic study of the manifestations of the sentiments. Meanwhile, a piece of work has been done in their allied but narrower quasi-pathological field by the psycho-analysts. We may well look with suspicion upon psychoanalytical theories, but the facts are firmly established, and they confirm this portion of Pareto's work.

The second part of the book includes a definition, description, and classification of residues and derivations. At this point Pareto has set up two technical terms, hoping to escape the tricks that old terms can play. A residue is the manifestation of a sentiment. A derivation is a nonlogical argument, explanation, assertion, appeal to authority, or association of ideas or sentiments in words.

Residues and derivations are found in the verbal utterances and the accompanying actions of men. They are obtained from the concrete phenomena by analysis and abstraction. We need an example. Here is one: Christians practise baptism to efface sin. The ancients used lustral water for ceremonial purifications. Others have similarly used blood; and there are innumerable practices known to anthropologists that are believed to restore the integrity of an individual when it has been injured by the violation of a taboo. In these phenomena there are manifested at least two sentiments; the sentiment of integrity of the individual and the sentiment that actions favorable to this integrity can be performed. These are residues. They may be conceived as the residuum left after the variable features of the phenomena have been put aside. But the phenomena also include an endless variety of ritual practices and the explanations of them. These explanations are derivations. They may be conceived as derived from the sentiments that find expression as residues. The importance of residues far exceeds the importance of derivations.

Theology and metaphysics and parts of law consist, in great measure, of systematic and extensive derivations from certain very important residues like those involving the words justice, duty, sanctity, and absolute. Some of these residues are not only important, but very useful and probably necessary for the survival of a social system. The complexes of psycho-analysis, or strictly speaking the manifestations of the complexes, include another important group of residues. A rationalization is one kind of derivation.

These things, residues and derivations, must be classified to be known, and Pareto has classified them; the residues with mediocre success, the derivations very acceptably. The residues fall into six classes. He calls the first class the residues of combinations and the second, the persistent aggregates; and these two classes serve his purpose well. Residues of the first class are attributes of inventors, speculators, politicians, and skilful leaders. Residues of the second class are found among those who are devoted to family, caste, church, and the community, in *rentiers*, and in good subordinates. The remaining four classes provide useful labels for the facts and hardly serve any other purpose. However, I venture to suggest that long experience in the natural sciences has taught the inestimable advantage of any classification over none, and I think that Pareto knew well what he was about when he made shift with a classification that did not please him, as an aid in a wide survey of facts.

The classification and description of derivations is perhaps the most finished portion of the whole work. At this point some of the leading ideas may possibly have arisen from Bacon's "Idols" or from other sources; but the hard substance of this remarkable study is Pareto's. Like Bacon, he, too, was a man of the world and a scholar. If he was not a lord chancellor, he had other advantages as an engineer and scientist, and behind him were three hundred years more of experience. In his study of the derivations he knew how to exploit all his advantages.

The last half of the book is synthetic, but like all the rest it is enriched with a profusion of diverse and well chosen facts. Pareto works up to his system, then defines it, and finally tests it in a survey of important aspects of the history of Europe. We can no longer follow him here, for these eight hundred pages are incompressible. To some readers they will seem to be prolegomena to a philosophy of history. But this view would be misleading, for they are chiefly the result of Pareto's singularly pertinacious effort to make use of his instrument and method in the study of the actual social systems that were known to him. So far as he was able, he approached this task in the spirit of a scientific investigator.

Long before, he had written:

> Each of us has within a secret adversary who tries to prevent him . . . from abstaining from the mixture of his own sentiments with logical deductions from facts. In noting this general defect, I well know that I am not exempt. My sentiments lead me to favor freedom; therefore I have taken pains to react against them. But it may be that I have gone too far and, fearing to give too much weight to the arguments in favor of freedom, have not given them enough weight. . . . In any case, since I am not quite sure that this source of error is absent, it is my duty to point it out.

Such was Pareto's position when he began his sociological studies. It never changed. But one of the most valuable results of these studies was a complete demonstration of the well-nigh universal presence, except in the most austere sciences, of derivations in the writings of men; we may recall with a change of reference, *quod ab omnibus, quod ubique, quod semper*. Thus from long frequentation and familiarity Pareto became even more amply aware of the danger, and, like an experienced physician, almost intuitively aware of it. Nevertheless, in the course of his labors he often lightened his effort and permitted himself the relief of parenthetical expressions of certain sentiments. But these interjections are no more than asides that leave the substance of the work unchanged. On the other hand, it is probable that he had not acquired complete immunity, and that from time to time he unconsciously fell into errors of the kind that he so well describes. Indeed he has, I think, demonstrated that complete immunity to non-logical thinking is impossible.

I hope that it will now be clear that the prevalent description of Pareto as the Karl Marx of the bourgeoisie or of fascism is nothing more than a derivation. It is a fact that Signor Mussolini has attributed his abandonment of socialism to the teaching of Pareto. It is also true that among the Fascists and the Nazis, Pareto's work is much esteemed, though perhaps not always understood. But his writings are no less applicable to France, England, the United States, and Russia than to Italy and Germany, and Pareto himself preferred to all other governments those of some of the smaller Swiss cantons.

On some persons this book has an effect like that frequently produced by the works of Machiavelli. For similar reasons, similar sentiments are stirred. Among these reasons the chief is that both Machiavelli and Pareto "write what men do and not what they ought to do." In order to understand this it is necessary to distinguish between subjects that include the residues and derivations of others and writings that exhibit the author's own residues and derivations.

It is often said that this work is anti-intellectual. If the term anti-intellectual is defined so as to make the statement true, it is true. Pareto held that a scientist's own residues and derivations are out of place in science. He demonstrated the abundant presence of certain kinds of residues and derivations in the writings of social scientists and explained how this condition interferes with the advancement of learning. He also held that the influence of these particular residues and derivations in the determination of public policy is disastrous. He says, "Like Chinese mandarins European 'intellectuals' are the worst of rulers; and the fact that European 'intellectuals' have played a less important role than mandarins in government is one of the numerous reasons why the fate of the peoples of Europe has been different from that of the Chinese." Does this perchance classify the failure of Woodrow Wilson and his intelligent advisers or of Mr. Hoover's Commissions and surveys, on the one hand, and the success of the nineteenth century English policy of muddling through, on the other?

Pareto's whole life was devoted mainly to science, and few have surveyed science more broadly, or more shrewdly analyzed it. His "Sociology" is the culminating work of this long life, a synthesis of his wide experience. Industry, skill, method, encyclopedic knowledge, initiative, originality, stubborn consecutive continuous thought are terms that describe it. It is a scientific treatise.

This book bears all the marks of early scientific work. Therefore, no sensible and experienced man will suppose that it is free from numerous and important errors of fact, or from mistakes of inference and judgment. Above all, it is inconceivable that the treatment of such a subject should be complete and exhaustive. But Pareto's errors and omissions will come to light if the work is continued, and this work is of the kind, being scientific, that can be continued by others. Thus sooner or later, it will be superseded in use by that which will rest upon it as a foundation. No one knew this better than Pareto, who took pleasure in saying that the sooner his "Sociology" was supplanted, the greater its success would be. Meanwhile, it is an indispensable book.

5

THE RELATION OF MEDICINE

TO THE FUNDAMENTAL

SCIENCES

1935

Editorial note: Reprinted by permission from *Science* 82 (1935):
477–81. This article and the next one show Henderson's long-standing
interest in the relations of medicine to the natural and social sciences.
Although Henderson was trained in medicine, he never practiced it.
He greatly admired the skilled physician as one who successfully combined theory and practice. This first article presents a fundamental
rationale for a sociological history of medicine and for a sociology of
medicine. It is itself an important chronicle for the kind of sociological
history of medicine in the United States that will someday be written.

THE PRACTICE, teaching and science of medicine have
never been isolated from the other affairs of men, but have modified them and been modified by them. My subject is this interaction, for I have been commanded to speak of it as it exists now
and especially as it exists here at Harvard at the end of Dr. Edsall's
administration under the influence of changes that he has directed.
These changes are the consequence of forces and tendencies that
Dr. Edsall has controlled and utilized. The changes are great, the
forces strong, the tendencies by no means superficial. All three are
manifestations of important intellectual and social processes which
concern the university as a whole as well as its parts, and which
involve both private affairs and the state itself.

Familiar facts suggest that in order to fix our ideas we may
speak loosely of three periods of the interaction from and toward
medicine; the first, a very long one when the influence was directed
chiefly from medicine outward; the second, a period of transition
strikingly marked by the influence of biology, of chemistry and of

physics upon medicine; and a third recent period when actions and reactions between medicine and other human affairs are so numerous, so prompt and so intricate that we can hardly follow the chains of cause and effect. These periods are by no means distinct, but it is clear that we are living in the third.

In the beginning and until recent times the action was, as I have said, outgoing; but it took many forms, so many that we can no more than sample the facts. Under the influence of his early medical environment Aristotle turned from the philosophy of his master, Plato. Here at the outset is one action that has never ceased. Like Aristotle, Darwin was the son and grandson of physicians and it is thought that he, too, received the tradition. Also, he, like his cousin Francis Galton, or, to go to another extreme, like the critic Sainte Beuve, pursued medical studies, and in all three the influence of these studies has been noted. Again and again medicine, like the church, has provided a livelihood and so made possible an intellectual life, as it did for Rabelais, for Cardan the mathematician and for Helmholtz.

In an earlier day the path to other fields often led through the study and practice of medicine. Gilbert investigated the magnet, Redi the generation of insects, Stensen geological stratification. John Locke passed from medicine to a psychological epistemology; Sir William Petty, one of the most intelligent of seventeenth century Englishmen, to statistics and economics; Quesnay, the best of the physiocrats, to economic theory guided by an idea of economic circulation borrowed from physiology. In the seventeenth century physicians contributed more than their share to a movement of the first importance in the evolution of science—the founding of academies.

The needs of medicine have created new sciences. They directed the attention of Vesalius to the systematic renewal of the science of human anatomy, of Harvey to his researches on the circulation of the blood and, still farther afield, to embryology. They led to the foundation in Paris of the garden for medicinal plants that finally developed into the Muséum—for one long period the greatest center of natural history in the world. They led Joseph Black, a professor of medicine and chemistry at Edinburgh, to his memorable work on carbon dioxide and on calorimetry. Medicine has also provided the stimulus to new developments. For instance, it was an accidental clinical observation that suggested to Julius Robert Meyer the principle of the conservation of energy.

Medicine has formed the background of the life and thought of humanists like Linacre and of physicists like Young. In other instances, for example, in the political careers of Marat and Clemenceau, we remain in doubt and can but guess about the nature of the influence. Finally, we may note the familiar and characteristic type of the physician-man of letters. At Harvard this brings to mind the elder Oliver Wendell Holmes in the past and, in the present, Harvey Cushing and Hans Zinsser.

Gradually the influence of the more abstract sciences upon medicine restored the balance of a one-sided action from medicine to other things and then, while some of the older tendencies waned, for a time became preponderant. The ancient world hardly knew this movement, and as late as the beginning of the seventeenth century the pseudo-science of astrology was still studied by medical students and applied in practice. For this reason the medical students of Padua, among them perhaps Harvey, attended the astronomical lectures of Galileo. Thereafter the change is unmistakable. It is implied in the work of Galileo himself and in the theoretical physiology of Descartes. It becomes manifest in the work of Sanctorius and of Stensen, as well as in Borelli's systematic application of Galileo's mechanics to physiology. It appears again and again in the seventeenth and eighteenth centuries; in the applications of the pendulum, of the thermometer and of the microscope, largely under Galileo's influence, and later in the application of the manometer to the study of blood pressure by Stephen Hales. Early in the seventeenth century the physiology of vision was renewed by Kepler and Descartes. Later the physical scientists Boyle and Hooke instituted at Oxford the study of respiration. Meanwhile, step by step, applicable chemical knowledge was acquired, and finally the discoveries of Lavoisier and of Lavoisier and Laplace established the science of metabolism on a secure foundation.

The effect of the abstract sciences on medicine was accelerated in the nineteenth century and at length became, or at least now seems to have become, the most characteristic feature of the time. In its course it has grown too complex for simple description, but I think the historical implications of the single name of Pasteur will bear out my assertion.

When some, I hope I may still say many, of us were students, the words "physics," "chemistry," "botany," "zoology" and "physiology" were safe and comfortable terms that caused no concern. We knew what they meant, and, long before Bridgman had instructed us, even possessed intuitively an operational definition of them. Physics was what B. O. Pierce and others of his guild did and taught and physiology what Henry Bowditch and his guild did and taught. There were indeed signs of change, but they passed unheeded. Thus the growth of the science of physical chemistry seemed to be nothing more than an immigration into a new field that was destined to preserve its independence. Perhaps, among our elders, the word "biology" was already giving some concern to conservatives, for Farlow, a doctor turned botanist and a great Harvard worthy, used to say, wittily and not without feeling, that a biologist is a zoologist who teaches botany or a botanist who teaches zoology. But the sciences still seemed to be independent. They are so no longer; *laissez faire, laissez passer* is the order of the day in science, and the skilful workman may construct what he pleases and seek his materials almost at will. For instance, organic chemists, under the influence of physiology, have returned to the study of natural products. Not without certain temporary inconveniences the guild economy of science is decaying and is being replaced by a system that is more free and, in some few respects, less disciplined. Perhaps the chief cause of this change is that the frontiers of science, formerly several and natural like our early western frontier, have become joint and artificial like those of Europe, and that real interests and prejudices which tend to preserve them are weaker than the opposing forces of initiative and invention.

Nevertheless, the separation of the sciences remains and it is hardly conceivable that it can disappear. The indispensable needs of skill and method endure and I think we may count upon them not only to preserve in the future much that is left of the guild system, but also to restore the discipline that may have been occasionally lost with the disappearance of certain elements of the older traditional training and standards of our fathers.

Let us not, however, prophesy. We are interested in facts, and the novel relations between the sciences are very imperfectly described by what I have said, for these relations are by no means of a random character. On the contrary, they will manifest, with all their increasing complexity, the trend that was so plainly evident during the nineteenth century, and they are in general only weakly transitive.

I am concerned to make this clear and therefore ask you to consider the following list of subjects: mathematics, physics, chemistry, physiology, pathology, medicine, epidemiology, hygiene. Is it not evident, in fact, does not every one know, that on the whole, and saving the exceptions, the influences that now exist are, as they have been in the past, in one direction rather than the other in the order of the list; from chemistry to physiology, pathology and medicine rather than the reverse? Is not the above-mentioned influence of physiology on organic chemistry a little different from the usual run of events? Further, is not the influence frequently from one subject to the *next* following subject, rather than directly to a later subject? Is it not from chemistry to physiology rather than to pathology or to medicine directly? Moreover, is it not in general from a more abstract to a less abstract subject, and again from an older and more highly developed science to one that is younger and less developed, and finally, of course, from a pure science to an applied science?

In short, there is activity everywhere and in every direction actions and reactions run on. This is all very confusing, but yet we see clearly enough that the actions, if far from uniformly, are on the whole, or at least in many cases, polarized and that there are several predominant tendencies which result in this polarity: actions from the pure to the applied sciences, from the older to the younger, from the developed to the undeveloped, from the abstract to the concrete, from one neighboring science to another. So much we can see, but we can hardly foresee the particular actions and reactions of even the immediate future, least of all perhaps in the domain of medicine and the medical sciences.

Such conditions make the task of guiding the evolution of medicine in a university difficult. They also impose limits within which it is probably bound to proceed.

In 1918, when Dr. Edsall took over the work of dean, many of these new conditions, especially the immaterial and intellectual conditions, in which the practice, the teaching and the science of medicine are evolving, were already present. But great organizations change slowly, and the formal structure of the University and of the Medical School still corresponded, in part and especially in externals, to the obsolescent guild economy of science. Material signs of this were and still are the isolation of the Medical School from the rest of the University and the planned isolation of the departmental laboratories within the school. But such external obstacles to free intercourse are no more than inconveniences when other conditions are favorable. What was important was the accompaniment of no little intellectual isolation which had already become a sensible disadvantage.

The new dean was well prepared to feel, and therefore to perceive, the effects of this state of affairs, for he had already experienced them concretely in his own work in medicine, especially in the application of chemical methods beyond the routines of diagnosis, in experimental clinical studies in the hospital, and in the application of the methods of experimental medicine to the study of industrial hygiene when pursuing investigations of occupational diseases in the factories and plants where they originate. This experience must have been of good service, while he was making decisions and working out the main lines of an administrative policy that has been from beginning to end realistic, empirical and intuitive, and has therefore led to a continuous adaptation to the changing conditions and needs of the times. Happily the great DeLamar bequest, munificent grants from the Rockefeller Foundation and many other gifts have made possible the execution of this policy.

One of the early results of his action as dean was the School of

Public Health, a new department, which from its foundation has borne a relation to the Medical School and other parts of the University that might easily be mistaken for the result of a long period of adaptation rather than of a new establishment. Let us look at the facts. Administratively a separate faculty, this school has never, from the very beginning, been really cut off from the Medical School in respect of staff and researches; for administrative independence, while preventing undesirable constraints, has favored desirable connections and facilitated all sorts of mutual aid. Thus, an ever-changing nexus of connections has grown up. This has extended farther afield, in a manner suggestive of the Hippocratic treatise on "Airs, Waters and Places," to the Children's Hospital, for example, in the study of the hygiene of infants; to the Fatigue Laboratory, for example, in the study of the effects of temperature and pressure; to the Dental School, for example, in the study of nutrition; and, notably, to the Engineering School, where conditions have arisen that well illustrate some of my introductory remarks.

Sanitary engineering has reduced the control and protection of the water supply to a routine, and even in part crystallized the routine in rule of thumb. It is now turning its attention to the air. The problems thus raised have led to a valuable collaboration in research between the Schools of Public Health and Engineering, and in the application of both the physical and the biological sciences to the problems of hygiene in a manner that is obvious enough. But it has also led to other interactions and collaborations of a character that could hardly have been foreseen. Such results, I repeat, depend upon the absence of constraints of the kind imposed by rigid organization and the guild system of science, and upon the presence of connections that grow up spontaneously when conditions favor free intercourse. It is an induction from experience that a necessary condition for the best kind of collaboration in scientific work, except in the relations of master and apprentice, is that those concerned should desire to study a problem and that, because of its nature and scope, they should be unable to do so severally and independently.

In the prosecution of research the relations between the Medical School and the School of Public Health are similar but far more extensive than those that have been established between the latter school and the School of Engineering. They are the sign of a new period within the Medical School as well as in its wider relations.

For some years there has existed at Harvard a Committee on Industrial Physiology, appointed by the corporation. Dr. Edsall has been the chairman, and among the members have been the dean of the Business School and the former dean of the Bussey Institution. This committee is charged with the administration of a large grant from the Rockefeller Foundation. Its authority is derived directly from the corporation. It carries on independently of all faculties and departments of the University and its sole responsibility is to see to it that the work done under its supervision shall be well done and that it shall be of such a character as to conform to the liberal terms of the gift.

This committee has voted funds in support of certain researches that are now going on in the University, such as those of the functional anthropologists, of the Psychological Clinic and of the International Expedition to Chile led by Dr. Dill. The committee administers all the funds of Professor Mayo's Department of Industrial Research in the Business School and all those of the Fatigue Laboratory.

In making plans that led to the establishment of this broad undertaking Dr. Edsall took a decisive part and I think that we can see how these plans are the outgrowth of his earlier policies and experiences. His own studies of industrial medicine were a first step in the direction of sociology and the foundation of the School of Public Health went much further in the same direction. Now these are the common features of the studies that have been supported by the Committee on Industrial Physiology; they are all concerned with problems that may be considered, in the broadest sense, sociological, or else with problems whose solutions appear to be necessary as a means of making progress in understanding the conditions within which social phenomena occur. In each instance the work is carried on by men who have acquired some special skill in the use of appropriate scientific methods, including statistical, chemical, physiological, psychological, anthropological and clinical methods. In every case these men have come, independently, to desire to investigate the problems in question. In general, each is interested in the work of many of the others, so that there is much intercourse and every useful mutual aid and collaboration. Evidently all this work is, on the one hand, the outcome of the special scientific interests of those concerned and, on the other hand, a result of the many unforeseeable interactions between the different sciences that are so striking a feature of our times. Also, it is, so far as I know, in no single instance something imposed as a deduction from a great rationalized project. I believe that it is for these reasons that the results have been thus far satisfactory to the investigators and not uninteresting to others. The influence of this work has extended into the Business School and into the Cambridge departments of anthropology, psychology and sociology.

Meanwhile, the opportunity for direct influence of the more abstract sciences on those of the Medical School has been provided. Ever since the foundation of the School of Public Health a professional mathematician and mathematical physicist has held the chair of vital statistics. Also, an experimental physicist has been a regular officer of the Cancer Commission. Many other factors have strengthened the influence of the abstract sciences. A department of physical chemistry has been established in the Medical School, Professor Fiske's laboratory has become almost a laboratory of organic chemistry and chemistry has infiltrated at other points. Finally, there has been no little collaboration with members of the Division of Chemistry of the Faculty of Arts and Sciences.

The relations between the Medical School and the Division of Biology of the Faculty of Arts and Sciences are somewhat different, because the various fields of biology at Harvard, as in most other universities, were formerly divided between the two faculties. This separation, which long remained as an anachronism, has now been largely overcome. The growth of medical zoology and the importance of the ecological and other aspects of tropical medicine on the one hand, and, on the other hand, the presence of Professor Redfield, for years a professor in the Medical School and now director of the Biological Laboratories in Cambridge, the presence of others from the Medical School and the rapid growth of physiology in Cambridge have established intimate relations where once there was almost none. Lastly, we may note the recent addition of an economist to the Faculty of Medicine.

Meanwhile the relations between the laboratories of the Medical School and those of the great Boston hospitals have been almost transformed. Where formerly little more than routine pathological anatomy supplemented clinical observations, now clinical researches employing refined chemical and physiological methods are the rule. To mention only one instance, the investigations of Professor Gamble have contributed not only to medicine and human physiology, but also to general physiology.

The influence of these developments upon the practice of medicine is great. They are known to most of you better than to me. But what of medical education? From the beginning of his administration President Lowell was interested in changes in the course of study and methods of teaching and examining in the Medical School which have been slowly adopted and which are the expression of the very tendencies that we have been considering. To this I can testify because I clearly remember parts of a conversation with him that is now more than a quarter of a century old. Some of these changes were accomplished before Dr. Edsall became dean. The others, entirely accordant with the dean's sentiments and opinions, were accomplished with the president's support, for here as in other respects, there was perfect accord between the two executives.

In another direction the initiative came from Dr. Edsall. Since it is the growth of the sciences that has given rise to all the changes that we have considered, it is not surprising that the same cause should have modified the problems of college education for the future medical student. Signs of the new conditions became clear long ago, and I remember a still earlier conversation with President Eliot, when as a young instructor I tried, prematurely and probably with little success, to argue that college undergraduates had need of information about the new relations between chemistry and biology and medicine. At the beginning of the century little was to be done, but by the twenties the problem had become serious. Nearly ten years ago it led, on the initiative of Dr. Edsall, to the establishment in Harvard College of tutorial instruction that was carefully designed to meet the need. This experiment has prospered, and from the early years of college to the end of their medical education, it has already enabled many students to prosecute and organize their studies more broadly and with a better understanding of their needs and of their intellectual interests. Moreover, the presence of a group of young and able medical men among the corps of tutors in Harvard College has greatly strengthened the interactions between the two faculties. It has also established a balance among the biological activities of the Faculty of Arts and Sciences that American physiologists have long admired and envied in the University of Cambridge and that formerly was unattainable here. The appointment of one of the tutors, Professor Ferry, as Master of Winthrop House, is a significant result of this change.

So much by way of chronicle. But the chronicle is not enough, for in ending we must try to seize the continuous threads that run through the events.

Edsall's administration is a period of transition. I have tried to suggest that it is especially marked by the application to University policy of the two principles of *laissez faire* and of *laissez passer* that were already evident in the evolution of medical science. A conspicuous result has been the strengthening of old relations and the formation of many new relations within the University. The influences of *laissez faire* are, perhaps, chiefly attributable to spontaneous forces, but it is in great part the dean who, by applying the principle of *laissez passer*, has made the intercourse and the interrelations possible and, above all, it is the man himself who has promoted that spirit of good will and mutual aid in collaboration which is to-day one of the most fortunate traits of Harvard.

6

PHYSICIAN AND PATIENT

AS A SOCIAL SYSTEM

1935

Editorial note: This article is reprinted by permission from *New England Journal of Medicine* 212 (1935): 819–23. Although it is now a commonplace in the sociology of medicine, the notion of taking the physician and patient as a social system was new in Henderson's day. This paper has had considerable influence on the sociology of medicine, particularly through its influence on Talcott Parsons.

MEDICINE is to-day in part an applied science. Mathematics, physics, chemistry, and many departments of biology find applications in this hospital and in the practice of all skillful physicians. Meanwhile, the personal relations between the physician and the patient remain nearly what they have always been. To these relations, as yet, science has been little applied, and it is unlikely that the men in this room are upon the whole as much concerned about their personal relations with patients as a similar group of Boston doctors must have been in the days of James Jackson. A multitude of important new facts and theories, of new methods and routines, so far absorb the physician's attention and arouse his interest that the personal relations seem to have become less important, if not absolutely, at least relatively to the new and powerful technology of medical practice. This condition, for which nobody is to blame, might perhaps be modified if it were possible to apply to practice a science of human relations. But such a science is barely growing into the stage where applications are possible.

The psychologists and sociologists are the professional custodians of what little scientific knowledge we possess that is conversant with personal relations. But from them we have, as yet, little to learn, for they are in general little aware of the problem of practicing what they know in the affairs of everyday life. Indeed, skill in managing one's relations with others is probably less common among professional psychologists and sociologists than among the ablest men of affairs or the wisest physicians. So the personal relations of the physician with his patients and with their families are still understood, when they are understood, at the empirical level, as they were in the days of Hippocrates. Such skill is not only empirical but it is also, as we vaguely say, intuitive. Sometimes in those favored persons whose perceptions and sensibilities are well suited to the task, it results in patterns of behavior that are among the most interesting and, if I may use the word, beautiful that I know. As I came into this room, I was saying that if Dr. Frederick Shattuck could only be here he, who knew so much more about my subject than I shall ever know, would have been able after I had finished to say many things to you and to me. Doctors like him have always existed and will always exist, but their skill dies with them except when their apprentices have learned in some measure to imitate them.

The necessary condition for the effective transmission of acquired knowledge seems to be scientific formulation, and for this purpose some kind of theory, working hypothesis, or conceptual scheme is necessary. In this way the natural sciences are preserved and transmitted, and the rôle of scientific laws and generalizations is seen to be not merely economy of thought, as Mach said, but also the effective remembering of the successful and economical thought of the past. A well learned theory is remembered in the right place at the right time, and this is a necessary condition for its use. Accordingly my first subject is the theory of the relation between physician and patient.

Four centuries ago, Machiavelli was thinking of certain great problems of human society and writing two famous books. In so doing, he reached scientific generalizations about the influence of the sentiments upon the actions of men and, through these actions, upon the fate of human societies. As a whole, these conclusions stand; but from this great and ingenious work of Machiavelli's almost no developments have followed. The science of statecraft and of the influence of the sentiments upon human behavior is little different to-day from what it was in Florence in the 16th century.

In the following century, another Florentine, Galileo, published his "Dialogues on Two New Sciences." From this work a great part of modern science has grown out. The two men were perhaps equal in ability and in originality. Why has the influence of one been small and that of the other inestimably great?

In seeking a partial answer to this question, I ask you to consider the names of the subjects that are taught in modern universities, and to divide them, so far as may be, into two classes: first, history, politics, economics, sociology, law, literature, etc.; secondly, logic, mathematics, physics, chemistry, biology, grammar, harmony, etc. Most subjects will fall well enough into one or the other of these two classes. Next I ask you to consider the behavior of the professors who cultivate the two classes of subjects. Those who are adepts of subjects of the second class, when they differ, commonly do so at the frontiers of knowledge, where growth occurs. Moreover, their differences are ordinarily settled by observation, experiment, mathematical calculation, and logical analysis. But in the subjects of the first class differences of opinion occur at all points, and frequently they cannot be resolved. The differences and the disputes seem to be interminable, and there is often no accepted method of reaching a conclusion.

Such a contrast between the behavior of the skilful devotees of the two classes of subjects must depend in part upon differences in the nature of the two classes of subjects, for we cannot admit that a natural selection of professors so nearly perfect as to produce this striking result should occur. Now there is, in fact, one difference between the two classes of subjects which, as I think, is sufficient in a rough approximation to explain the phenomenon. The subjects of the second class do not, in general, consider the interrelations of two or more persons. The subjects of the first class always consider the interrelations of two or more persons. Thus in history, politics, economics, sociology, law, literature, etc., the interrelations and interactions of people are always concerned, but in logic, mathematics, physics, chemistry, biology, grammar, harmony, etc., except perhaps in certain subjects on the borders of biology, they are ruled out. Perhaps this distinction also goes far to explain the curious condition of psychology in our own time. At any rate I am persuaded that it goes far to explain why we have little more than empirical knowledge about the relations of physician and patient.

Willard Gibbs's generalized physico-chemical system is possibly the most famous piece of scientific work that has been done by an American. According to Gibbs, any arbitrarily isolated portion of the material universe may be regarded as a physico-chemical system. In a first approximation, it may be characterized as follows: A physico-chemical system is made up of components. Components are individual chemical substances such as water, salt, etc. They exist in phases. Phases are physically homogeneous parts of the system, either solid, or liquid, or gaseous such as ice, a salt solution, or air. The system is further distinguished by the concentration of the components in the phases, by its temperature, and by its pressure. For many purposes no other factors need be considered.

The Italian sociologist, Pareto, formerly professor at the University of Lausanne, has described a generalized social system which may be usefully compared with Gibbs's physico-chemical system. Pareto's social system is made up of individuals. They are perhaps analogous to the components of Gibbs's system. The individuals are heterogeneous, that is, unequal. They are unequal in size and in age. There are two sexes. They have different educations. They belong to different social and economic classes, to different institutions, to different social structures. They suffer from different pathological conditions, and their mental differences are different far beyond our computation and description. This heterogeneity suggests the heterogeneity of solid, liquid, and gaseous phases in the physico-chemical system.

These individuals possess, or at least manifest, sentiments. I implore you not to ask me to define the word sentiment, but to permit me to use it without definition to include in its meaning a variety of mental states. For example, I desire to solve a problem;

that is a sentiment. You have a feeling that the constitution of the United States should be preserved; that is a sentiment. Affection for the members of your family is a sentiment. The feeling of personal integrity is a sentiment. The desire to express your gratitude for a kindness is a sentiment. The sexual complexes of psychoanalysts, even though they may be unconscious, are for my purpose sentiments.

The individuals who make up social systems also have economic interests, and they have and use language. This use of language is sometimes a non-logical manifestation of sentiments. For example, I read the other day the following title of a sermon, posted up in front of a church in a New England town, "One on God's side is a majority." Language is also sometimes used, though less often than we fondly suppose, to perform logical operations and to express their results.

A physician and a patient make up a social system. And that is my first point.

Many of you, I fear, will think this introduction singularly irrelevant to the subject of my discourse, and so vague and general that it can hardly be of any use in the premises. To them I venture to suggest that it is possible that they may be mistaken, and I ask them to try to follow what I now have to say receptively, postponing criticism until they have received my whole statement.

Two persons, if no more are present, make up a social system. These individuals are heterogeneous. They have and are moved by sentiments and interests. They talk and reason. That is a definition. I shall now state a theorem. In any social system the sentiments and the interactions of the sentiments are likely to be the most important phenomena. And that is my second point. Sometimes the interaction of the sentiments of the individuals making up a social system is hardly less important than gravitational attraction in the solar system.

In the eighteenth century, before a wave of sentimentality swept over the western world, some people saw human relations pretty clearly. They had not been brought up on Rousseau and others whose writings have continued down almost to the present time to influence the intellectual atmosphere in which men have formed this habit of thought. Among the more successful eighteenth century observers of the mechanism of human behavior was Lord Chesterfield. From one of his letters to his son I venture to quote:

I acquainted you in a former letter, that I had brought a bill into the House of Lords for correcting and reforming our present calendar, which is the Julian; and for adopting the Gregorian. I will now give you a more particular account of that affair; from which reflections will naturally occur to you, that I hope may be useful, and which I fear you have not made. It was notorious, that the Julian calendar was erroneous, and had overcharged the solar year with eleven days. Pope Gregory the Thirteenth corrected this error; his reformed calendar was immediately received by all the Catholic Powers in Europe, and afterwards adopted by all the Protestant ones, except Russia, Sweden, and England. It was not, in my opinion, very honourable for England to remain in a gross and avowed error, especially in such company; the inconveniency of it was likewise felt by all those who had foreign correspondences, whether political or mercantile. I determined, therefore, to attempt the reformation; I consulted the best lawyers and the most skilful astronomers, and we cooked up a bill for that purpose. But then my difficulty began: I was to bring in this bill, which was necessarily composed of law jargon and astronomical calculations, to both which I am an utter stranger. However, it was absolutely necessary to make the House of Lords think that I knew something of the matter; and also to make them believe that they knew something of it themselves, which they do not. For my own part, I could just as soon have talked Celtic or Sclavonian to them, as astronomy, and they would have understood me full as well: so I resolved to do better than speak to the purpose, and to please instead of informing them. I gave them, therefore, only an historical account of calendars, from the Egyptian down to the Gregorian, amusing them now and then with little episodes; but I was particularly attentive to the choice of my words, to the harmony and roundness of my periods, to my elocution, to my action. This succeeded, and ever will succeed; they thought I informed, because I pleased them; and many of them said, that I had made the whole very clear to them; when, God knows, I had not even attempted it. Lord Macclesfield, who had the greatest share in forming the bill, and who is one of the greatest mathematicians and astronomers in Europe, spoke afterwards with infinite knowledge, and all the clearness that so intricate a matter would admit of: but as his words, his periods, and his utterance, were not near so good as mine, the preference was most unanimously, though most unjustly, given to me. This will ever be the case; every numerous assembly is *mob*, let the individuals who compose it be what they will. Mere reason and good sense is never to be talked to a mob; their passions, their sentiments, their senses, and their seeming interests, are alone to be appealed to. Understanding they have collectively none, but they have ears and eyes, which must be flattered and seduced; and this can only be done by eloquence, tuneful periods, graceful action, and all the various parts of oratory.

It is not only to a mob that reason and good sense cannot effectively be talked. A patient sitting in your office, facing you, is rarely in a favorable state of mind to appreciate the precise significance of a logical statement, and it is in general not merely difficult but quite impossible for him to perceive the precise meaning of a train of thought. It is also out of the question that the physician should convey what he desires to convey to the patient, if he follows the practice of blurting out just what comes into his mind. The patient is moved by fears and by many other sentiments, and these, together with reason, are being modified by the doctor's words and phrases, by his manner and expression. This generalization appears to me to be as well founded as the generalizations of physical science.

If so far I am right, I think it is fair to set up a precept that follows from all this as a rule of conduct: The physician should see to it that the patient's sentiments do not act upon his sentiments and, above all, do not thereby modify his behavior, and he should endeavor to act upon the patient's sentiments according to a well-considered plan. And that is my third point.

I believe that this assertion may be regarded as an application of science to the practice of medicine, and that as such it will bear comparison with the applications of physics, chemistry, and biology to practice. However, in this case the application of science to practice is peculiarly difficult. If I am to speak about it, I must in the first place beg explicitly to disclaim any skill of my own. It is not my business to deal with patients, nor has it been my business to perform that kind of operation that Chesterfield so well describes in his letter. Accordingly, what I am now to say to you is, in the main, second-hand knowledge that I have cribbed from others.[1] It represents, so far as I can understand what I have seen and heard, the soundest judgment, based upon experience, skillful performance and clear analysis in this field. In order to be brief and clear, I shall permit myself the luxury of plain assertion.

In talking with the patient, the doctor must not only appear to be, but must be, really interested in what the patient says. He must not suggest or imply judgments of value or of morals concerning the patient's report to him or concerning the patient's behavior. (To this there is one exception: When the patient successfully presents a difficult objective report of his experiences, it is useful to praise him for doing well what it is necessary that he should do in order to help the physician to help him.) In all those matters that concern the psychological aspects of the patient's experience few questions should be asked and, above all, no leading questions. There should be no argument about the prejudices of the patient, for, at any stage, when you are endeavoring to evoke the subjective aspect of the patient's experience or to modify his sentiments, logic will not avail. In order to modify the sentiments of the patient, your logical analysis must somehow be transformed into the appropriate change of the patient's sentiments. But sentiments are resistant to change. For this reason, you must so far as possible utilize some part of the sentiments that the patient has in order to modify his subjective attitude.

[1]   I owe my information to my colleagues, Professors Elton Mayo, F. J. Roethlisberger, and their associates. The theory and practice of interviewing developed by Mayo were applied and adapted with the advice and collaboration of the Harvard Department of Industrial Research by the Western Electric Company in the course of an elaborate investigation at the Hawthorne Works of the Company. A valuable description of these Western Electric methods of interviewing may be found in Bingham and Moore's *How to Interview*, New York, 1931; Second Edition, 1935. In all this it is possible to discern more than traces of the methods of psychoanalysis, divested however of the usual theoretical and dogmatic accompaniments, and therefore considerably modified.

When you talk with the patient, you should listen, first, for what he wants to tell, secondly, for what he does not want to tell, thirdly, for what he cannot tell. He does not want to tell things the telling of which is shameful or painful. He cannot tell you his implicit assumptions that are unknown to him, such as the assumption that all action not perfectly good is bad, such as the assumption that everything that is not perfectly successful is failure, such as the assumption that everything that is not perfectly safe is dangerous. We are all of us subject to errors of this kind, to the assumption that quantitative differences are qualitative. Perhaps the commonest false dichotomy of the hypochondriac is the last of those that I have just mentioned: the assumption that everything not perfectly safe is dangerous.

When you listen for what the patient does not want to tell and for what he cannot tell you must take especial note of his omissions, for it is the things that he fails to say that correspond to what he does not want to say plus what he cannot say. In listening for these omissions, which is a difficult task, you must make use of every aid that is available. Among the available aids are the results of psychoanalysis. Many of them are well established; but if you wish to preserve a scientific point of view, you must beware of psychoanalytical theories. Use these theories, if you must use them, with skepticism, but do not believe them, for they are themselves in no small measure rationalizations built up by an eager group of enthusiastic students who are unquestionably seeking new knowledge, but whose attitude is strangely modified by a quasi-religious enthusiasm, and by a devotion to the corresponding quasi-theological dogmas. As a useful corrective for undue confidence in the importance of such theories, it is well to recall Henri Poincaré's judicious and skeptical remark: "These two propositions, 'the external world exists,' or, 'it is more convenient to suppose that it exists,' have one and the same meaning." In truth, all theories, but above all others those that refer to the sentiments of men, must be used with care and skepticism.

Therefore, beware of your own arbitrary assumptions. Beware of the expression of your own feelings. In general, both are likely to be harmful, or at least irrelevant, except as they are used to encourage and to cheer the patient. Beware of the expression of moral judgments. Beware of bare statements of bare truth or bare logic. Remember especially that the principal effect of a sentence of confinement or of death is an emotional effect, and that the patient will eagerly scrutinize and rationalize what you say, that he will carry it away with him, that he will turn your phrases over and over in his mind, seeking persistently for shades of meaning that you never thought of. Try to remember how as a very young man you have similarly scrutinized for non-existent meaning the casual phrases of those whom you have admired, or respected, or loved.

Above all, remember that it is meaningless to speak of telling the truth, the whole truth, and nothing but the truth, to a patient. It is meaningless because it is impossible;—a sheer impossibility. Since this assertion is likely to be subjected to both objective and subjective criticism, it will be well that I should try to explain it. I know of no other way to explain it than by means of an example. Let us scrutinize this example, so far as we may be able, objectively, putting aside all our habits of moralistic thought that we acquired in early years and that arise from the theological and metaphysical traditions of our civilization.

Consider the statement, "This is a carcinoma." Let us assume in the first place that the statement has been made by a skillful and experienced pathologist, that he has found a typical carcinoma—in short, that the diagnosis is as certain as it ever can be. Let us also put aside the consideration that no two carcinomas are alike, that no two patients are alike, and that, at one extreme, death may be rapid and painful or, at another extreme, there may be but a small prospect of death from cancer. In short, let us assume, putting aside all such considerations, that the statement has nearly the same validity as the assertions contained in the nautical almanac. If we now look at things, not from the standpoint of philosophers, moralists, or lawyers, but from the standpoint of biologists, we may regard the statement as a stimulus applied to the patient. This stimulus will produce a response and the response, together with the mechanism that is involved in its production, is an extremely complex one, at least in those cases where a not too vague cognition of the meaning of the four words is involved in the process. For instance, there are likely to be circulatory and respiratory changes accompanying many complex changes in the central and peripheral nervous system. With the cognition there is a correlated fear. There will probably be concern for the economic interests of others, for example, of wife and children. All these intricate processes constitute the response to the stimulus made up of the four words, "This is a carcinoma," in case the statement is addressed by the physician to the patient, and it is obviously impossible to produce in the patient cognition without the accompanying affective phenomena and without concern for the economic interests. I suggest, in view of these obvious facts, that, if you recognize the duty of telling the truth to the patient, you range yourself outside the class of biologists, with lawyers, and philosophers. The idea that the truth, the whole truth, and nothing but the truth can be conveyed to the patient is an example of false abstraction, of that fallacy called by Whitehead, "The fallacy of misplaced concreteness." It results from neglecting factors that cannot be excluded from the concrete situation and that have an effect that cannot be neglected. Another fallacy also is involved, the belief that it is not too difficult to know the truth; but of this I shall not speak further.

I beg that you will not suppose that I am recommending, for this reason, that you should always lie to your patients. Such a conclusion from what I have said would correspond roughly to a class of fallacies that I have already referred to above. Since telling the truth is impossible, there can be no sharp distinction between what is true and what is false. But surely that does not relieve the physician of his moral responsibility. On the contrary, the difficulties that arise from the immense complexity of the phenomena do not diminish, but rather increase, the moral responsibility of the physician, and one of my objects has been to describe the facts through which the nature of that moral responsibility is determined.

Far older than the precept, "the truth, the whole truth, and nothing but the truth," is another that originates within our profession, that has always been the guide of the best physicians, and, if I may venture a prophecy, will always remain so: So far as possible, "do no harm." You can do harm by the process that is quaintly called telling the truth. You can do harm by lying. In your relations with your patients you will inevitably do much harm, and this will be by no means confined to your strictly medical blunders. It will arise also from what you say and what you fail to say. But try to do as little harm as possible, not only in treatment with drugs, or with the knife, but also in treatment with words, with the expression of your sentiments and emotions. Try at all times to act upon the patient so as to modify his sentiments to his own advantage, and remember that, to this end, nothing is more effective than arousing in him the belief that you are concerned wholeheartedly and exclusively for *his* welfare.

What I have said does not conform in my manner of saying it to the rules that I have suggested for your relations with patients. I have tried to talk reason and good sense to you, following, so far as I have been able, the habits of a lecturer upon scientific subjects. With some of you I have surely failed to accomplish my object. To them I suggest that this failure is an excellent illustration of the phenomena that I have been describing, for, unless I am mistaken, if you dislike what I have said, it is chiefly because I have failed to appeal to and make use of your sentiments.

7

THE EFFECTS OF

SOCIAL ENVIRONMENT

1936

Editorial note: Reprinted by permission from L. J. Henderson and Elton Mayo, "The Effects of Social Environment," *Journal of Industrial Hygiene and Toxicology*, 18:401–16; copyright 1936, The Williams & Wilkins Company, Baltimore, Maryland.

This paper was read before the symposium "The Environment and its Effects on Man" at the Harvard Tercentenary Celebration in 1936. It is an early account of the research at the Hawthorne Plant of the Western Electric Company, research which became famous in social science through F. J. Roethlisberger and W. J. Dickson's *Management and the Worker* (Cambridge: Harvard University Press, 1939). This book's influence is perhaps indicated by the fact that it is the book most frequently cited in the *International Encyclopedia of the Social Sciences* (New York: Macmillan and Free Press, 1968). The authors of this book gratefully acknowledge the help of, among others, Henderson, who "must be considered to have been actively participant in the research from the beginning." Henderson was probably particularly pleased with this important research because it demonstrated so clearly that social systems also existed where previously only physiological and economic systems had been "seen."

THE HUMAN ASPECT of modern industrial organization attracted no great attention from industrialists until the advent of the European War of 1914; after the outbreak of hostilities the need to accelerate and to maintain production of various necessities quickly provoked a formulation of the problem. Apparently no one had ever sufficiently considered the enormous demand upon industry that would be made by a war-machine organized upon so heroic a scale, for armies counted in millions were a gigantic innovation. Nor had anyone considered the effect of the strenuous and sustained exertion imposed upon those who worked to provide supplies. The authorities in England speedily became aware of a "national lack of knowledge of the primary laws governing human efficiency." In particular, there was "need for scientific study of the hours of work and other conditions of labor likely to produce the maximum output at which the effort of the whole people was aimed." The actual conditions of work set in the munition factories were, in the early days of the struggle, admitted to be progressively detrimental to the worker and consequently unfavorable to that maintenance of output for long periods upon which success in large part depended. Inquiries undertaken by Dr. H. M. Vernon and others appointed by the *British Health of Munition Workers Committee* were effective; the introduction of shorter hours of work, of rest pauses and of other humane innovations resulted in the restoration of morale and the maintenance of production.

The stimulus to inquiry provided by this situation has continued to operate in the years that have elapsed since 1918, and much has been learned of the human factors that are involved in industrial organization for work. Another paper given at this symposium, by Dr. D. B. Dill, will present some of the most recent and interesting findings by physiology in the problem of fatigue. In addition to physiology, psychology has been summoned by industry to aid its determination of appropriate working conditions for the human being in action. In many of these inquiries, and rightly, the worker is considered and studied as an individual. Up to the present there have been few attempts to study the social conditions of work—that is to say, the effect upon morale and production of the situation created by the interrelation of several human beings in an industrial department. This paper is designed to give a brief account of two experiments at the Hawthorne Plant of the Western Electric Company which in a sense stumbled upon this problem as an exceedingly important aspect of industrial administration.

Officers of the Western Electric Company were probably moved to begin the researches of 1927 at Hawthorne by two chief influences. The one may be described as a general interest in the problems of the incidence of "fatigue" and "monotony" in factory work. This took its rise, remotely, in the publication by the English Industrial Health Board of its studies of the conditions of work in munitions factories and other industrial plants during and after the War. The other influence may be attributed to the fact that, as good engineers, these same officers were aware that Company policies with respect to human beings were not so securely based as policies with respect to materials and machines. Mechanical processes, the type and quality of materials used, were based upon carefully contrived experiment and knowledge; the human policies of the Company, upon executive conceptions and traditional practices. In determining the human policies, the Company had no satisfactory criterion of the actual value of its methods of dealing with people. A mechanical process as studied in a modern factory will in some way reveal an inefficiency; a traditional method of handling human situations will rarely reveal that it is rooted in mere use and custom rather than knowledge. The hope that an experimental method of assessing the human effect of different working conditions might be discovered must be regarded as counting for something in the development of the experiment. The object was not to increase production but to discover facts. Where production could be accurately observed, records were kept; but this was arranged merely as an essential part of the experimental procedure.

The original "test room" was installed in April, 1927, and continued to operate until 1932, when, for reasons not connected with the experiment, it was abandoned. The principal results here presented have been described by T. N. Whitehead.[1] The operation selected for study was that of the assembly of telephone relays. Five girl workers were transferred from their usual work surroundings into an experimental room, within which their work was supervised by specially appointed observers. Arrangements were made for the continuous and accurate record of individual output and for other observations that were considered appropriate. It will suffice for our present purpose if we say that the output of the test room workers continued to rise slowly for a period of years. In its

---

1 Social Relationships in the Factory: A Study of an Industrial Group. T. North Whitehead. The Human Factor, *9*, 381 (1935). We have here summarized and paraphrased a large part of this paper.

upward passage this major gain ignored almost completely experimental changes arbitrarily introduced from time to time by the officers in charge of the experiment, including modification of the hours of work, the introduction of rest periods, etc., except those that modified the social organization of the group.

Thus it became evident that the group was performing two distinguishable, but mutually dependent, functions. On the one hand, the group was performing its technological, or economic, function; on the other hand, the activities of the group were being so modified and controlled as to heighten the social solidarity of the group within itself, and also to stabilize its relations with other groups.

As time went on, the interplay between the economic and the social functions of industrial groups became the central subject of the Western Electric researches. Although the girls' work itself was not altered, the general conditions in the test room differed in a number of respects from those to which the girls had previously been accustomed. They were informed as to the nature of the experiment, and their coöperation was invited. The girls were paid, as before, on the same system of group piece work; but their previous group had contained over a hundred individuals, while in the test room the group, for purposes of payment, consisted of only five members. They were told to work at a comfortable pace, and no emphasis was laid on achieving any given level of output; in fact, they were warned against "racing" or forced output in any form. Conversation was permitted; on occasion it was general, while at other times it was confined to pairs of neighbors. In addition to these innovations, certain other experimental changes were introduced from time to time. The length of the working day was varied, as were also the number of working days in the week, rest pauses were introduced, and so forth.

Numerous records were kept by the supervisor in charge. Since an automatic instrument recorded, to a fraction of a second, the instant at which each girl completed every assembled relay, we have the minute-to-minute output of each individual over a period of 5 years. Other records relate to quality of output; reasons for temporary stops; the length of time spent in bed every night; periodical medical reports, and so on. Room temperatures and relative humidities were taken hourly and the Chicago Weather Bureau has supplied similar records for outside conditions. In addition to these, a number of other records were kept.

The supervisor and his assistants made extensive daily notes of conversation, and of the relations developing between the workers. The workers were also separately interviewed by an experienced person on a number of occasions in another room. In all, we have volumes of contemporary observations bearing on the characters and dispositions of these girls, their mutual relations, their conversations and attitudes, their home situations, and their leisure hour acquaintances and activities. All this information was collected with the knowledge and consent of the girls themselves; and, as evidence that this consent was real, we may add that two suggested records were vetoed by the girls and so were never kept.

Figure 1 shows the weekly output rates for each of the girls in the test room. Each point, or short horizontal bar, indicates the average number of relays assembled per hour by the worker for the given week.

It will be noticed that girls Nos. 1 and 2 did not enter the test room until the beginning of 1928, when they replaced the original girls 1A and 2A. Similarly, No. 5 left the Company in the middle of 1929, and returned about 10 months later. During this interval her place was taken by No. 5A. In this short account no further mention will be made of Nos. 1A and 2A, but No. 5A entered into the life of the group too vitally to be ignored, and she will be referred to in due course.

All these girls were experts at relay assembly, having already had several years' experience, but it is noticeable from the figure that in every case their output rate increased substantially, the average increase being somewhere in the neighborhood of 30 per cent.

Of great interest are the wave-like irregularities exhibited by each graph. Some of these "waves" last for months, and others only for a week or two. Moreover, the available output figures show that similar irregularities occurred with durations of as little as a minute or two upwards. At first it was supposed that these variations in working speed might be related to the experimental

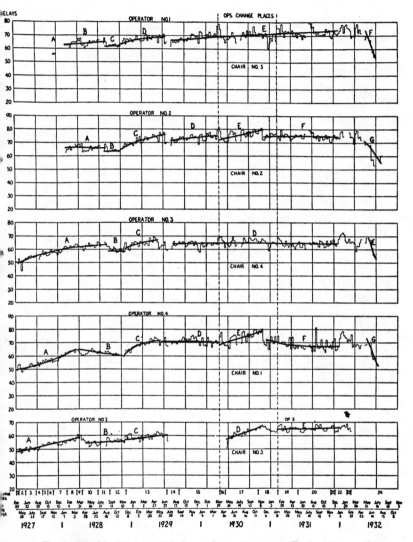

Fig. 1. Weekly output rates for girls in test room. Each point or short horizontal bar indicates the average number of relays assembled per hour by the worker for the given week.

changes deliberately introduced, or possibly to other changes in physical circumstance, such, for instance, as temperature, or the worker's own physical state. But a careful analysis of the data forced us to the surprising conclusion that irregularity in speed of work substantially failed to correlate with any changes of physical circumstance. This applied equally whether experimental changes, irregular changes of natural circumstances, or those cyclical changes involved in the passage of time were considered.

Since working speed was in fact very variable, and yet so insensitive to changes in physical circumstance, changes in the girls' social relations were next examined as being possibly connected with variations in working speed. And this time positive results were obtained. Speed of work varied markedly with changes in the sentiments entertained by the workers towards each other, towards their supervisors, and towards the group as such. To give a social history of the test room from 1927 to 1932 would be to give an explanation of the major trends shown in these graphs.

We have already remarked that these graphs show an average increase of speed of about 30 per cent. In any ordinary sense they are not learning curves, for the workers all had several years' experience in this particular work, and they had reached a more or less steady state as regards speed and skill.

Nevertheless the plateaux and spurts are decidedly suggestive. It was the organization of human relations, rather than the organization of technics, which accompanied spurts in these cases. This illustrates the futility of attending exclusively to the economic motivation of workers, or to their physical conditions of work. These things are of high importance; but no group of workers can be expected to remain satisfied, or to cooperate effectively unless their social organization and sentiments are also protected.

In looking at figure 1 once more, each graph can be imagined as the resultant of a number of wave-like disturbances of differing wave-lengths each superimposed upon the other. An ocean, such as the North Atlantic, only too frequently provides us with an analogy. So often it is simultaneously disturbed from shore to shore by ripples, waves, oceanic rollers, and by tides—four different types of wave-like disturbances, differently produced, and each with its characteristic range of wave-lengths. In similar fashion a work speed graph can be thought of as simultaneously disturbed by superimposed fluctuations of very different wave-lengths, or better, *time-spans*, for in this case the length of the wave is measured in units of time.

By means of a statistical device it is not difficult to break down a work speed graph into a family of curves, each curve containing only those fluctuations lying between certain limits of wave-length, or time-span, and such that, if the ordinates of all these curves be added together, the original graph results. This has nothing to do with harmonic analysis; it is just a device for examining all disturbances of approximately similar time-spans in isolation from the others.

This analysis has been performed by Whitehead for each of the work speed graphs in figure 1. For instance, among others, one curve has been prepared for each girl, showing all those fluctuations of speed whose time-spans lie between 1 and 4 weeks—all other fluctuations have been eliminated from these particular curves. And these 1–4 week time-span curves have been compared with one another to see in what degree the speed fluctuations of one girl correspond with those of another.

The accompanying figures give this information for typical dates throughout the experiment. Figure 2 refers to April, 1928.

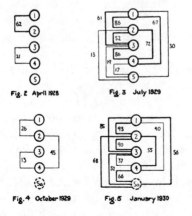

Fig. 2 April 1928   Fig. 3 July 1929

Fig. 4 October 1929   Fig. 5 January 1930

FIGS. 2–5. Correspondence in output fluctuations.

The five circles represent the five relay assemblers in the order in which they sat, the distinguishing number of each girl being placed within her circle. When the speed fluctuations of two girls show a significant correspondence in the 1–4 weeks time-span, then the pair in question are joined by a line; for example, the pairs 1–2 and 3–4. The figures against the lines indicate the strength of the correspondence stated in percentages, and when this correspondence amounts to 50 per cent or more this is indicated by a thick line. These figures do not refer to correlations (r), but to the squares of correlations (r^2), and are called "determinations."

Determinations have certain theoretical and practical advantages as compared with correlations; but the point to remember is that a determination is always numerically smaller than its corresponding correlation. Thus a correlation of 0.8, or 80 per cent, corresponds to a determination of 0.8^2, or 64 per cent. All the determinations shown in the following figures are positive unless otherwise indicated.

With this preliminary explanation let us examine figure 2. The relay test room had been running for about a year, but Nos. 1 and 2 had been members of the group only for the last 3 months of that time. As the figure shows, these two girls "determinated" quite strongly. No. 2, of Italian origin, was undoubtedly the leading member of the group. She was the fastest worker, showed the highest score in an intelligence test, and possessed the most forceful character in the room. This girl was ambitious and at times hoped to obtain a secretarial post, but circumstances had prevented this. At the date in question, April, 1928, her mother and sister had recently died, and No. 2 ran her father's house, looked after her younger brothers, and was the principal wage-earner of the family. In the main shop, No. 2 had found little scope for satisfaction, but the test room seemed to offer a greater outlet for her ambitions and energies, and she threw herself into the new situation with vigor. Her friend, No. 1, of Polish origin, possessed a more placid disposition and contentedly followed her strong-minded neighbor. This friendship lasted throughout the 5 years of the experiment.

Workers 3 and 4, both of Polish origin, had been friendly since the beginning of the experiment, although they had little in common except their chance propinquity. Neither possessed conspicuous qualities of leadership, though it appears that, in the absence of No. 2, No. 4 might possibly have assumed a dominant position in the group.

Characteristically, No. 5 shows no correspondence in her speed fluctuations with any of the others. A Norwegian by birth, she had lived in the States only a few years and spoke English with difficulty; and this, combined with the fact that she was married, older than the others, and of a phlegmatic disposition, prevented her from entering fully into the life of the group.

So figure 2 shows determinations between two pairs of friends, but nothing that could be described as a general state of mutual influence as between the five girls.

Figure 3 illustrates the state of affairs 15 months later, in July, 1929. Here every girl "determinates" significantly with every other girl, and in many cases the degree of determination is decidedly great. It will be noticed that every determination exceeds 50 per cent, except those involving No. 5 which never exceed 00 per cent.

During the 15 months separating figures 2 and 3 the group had been acquiring common activities, interests and loyalties. To a large extent the group had taken their discipline out of the hands of the supervisor and were performing this function for themselves. To give only one instance: when a girl wished for a half day's leave of absence she had to obtain permission from the supervisor. But a custom had become established by which no girl could ask for such permission unless the group sanctioned it. This leave was seriously debated by the group and not always granted, and we do not think the supervisor ever reversed the decision of the group in this matter. Group solidarity had developed with No. 2 as the unofficial but acknowledged leader; and figure 3 shows the extent to which the girls were influencing each other in respect to speed fluctuations in a particular time-span.

Figure 4 shows an almost complete collapse of group solidarity only 3 months later, in October, 1929. In the interval between figures 3 and 4, No. 5 had left the Company's employment of her own free will, and had been replaced by another relay assembler,

No. 5A. This last girl was selected at the request of No. 2, the two having been close friends for some years.

No. 5A was in all respects more congenial to the group than her predecessor; she was of the same age as the others, unmarried, good tempered and coöperative. Nevertheless, No. 5A was unaccustomed to working with her new associates and quite unused to the type of integrated group activity of which she had no previous experience. The result was that, in the 1–4 weeks time-span, she "determinated" with no one. But, even more significant, other pairs not involving No. 5A also failed to show much mutual influence. Solidarity had fallen all round in consequence of an unassimilated social element, and this in spite of the fact that No. 5A was more popular than her predecessor.

However, this state of affairs did not last long, and 3 months later (figure 5) we find the highest state of integration ever observed in the group in this particular respect. No. 5A had established herself as a participating member of the group and being better adjusted in her surroundings than No. 5, determinations are higher. Every individual determinates with every other; the mean value of all the determinations is 64; and the least is 37, corresponding to a correlation coefficient of 0.6.

Taking figures 3 and 5, the only cases here presented of complete determinations, the mean values of the determinations for neighbors are 66; for two individuals separated by one other, 57; for those separated by two others, 47; for those separated by three others, 43.

Figure 6 shows another change by June, 1930, 5 months later. Two events occurred to account for this. In the first place the girls had changed seats, as can be seen from the figure.

This rearrangement was introduced for experimental reasons in April of 1930, and was maintained for 10 months. A change in seating may not seem important to those whose occupation permits them some liberty of bodily action during working hours, but it made a great difference to the relay group. Their work necessitated some degree of visual attention, as well as continuous finger and arm action; it thus determined the position of the body with respect to the work-bench. So, of necessity, intimate conversation

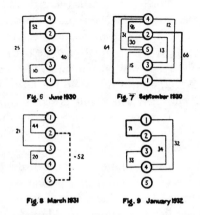

Fig. 6   June 1930   Fig. 7   September 1930

Fig. 8   March 1931   Fig. 9   January 1932

Figs. 6–9. Correspondence in output fluctuations.

could only be carried on between neighbors, although general conversation in a raised tone of voice was not uncommon. Thus a change of seating order involved new associates, an entirely different perspective of the whole group and consequently the need for a new orientation.

Shortly after this change No. 5 requested the Company to take her back and to place her again in the test room. The circumstances surrounding this request were pathetic and the request was granted. But the responsible official had not realized the extent to which this action would be resented by the remainder of the group. The fact was that No. 5A was decidedly popular and was supporting an invalid father. Her removal from the test room resulted in a small drop in her wages (she was given a somewhat different occupation), and it was supposed to increase her chance of being laid off as a result of the industrial depression, which was then in its early stages. For both these reasons the reinstatement of No. 5 was disliked by the group, and this dislike was transferred to No. 5 herself. In figure 6 No. 5 has no relations with anyone, and other determinations are few and relatively weak. However, by September of 1930, three months later, the group began to show signs of reintegration (figure 7). How far this might have gone it is impossible to say, for shortly afterwards the girls were put back into their original order of seating. The result is shown in figure 8. Not only has integration in this respect collapsed, but Nos. 2 and 5 show a marked negative determination (the corresponding correlation equals —0.72). It will be remembered that No. 5A was a close friend of No. 2, and at this time the latter rarely spoke to No. 5 except to snub her. The result is seen in the variations of their working speeds; when one worked faster the other worked slower. Their speeds varied in antiphase. This is the only instance of a negative correlation in the 1–4 weeks' time-span, though more frequent instances are found in some of the other spans.

The occurrence of this one negative determination involving No. 2 should perhaps be considered in connection with the fact that the total of her determinations contributed about 40 per cent more than their proportional share to the total of all the determinations of figures 2–9. In other words, determinations in which No. 2 is involved are approximately twice as great as those in which she is not involved. This presumably is the mark of her leadership, and it is possible that the one negative determination may be partly due to the same influence.

Finally, figure 9 shows the situation about 10 months later, in January, 1932. By this time the depression was at its height, many employees had been laid off and quite evidently the process was bound to continue. For this reason, as well as others, the tone of the relay group had been gradually changing from optimism to resignation. The future was a matter for dread rather than hope and No. 2 in particular was again restless in the feeling that her ambitions were not being realized. The self-discipline of the group showed signs of deteriorating, and the 10 months separating figures 8 and 9 resulted in little growth of solidarity. The group had lost its spring. No. 5 was no longer the object of active resentment, but she was effectively outside the common life and practically never spoke to any of the other girls.

We have briefly compared synchronization of fluctuations, in the 1–4 weeks time-span, with the social sentiments of the workers themselves; and it appears that these two factors tend to vary in close accord with one another. This accord was considerably more detailed than has been explained. Moreover, the story is much the same whatever time-span be considered. For fluctuations have been examined with individual endurances of a minute or two, at one end of the scale, up to those having endurances of nearly 3 months at the other extreme.

In every case, the degree in which the speed fluctuations of two workers correspond relates itself in some fashion to their mutual sentiments; though the type of social sentiment involved does depend somewhat on the length of the time-span chosen.

The second experiment we report has been fully described in a monograph entitled "Management and the Worker" by F. J. Roethlisberger and W. J. Dickson. A study of a bank-wiring room, it constituted the final experimental phase at the end of 5 years' inquiry at the Hawthorne plant. "The method of study was novel in that it utilized two types of investigation simultaneously. One type consisted of an indirect conversational interview, the other of direct observation. The interviewer remained as much as possible an outsider to the group, and the interviews were held by appointment in a private office. The observer was stationed with the group in the rôle of a disinterested spectator. His function was to keep records of performance, and of events and conversations which he considered significant. . . . The attention of both investigators was fixed upon the same group, and the one simply attempted to get information which the other could not get as well, or could not get at all."[2]

The situation that was revealed in this method of study was very different from that which obtained in the relay assembly test room. Whereas in the test room the collaboration of workers with management was at a high level and the aims of the two groups apparently in perfect accord, the situation in the bank-wiring observation room was quite otherwise. The spontaneous social organization of the latter group seemed to order itself about a certain sentiment of fear or doubt with respect to managerial intention. The group had arrived at a conception of a day's work which was

[2]   Actual Behavior in a Shop. W. J. Dickson. Paper read to Personnel Research Foundation, January 25, 1935.

less than the "bogey" set for the department. This decision was not the result of careful consideration or logical process; it had "just happened." And the output records showed a "straight-line" production which was closely in accord with the group conception of a day's work. There were a variety of methods by which group discipline was enforced; no individual escaped the group decree. As a result of these practices the departmental efficiency records did not reflect the actual situation. The official incentive plan was not functioning as it was intended. The group had so organized itself—in a purely spontaneous fashion—that the intentions of the engineer organizers were defeated.

To show how completely the informal organization of the group had defeated the official plan, we quote certain findings made by W. J. Dickson, the officer in charge of the investigation. In the original test room experiment, study of the performances of the girl workers after a period of years showed that the comparative achievements of the individuals in respect of output gave a ranking order that coincided very closely with the order assigned by intelligence and vocational tests. Quite a contrary situation revealed itself in the bank-wiring room. The relative rank in output of the various workers was compared with their relative rank in capacity as measured by tests of intelligence and dexterity. "This comparison showed that there was no relation between their ability as measured by these tests and their actual performance. The lowest producer ranked first in intelligence and third in the dexterity tests. The man who scored highest in the dexterity test ranked seventh in intelligence and seventh in output. The man who scored lowest in the dexterity test shared first place in intelligence and ranked fifth in output. This then was a situation in which the native capacities of the men were not finding expression in their work. In order to see whether differences in earnings accounted for difference in output, these two factors were then compared. Here again no relation was found. The man who ranked first in earnings ranked fourth in output, and the man who ranked lowest in earnings ranked fifth in output. Two of the men received the same wages, yet one produced an average of 16 per cent more work."[3]

[3]   Op. cit., W. J. Dickson.

Dickson goes on to point out that careful analysis of all the available data showed that these differences in output related themselves approximately "to the individual's position in the group." That is to say, differences in output related themselves to the social controls established by the informal grouping and not to individual capacity or to economic or logical considerations. Dickson's conclusions, briefly summarized, follow. He expresses a caution that these conclusions apply specifically to the group under observation and are not to be interpreted as generalizations.

1. Output for these operators was a form of social behavior. Their own peculiar concept of or feeling about a day's work was the idea about which the informal grouping was organized. Individual differences of performance were related rather to the individual's position in the group than to his actual capacity.

2. In this situation the supervisory controls established by management had failed. The whole logic of the technical organization was implicated in this failure.

3. The problems encountered were not due to a logical insufficiency in the wage plan. Such plans assume that a worker is primarily moved by economic interest and that he will act logically. The study shows that social considerations outweigh the economic and logical; the workers' actions were based upon nonlogic and sentiment—in other words, upon social routine procedures.

4. The study has some interest for vocational work in selection. In the conditions described, scientific selection and placement do not ensure a corresponding efficiency.

5. The conflict of loyalties involved in the dissonance between the official and the actual organization leads to worry and strain, not only for the supervisor but also for the workers. There is reason to believe that the girl workers in the test room, whose work closely reflected their capacities, experienced a feeling of release from this type of strain.

Roethlisberger and Dickson have elsewhere pointed out[4] that situations such as that described are commonly misinterpreted. It

[4]   Management and the worker, technical vs. social organization in an industrial plant. Harvard Business School, Bureau of Business Research, Boston, 1934.

is supposed, for example, that there is a necessary hostility somewhere implicit in the relations between management and the worker, and that restriction of output is consciously contrived. But this type of explanation misses "the essentially non-logical character" of the situation. It is only those who assume that economic interests dominate the individual and that clear logical thinking serves these interests who can argue thus. And it is the assumption, and not the fact, that drives them in this direction. "Logically it could be argued, for example, that it was to the economic interest of each worker to produce as much as he could and to see that every member of his group did the same. But, in actuality, the workers saw to it that no one's output ever exceeded a certain limit. Had they been asked why they limited their output in this way, they would probably have expressed fears of a possible 'rate reduction.' *Yet none of the men in the bank-wiring observation room had ever experienced a reduction of rates. But they acted as though they had.* This behavior was not directly in line with their economic interests, nor was it based on the facts of their own experience with the company."

There are other observations which make the hypothesis of a necessary hostility between management and workers untenable. The Western Electric Company has a long and consistent record of fair dealing with its employees. Both overtly in a very low labor turnover and verbally in the interviewing program, employees have shown a manifest appreciation of the company's attitude. "In the interviews of 1929, when over 40,000 complaints were voiced, there was not a single unfavorable comment expressed about the company in general." It seems to be clear that the hostility hypothesis is an inference from the insufficient assumption of economic interest and logical thinking as fundamentals of human association; it is not an inference from the facts.

"Upon examining more closely the behavior of employees," it became evident that "many of their actions were of the nature of mechanisms to resist too rapid changes in their environment." The opposition to change was not only reflected in all their tactics to keep output constant, but was also implied in all the reasons they gave in justification of their actions. Roethlisberger and Dickson, therefore, conclude that the chief function of the informal groupings which organize themselves on the working line is "resistance to change or any threat of change in their established routines of work or of personal interrelation." This is a very ancient and well-known character of human association.

Scientific management has preferred to work with explanations or hypotheses that are simple and logical. This would be admirable, if one were not guilty of what A. N. Whitehead terms "the fallacy of misplaced concreteness."[5] But no study of human situations which fails to take account of the non-logical social routines can hope for practical success. Roethlisberger and Dickson give two reasons for the failure of the technical plan in the bank-wiring department. They begin by distinguishing between the technical organization and the informal social organization of the employees. The technical organization is chiefly remarkable "for its logically contrived character" which makes for rapid change. And, just as capacity for change characterizes the technical organization, so resistance to change characterizes the informal employee groups. As a result the employee groups feel that they are constantly under fire—in the sense that it is as if the technical experts were constantly battering to pieces any routines of collaboration that the workers develop. This rouses resistance, first, because "the worker is at the bottom level of a highly stratified hierarchy. *He is always in the position of having to accommodate himself to changes which he does not initiate.*" Second, "many of the changes to which he is asked to adjust rob him of the very things that give meaning and significance to his work. His established routines of work, his personal relations with fellow-workers, even the remnants of a cultural tradition of craftsmanship—all these are at the mercy of the technical specialist. He is not allowed either to retain his former traditions and routines or to evolve new ones of any probable duration. Now, the social codes which define a worker's relation to his work and to his fellows are not capable of rapid change. They are developed slowly and over long periods of time. They are not the product of logic, but of actual human association; they are based on deep-rooted human sentiments. Constant interference with such

5   Science and the modern world. A. N. Whitehead. The Macmillan Company, New York, 1926.

codes is bound to lead to feelings of frustration, to irrational exasperation with technical change in any form." Ultimately, therefore, the disrupted codes revenge themselves by giving rise to informal employee organizations which are opposed to the technical authority.

Scientific management has developed a logical flexibility which in itself is admirable. As applied to industrial organization, however, this flexibility perhaps creates more problems than it solves; it is at least true that social sentiments and routines of association find difficulty in adjusting themselves to the rapid "shift." But scientific management has never studied the facts of human social organization; it has accepted the nineteenth-century economic dictum that economic interest and logical capacity are the basis of the social order. It would seem possible, therefore, that scientific management has itself done much to provoke that hostility between management and workers which now so inconveniently hampers every development towards "rationalization."

There remains comfort, however, to be drawn from the series of experiments at Hawthorne. These experiments—

1. Have called attention to an important group of facts—the facts of spontaneous social organization at the working bench. These facts are of such a nature that they escape the notice of physiological and psychological inquiry.

2. The experiments strongly suggest that the excellent results obtained in the original test room were largely due to the achievement of a comfortable equilibrium between the technical organization, or plant authority, and the spontaneous social organization of the workers themselves. This equilibrium is not generally found in working departments or in other factories.

The facts that we have been considering have revealed and have led us to describe certain characteristics of two social systems, one experimentally (though accidentally) produced, the other a spontaneous formation whose existence had been ignored. Now there can be little doubt that any group of people who work together sooner or later take on some of the characteristics of such a system, and thereafter so act that their behavior can only be conceived as the resultant of social forces as well as of economic forces and of those psychological forces that are private to the individuals. Social organization is, in fact, a human need; it is, in some measure, necessary and inevitable. Its mere existence disciplines the members and gives rise to sentiments, often very strong sentiments, of loyalty, of personal and group integrity, and not infrequently of pride. No. 2 of the test room, commenting after the event on the decline of output toward the end of the long experiment, at a time when the effects of the depression were at their worst, remarked, "We lost our pride."

Not infrequently the proprieties of the spontaneous social system call for more consideration than the strictly economic interests of the group or the psychological properties of the individual members of the system. This is because the social forces are nearly always strong, and sometimes dominant. Like that of the family, the social organization of any group is *felt* as a real thing, indeed as something far more real than the technical organization of a factory; and spontaneously formed human relations are felt to have a meaning and a value that are lacking in purely hierarchical relations or in those relations that are involved in merely working together in time and place, according to an arbitrarily determined plan.

These statements, assuredly, are platitudes; but they are platitudes that are nearly always forgotten by most men of action in action. Yet, it is urgently necessary that they should be always remembered,—remembered and acted upon. Whenever men work together search should be made to discover and to characterize the social systems that have spontaneously arisen, for these are the worlds in which the individual members feel themselves to be living, just as a mother feels herself to be living not so much in a particular house, in a particular street, in a particular town, as in her family

If you are talking with, giving orders to, planning for, making use of a man who is living in a world—or *feels* that he is living in a world—of which you are ignorant, whose existence you do not suspect, is it possible that what you say to him, what you command him to do, what you plan for him, what you use him for, will have for him the same meaning that it has for you? Is it not more probable that what seems to you good for him will to him sometimes seem bad, both for himself and for his fragile and insecure social system, which he values and which gives meaning and color to his life? And is there any ground for thinking that what is logical and reasonable to you will be so to him? If you do not know his axioms, it is probable that your axioms will not be his, and, besides, he cannot, in general, be persuaded by reason but only by an appeal to his sentiments. How shall you appeal to sentiments that you do not know?

The stability of the world in which he feels—however nonlogically, however irrationally—that he is living—however vague, however unanalyzed his feeling—is of first importance to every man. That world is largely made up of his human social relations and of the sentiments that habitually arise in the course of his habitual performance of the routines and rituals of daily life. Change too rapidly imposed from without, for him is evil, because his social system cannot change very rapidly without breaking; it is bound together by sentiments, which change slowly and resist change, because rapid change is destruction of routines and rituals, of habits and of conditioned behavior. Such change is painful even to a dog.

The social environment is what sentiments, routines and rituals make it. From the most perfect family in the world take away the sentiments, the routines and the rituals, and the residue will be unrelated individuals. No doubt the social environment (the various social systems) of a factory is in many ways less important and far less perfect than the social system of a good family. But in several respects it is the same kind of thing and, as experiment shows, it is in several respects so important that it cannot be neglected by anyone who wishes to plan wisely, or even merely to know what he is doing.

The environment is at once physical, chemical, biological, psychological, economic and sociological. As a rule, we all have the strongest feelings about its sociological properties and the least intellectual awareness of them. Often these are the most important properties of the environment. Let us study, weigh, modify and use them.

8

APHORISMS ON THE

ADVERTISING OF

ALKALIES

1937

Editorial note: Reprinted by permission from *Harvard Business Review*, Autumn 1937, pp. 17–23. In this piece, written, says Henderson, "for my own amusement," he explores some relations between medicine on the one hand and sociology, psychology, and not least of all, economics, on the other. The persistence of the phenomenon of medical fads indicates that "the logic of the sentiments," as Pareto called it, as well as commercial exploitation, still plays a considerable part in our lives. Note, in the conclusions, Henderson's raising of the important problem of a functional calculus, or the modes of measuring a net balance of favorable and unfavorable effects in a social system. His concern with social utility, which he learned much about from Pareto, is still a central concern of sociology which we find it hard to cope with satisfactorily.

ADVERTISING has lately experienced an obscure change and gone alkaline. Year by year the concentration of emphasis upon alkalies in the daily and weekly press, in posters, and even "on the air" has increased and still increases. All about us printed and spoken words, slogans and symbols, forms and colors announce to a receptive public the prophylactic and healing virtues of a multitude of alkaline remedies and prescribe their use.

EDITORIAL NOTE: The Editors of the *Harvard Business Review* in publishing the "Aphorisms on the Advertising of Alkalies" by Doctor Henderson have considered the fact that it varies from the present practices of the *Review* in regard both to presentation and to content. They have, however, judged it of value in a business journal since it presents the views of an eminent biochemist upon a subject which lies in his own field and also has a direct bearing upon advertising and selling practices in gen-

The mechanism of this change is not chemical, but economic and psychological. It is a complex mechanism, not altogether open to public inspection; and the reference to medicine is almost completely misleading. I have here tried to analyze and elucidate the process, in the hope that what I have written for my own amusement may find favor with others.

Medical Facts

I. The great Hippocrates held that drugs and medical treatment are not necessary to keep healthy people healthy. Apart from such practices as vaccination, this doctrine is just as good now as it was 2,300 years ago—and no less useful.

II. The natural defenses of the body against acids and the effects of acids (acidosis) are exceptionally well known. Like a dog's defenses against heat and cold, they are so strong and efficient and so prompt in action that the Hippocratic principle applies to them, if anywhere. In a fairly healthy person and in the vast majority of sick people the defenses need no reinforcement.

III. As a rule a healthy person may eat as much acid-forming food as he likes, and will not need to dose himself with alkali.

IV. There is ordinarily no connection whatever between drinking, unless it be drinking mineral acids, and the need of alkali. (Great alcoholic excess sometimes leads to a pathological state with which we are not concerned.)

V. Fatigue is relieved by rest and food, not by the use of alkalies or cigarettes. But sometimes it may be relieved by faith.

VI. The belief that colds are cured by the use of alkali should, on the whole, taking account of all considerations, be classed with the belief that carrying a horse-chestnut in the pocket wards off disease.

VII. Almost anything—real or imaginary; material or spiritual; solid, liquid, or gaseous, or merely verbal; animal, mineral,

---

eral. In addition to dealing directly with this particular subject matter, it presents views of broad bearing upon the social aspects of business practices.

or vegetable; acid or alkaline—may serve for a faith cure. This is not irony, but a plain statement of fact.

VIII. There are innumerable hypochondriacs and potential hypochondriacs; innumerable faddists and potential faddists. They are to be found in all places, at all times.

Psychological Facts

IX. One of the chief objects of the popular advertising of drugs and of the propaganda of medical sects is to exploit the hypochondriacs and the faddists and to form and exploit new hypochondriacs and new faddists. This object is often unconscious; but, whether conscious or unconscious, successes follow in an endless progression.

X. Examples of successful appeals to hypochondriacs: (1) Acidosis is not uncommon in severe chronic diseases. Alkalies neutralize acids in test tubes. Therefore, let us all, old and young, take alkali every day of our lives, as a precaution. (2) Some people suffering from ulcer of the stomach or from an irritation sometimes caused by great alcoholic excess find relief in the use of alkali. Let us, therefore, never fail to take a little alkali, as a precaution, whenever we "take a drink."

XI. The hypochondriacs are unhappy people. Their hypochondria is a misfortune, and may become a disaster to them, to their families, and to their friends.

XII. Of the faddists, those who escape hypochondria are perhaps generally not unhappy. They are more often people of little intelligence or judgment to whom their fads are a resource, a means of occupying their time pleasantly and of explaining their health, happiness, and good fortune. Like most men they feel the need of accounting for events, of "knowing why." But they lack the knowledge and intelligence to understand correct explanations and seek comfort in their own pseudo-explanations. They are often bores and often silly, but are probably not very harmful to others.

XIII. One of the chief objects of that part of the advertising of alkaline remedies which is addressed to physicians is to provide ready-made directions and suggestions for the treatment of patients. It is, or at least it may seem, an economy of time and effort for the doctor to follow blindly such directions and suggestions. Or again, to do so may be only moving along the line of least resistance. I suggest that this is why the advertising is profitable.

XIV. The advertisements of alkaline remedies are nearly always more or less and often very inaccurate. As a rule, this is probably due to the ignorance and indifference of the writers of the advertisements rather than to downright dishonesty. Thinking of the effect and the form, they are oblivious of the substance of their utterances, or perhaps merely indifferent. Some of these writers, no doubt, do their work with their tongues in their cheeks; many, however, are merely stupid people who own no other stock-in-trade than a pitiful technical proficiency, and who follow, sheep-like, wherever they are led. But whatever the explanation, the advertisements are in general misleading as to facts.

XV. The principal immediate conscious aim of advertisers is to appeal to sentiments rather than to reason. This practice rests securely on one of the great discoveries of modern business. Therefore, advertisers often make use of "slogans," of reiterated, irresponsible assertions, which sometimes take the form of mere pictures, of appeals to pseudo-authority, and of irrational accords of sentiments, prejudices, fads, and fashions.

XVI. The advertising of alkaline drugs and of alkali-forming foods shares all these traits. In its special characteristics it appeals chiefly to fears and to the desire for vague, oversimplified pseudo-scientific explanations. It also aims to give a feeling of assurance to those who crave this feeling.

Economic Facts

XVII. The principal direct economic effect of such advertising is to remove money from the pockets of the many fearful or unintelligent or ignorant people among the 125,000,000 living Americans, and to put it into the pockets of the relatively few shrewd advertisers and of the purveyors of advertising. Nobody knows what the indirect economic effects may be.

XVIII. Because newspapers and magazines receive large sums

in payment for the advertisements that they print, many of them are dependent upon the goodwill of advertisers and cannot freely publish facts and opinions about advertising. (This may be verified experimentally.) Thus economic forces give rise to something like a censorship of the press. However, these forces are opposed by another: the common need of editors and advertisers for readers. Now, success in the competition for readers depends upon getting and holding public confidence. Therefore, as this competition has grown keener, the power of editors to oppose the special interests of advertisers has grown stronger. The result is a balance of forces, a state of equilibrium that seems to be tending slowly toward greater freedom of the press.

XIX. Most of the advertised preparations of alkalies are sold at a price that is many, many times greater than their cost. So if you want some alkali, do as most doctors do, as many of them often do; go into the kitchen and take a little cooking soda. The price of a hundred-pound barrel is $1.75.

XX. The result of a careful estimate by a competent investigator: The cost of advertising a certain alkaline remedy is now much more than $1,000,000 a year.

Medical Effects

XXI. The physiological effects of the present widespread advertising of alkalies and of alkali-forming foods are probably not appreciably harmful. Indeed, the occasional use of a little bicarbonate of soda may be effectual in relieving slight gastric distress, and an increased use of alkali-forming fruits and vegetables may also be a benefit, in one way or another, to some persons. It is not likely to be harmful to many. In short, for the great mass of people in whom common sense is stronger than fads and fears, the frequent use of bicarbonate of soda or the habitual use, say, of orange juice is probably quite harmless and, in a small way, useful because at least comforting. (There are other properties of orange juice, aside from alkali formation, with which we are not here concerned.)

XXII. Because the defenses of the acid-alkali balance of the body, the ordinary ever-present automatic checks on acidosis and alkalosis, are very strong, even the prolonged use of alkalies in large amounts is generally much less dangerous than the use of many other popular or proprietary remedies. In fact, for most people the risks of alkalosis, like the risks of acidosis, are practically negligible. The very mechanism that makes treatment unnecessary makes it harmless. It is because alkalies have almost no physiological effect beyond bringing the protective mechanism into action that it is safe to advertise them.

XXIII. Experience shows, however, that harmful overdosing with alkalies is possible, at least in patients who really have something wrong with them. The condition is perhaps more often a result of the doctor's than of the patient's fad. Exceptionally, where a fad has become a fashion among doctors, it may be common.

XXIV. The psychological, sociological, and economic forces that produce hypochondriacs and faddists are many and strong. Therefore, it seems unlikely that all the advertising of alkaline remedies and all the talking about the danger of acidosis greatly increase their number. Probably a pretty large part of the American people are born with the preëstablished destiny of becoming hypochondriacs or faddists. If their destiny were not realized by acquiring a fear of acidosis or a fad for the use of alkalies, it would probably be more often than not worked out in some similar way. And if their money were not spent on alkaline drugs, it would perhaps be spent no more profitably on other drugs.

XXV. In many persons the capacity for fears and fads, if not infinite, is at least practically unlimited. In them the fear of acidosis or the fad for the use of alkalies is often not a substitute for some other fear or fad, but an addition to those that they already possess. In such cases the objects feared are of small importance; what is important is the habit of fearing. These persons belong to the pure or unmixed type of hypochondriac. *"Primus in orbe deus fecit timor."*

XXVI. Thus, a new question arises: What would be the result if all the advertising of drugs and of medical crazes, if all the warnings of life insurance companies and of the purveyors of foods and drinks, of hygienic appliances, and of so many other articles of commerce, were to cease? We do not know. It is conceivable that our yearly production of hypochondriacs and faddists would fall. But it is by no means certain. And the condition above stated must surely seem to a hard-headed man almost beyond the range of any conceivable attainment. Even under a dictator such things do not happen.

XXVII. It may be that, on the whole, more people are indirectly benefited than injured by fastening upon them a fear of acidosis or a fad for the use of alkalies, since they might otherwise adopt a more dangerous form of self-treatment.

XXVIII. Because the irrational fear of acidosis is possibly less intense than that of cancer, of heart disease, or of infection, it may be that acidosis-hypochondriacs are less unhappy than cancer-hypochondriacs or heart disease-hypochondriacs or infection-hypochondriacs. But this is very doubtful because the *intensity* of a hypochondriacs's fear has little and often nothing to do with the thing feared.

Conclusions

XXIX. In so far as the advertising of alkaline remedies leads to a net increase in the number of hypochondriacs and faddists, it may be said to be harmful to certain individuals. No doubt those others who profit from it directly or indirectly consider it beneficial to themselves.

XXX. I must leave it to others to weigh harm and good to the community, for the community is something more than and something different from the sum of the individuals who make it up, and a physiologist is not well acquainted with it. But we must not forget that most judgments of social utility are expressions of faith, not reasoned scientific conclusions, or perhaps more often just another form of advertising, like much that issues from Washington, London, and Paris or from Rome, Berlin, and Moscow.

XXXI. The influence of the prejudices and economic interests of advertisers probably brings about the exclusion of both nonsense and good sense from the pages of newspapers and magazines.

The net result is perhaps indeterminate, but neither uplifters nor advertisers are likely to admit it.

XXXII. I know no well-informed person who, unless he is amused by the human comedy, is not disgusted by the stupidity, the deception, and the misrepresentation that are manifest in the current advertising of alkalies. And in spite of the dictates of caution I do think that this disgust, at least, is socially useful.

XXXIII. In these aphorisms I have tried to present sufficient materials for a diagnosis which anyone can make for himself. Unhappily, I know nobody who seems to me qualified to make the prognosis or to prescribe the treatment of this affliction of the commonwealth.

Advertising in General

XXXIV. It is an error common among "New Dealers" and their like to extend some of the conclusions of these aphorisms and to apply them to any and every use of sentimental appeals in advertising. Such critics do not see that advertising must always appeal to the sentiments because all human relations involve the sentiments. One of the commonest and worst errors of "intellectuals" is to ignore this larger generalization. For this reason, especially, their rational Utopias, from Plato's to the New Deal, are not only impossible in fact, but inhuman. If they were possible, they would still be intolerable.

XXXV. The great, but by no means new, discovery of modern business to which I have referred is the clear recognition that advertising must use, indeed necessarily involves, sentimental appeals. Julius Caesar knew this well. Such appeals may be morally and socially good, bad, or indifferent. That is a question of fact (and in a measure of arbitrary preference) difficult to answer in any case; but impossible to answer in general, and indeed meaningless. The only possible answers must arise from the study of concrete instances, one by one, from case to case. The strength of the automobile industry seems to depend largely upon engineering and advertising. The engineering rests upon the skillful use of natural science, the advertising upon skillful appeals to people's sentiments. Who among us is wise enough to say that the one is more or less useful or harmful to the community than the other? And who cares?

Not a Conclusion

XXXVI. Many readers of these aphorisms will perhaps accuse me of vacillation and inconsistency; but I hope the accusation is false. If they do so, I believe it will be because they are accustomed to one-sided discussions of complex questions, to the methods of advocates and propagandists, and have mistakenly thought to find them here.

XXXVII. There are others to whom my conclusions may seem timid and overcautious. Accustomed to the security of the desk or the library, conditioned by debate with other men of words rather than by operations performed upon things, they do not hesitate to form easy judgments of right and wrong. They forget that, though words seldom burn fingers or break bones, things often do; that, as Bacon said, "The subtlety of nature is greater many times over than the subtlety of the senses and understanding," for they do not try their minds against things. They have not learned, by trial and much error, one of the professional secrets of the scientist and of the man of affairs: how to say cheerfully and contentedly, "I do not know." Not lightly or timidly or overcautiously, but deliberately and because I have often been wrong in similar premises, as well as for theoretical reasons, I have here said that I do not know.

XXXVIII. I have nothing to advocate, except that ancient maxim *caveat emptor* (which, interpreted, means: let every man take the responsibility of protecting his family and himself), the observation of which in all societies, under all forms of government, has always been honored as a source of self-respect in the individual and of strength in the community. And I can draw no single, firm, synthetic conclusion, but only many various conclusions that, like the different traits of a man's character, seem to involve a mixture of good and bad, and to defy synthesis.

XXXIX. If we stick to the facts, which few people do, we see that here, as in most human affairs, some point one way, some another. Therefore, a general conclusion, a plan of action, a policy, a law, is likely to be the expression of a prejudice and, because it ignores important facts, to lead to unexpected and undesired results, just as the prohibition amendment did. So the remedy is often worse than the disease.

Individual and Collective Utility

XL. Experience shows that the state may usefully protect both individuals and the community by enforcing very explicit and concrete laws or police regulations concerning the accuracy of weights and measures, the purity of foods, the labeling of drugs, the sale of poisons, and other things that can be objectively tested. But appeals to fears and sentiments cannot be objectively tested, so that here the welfare of individuals and that of the community are probably best served by individual actions and collective attitudes, rather than by putting meddlesome busybodies to work, who are pretty sure to try in vain to check indefinite abuses, and meanwhile interfere with honest men.

XLI. Observance of these well-worn precepts, which may be regarded as implications of the maxim *caveat emptor,* I think useful to the *individual:* Seek disinterested advice and trustworthy information. Learn to recognize facts; then act upon them. Avoid the influence of suggestion, of fears, and of fads. Look real dangers in the face. Despise vain apprehensions.

XLII. Countrariwise, it is harmful to a man to be ignorant, to be credulous, to yield to suggestion, to cherish fears, and to cultivate fads. It is alike harmful to ignore serious risks and to think most risks serious. Physicians know no greater source of unhappiness than the assumption, often unconscious, that imaginary or infinitesimal dangers are real and great, and there is no more characteristic symptom of hypochondria than the feeling that everything not perfectly safe is dangerous.

XLIII. Two things I hold useful to the *community,* and now explicitly reaffirm my belief in them; for I wish to be understood. One is indignation at conscious or unconscious misrepresentation or deceit. But without full and unprejudiced knowledge of facts and the rarest of foresight this is no safe ground for repression or prohibition. So experience teaches. The second is a strong, widely spread, and effective sense of individual responsibility, a disposition to protect one's own and one's self, an unwillingness to trust in our rulers, the time-serving politicians.

XLIV. As for what is harmful to the community, I cannot be explicit, but this I know, that I fear the "intellectuals," the sentimentalists, and the uplifters—to me they are all one—even as I do the politicians and the profiteers. If only, instead of heaping up evils, they could but neutralize each other, like alkali and acid!

9

WHAT IS

SOCIAL PROGRESS?

1941

Editorial note: This appeared in *Proceedings of the American Academy of Arts and Sciences* 73 (1941): 457–63. Henderson here expresses his convictions on how little sociology knows about social change and how glibly most men talk about social progress. Many liberals would probably call Henderson a conservative, but he probably thought of himself as an old-fashioned and *real* liberal.

The Word

IN THIS PLACE, addressing the Academy on this occasion, I feel constrained to take—or to try to take—a position that shall be logical and scientific. I feel thus constrained even though, or better because, the question "What is 'social progress'?" seems to me logically a meaningless question about things that admit of little precise analysis.

The question is meaningless because there are no procedures, either measurements or mere observations, that can be regarded as suitable for its investigation. The question is also meaningless because the term "social progress" is useless and worse than useless as a symbol in performing logical operations. The first of these assertions hardly requires further proof. Let us examine the second.

Oliver Wendell Holmes the younger, writing in his old age to a Chinese friend, once remarked:[1] "I have said to my brethren

[1]   *Justice Oliver Wendell Holmes: His Book Notices and Uncollected Letters and Papers.* Edited by Harry C. Shriver, New York, 1936, p. 201.

many times that I hate justice, which means that I know if a man begins to talk about that, for one reason or another he is shirking thinking in legal terms." I shall presume to make a single exegetical remark on Holmes's text: the phrase "shirking thinking in legal terms" may be generalized to read "shirking thinking in terms that can be used for even rough and ready logical purposes or for any sort of clear thinking." Holmes's remark is not new, but it is the opinion—the induction—of a man who through a long life had formed his opinions from experience under the burden of responsibility. The same opinion was earlier expressed by Montaigne, who remarked:[2] "We say, indeed, Power, Truth, Justice: they are words that denote something great, but that something we are quite unable to see and conceive." A general treatment of the matter, not modern or rigorous, but sufficient for many purposes, may be found in Bacon's theory of Idols.[3] Probably, in most ages, at least a few sensible men have always known what Montaigne, Bacon, and Holmes knew; that many words, for other uses indispensable, are useless for clear thinking.

Why are terms like justice and social progress useless for clear thinking? First I suppose because, unlike such a word as contract, they have no accepted, fairly clear meaning, and again because, unlike such a word as cathode, they can be given an arbitrary definition only at the cost of strong persistent emotional opposition. Consider, for instance, the probable attitude of many thousands of Nazis to a definition of "justice" that should make discharging hostile university professors unjust. Now consider a definition of "social progress" that should make this same action socially unprogressive. The effect must be, at least for many people, not logical thinking, but strife, because strong feelings associated with the word inhibit its logical use and demand its nonlogical use. I suggest that an arbitrary definition of "social progress" that should make, or should not make, the National Labor Relations Act an instance of social progress would, if the point were raised, arouse similar, if less violent, strife in this room tonight.

[2]   *The Essays of Montaigne*, translated by E. J. Trechmann, London, 1927, Book I, Chapter 23, pp. 103–120.
[3]   *Novum Organum*, Book I, Aphorisms XXXVIII–LXVIII.

Bury has said[4] that for Turgot the idea of progress "was an organizing conception, just as the idea of Providence was for St. Augustine and Bossuet an organizing conception, which gave history its unity and meaning." In plain English this means that for Turgot the facts of history were subordinate to and had to be forced into conformity with certain lofty sentiments and dogmatic beliefs. I suspect that Turgot's view is still the prevalent view.

In general, men feel that words like justice and progress must have a meaning, must correspond to some deep reality, but they agree in only one respect: each feels that this reality, this unknown thing, must fully accord with *his* sentiments. So discussion of the attitudes of justice or progress is like discussion of the attributes of God. It is the business of metaphysicians; it is clearly not the business of scientists. Therefore, if we are to pursue our subject, we must altogether abandon social progress as a logical symbol, or as a concept, or as an abstract metaphysical reality, and look at facts. Perhaps we may more easily reconcile ourselves to this lowly occupation by reflecting that the question "What is progress?" has been much debated, but without result, and that there is hardly any social change that has not been called progress by somebody.

The Sentiments

For Montaigne, power, truth, and justice—though they lack clearness—"denote something great"; and I do not believe that here Montaigne was speaking ironically. At all events, the social importance of the sentiments behind these words and of the words themselves as expressions of these sentiments is inestimable. Human societies have existed in which science and logic played only a small part, but there have been few indeed in which these sentiments did not have a great part. And in our own societies the words justice and truth themselves—the words themselves—have for thousands of years served to reinforce the sentiments, to arouse them, and perhaps even to instill them where they were lacking.

---

4   J. B. Bury, *The Idea of Progress*, London, 1920, p. 158.

Such words are indeed indispensable. But "progress" is a modern invention which only yesterday attained to the dignity of personification. Today Progress is the most youthful, though not the fairest, of the goddesses, pale and wan of face, but not for love. We fear for her. Perhaps it is that fear which has brought us together tonight.

I wonder whether the word progress—so unlike "truth" and "justice"—is a trustworthy vehicle for the deep and abiding sentiments of men, except only for hope, or others that may have been recently, and weakly, associated, and whether it is not much more a sterile intellectual construction, for the greater part a rationalization of the eighteenth century *philosophes* and their nineteenth century heirs, the good liberals, under the influence of economic, political, and social change and the increasing control and exploitation of the environment. I suspect, in short, thát for most of us the word progress suggests something less great than the words truth and justice do, for I believe that it expresses sentiments which are on the whole less deep in the human heart, because they have had a place there far less long. They seem not to have been a need of our forefathers. Unhappily this question—the social importance of the affective states, of the sentiments and emotions, associated with the word progress and with belief in progress—seems unripe for solution. I can but raise the question, express my doubts, and pass on.

The Rationalizations

The social importance of the *belief* in progress is another question. Considering this belief apart from the accompanying sentiments and emotions, as an intellectual influence, we may hazard the guess that its importance is small. For two centuries the belief has, no doubt, occupied the attention of political and social philosophers and of many others, but it is hard to see that much has come of this intellectual manipulation of the idea that has greatly changed human societies. On the one hand, the belief is difficult of application, being in no sense a scientific induction; on the other hand, it is perhaps only a quasi-religious dogma.

Social Changes

So we come to the question of the nature of social change. Social change is a fact. Here, however ignorant we may be, we stand on firm ground. Yet we are indeed most ignorant, and how unprepared to cope with the little we know! For there is nobody who has that intimate, intuitive familiarity with the phenomena which is the beginning of wisdom; and perhaps there can be nobody. Change is long, life short. Again there is nobody who has extensive systematic knowledge of social changes, for no good sociological classification of changes exists, to say nothing of broad information thus classified. And still again we have only just begun to think in terms of a generalized social system according to the example of the natural sciences, and what we can do with this social system or any other theory is but little. So in searching for the facts we must feel our way.

The Greek theory of recurrent world cycles, like the legend of the Golden Age, need not detain us. But there was also among the Greeks a theory of political cycles which, whatever its origin, came to be partly founded on observation. Polybius was a sensible man, and for Polybius, at least, it was an induction from experience that any form of government in due course takes on characteristics that lead to its destruction.[5] So another form arises, with a like result, and so after a time the first form returns. We may cautiously note this opinion, even though it seems likely that Polybius went beyond his facts, for many things that have lately been seen resemble the phenomena noted by Polybius and are consistent with his conclusions. Furthermore, old surviving constitutions are scarce today, and they seem to have been scarce also in times past.

From Vico to Spengler moderns have added their own to ancient speculations about historical cycles. Let us pass them by, for they seem to offer little that we can use. But meanwhile experi-

[5]   *Histories*, VI; 3, 1; 9, 14.

ence has been accumulating and it has gradually become plain that most things undulate. The πάντα 'ρεῖ of Heraclitus is sharpened for us by a half unconscious induction into πάντα 'ρεῖ καὶ ἀναρρεῖ. Tastes, doctrines, schools and forms in the arts and letters rise and fall as they do, often more quickly nowadays, in dress and in personal adornment. So they do in philosophy and in political and social theory. Is not the history of the theory of our subject a fair instance of this? So too economic processes ebb and flow.

In this one instance some progress (note the intrusion of our word) has been made in getting on from vague statement in phrases like those of the last paragraph to measurement and mathematical analysis; and we have, such as it is, the description and the theory of the business cycle. Clearly the phenomena are at least undulatory, even more than they are cyclical. Clearly the frequencies and the amplitudes of the waves of the business cycle seem to follow no simple rules. Clearly these waves seem to be, in general, unrelated by any simple laws to other undulatory processes. If all this were not so, some people, who have not, would have grown rich.

For many economists and for most men of affairs and politicians the waves of the business cycle are long waves, but for the historian of, say, three thousand years, they are short. Now there exists no more familiar, no more trustworthy historical generalization than this: During two historical periods, very vaguely defined, that are commonly referred to as ancient and modern times, there has been much intense activity in many of the affairs of European men; during an intervening period, sometimes called the Dark Ages, *in these same affairs* little intense activity. So the large-scale or long-period wave phenomena seem to be highly correlated.

The question arises: Considering that we find waves of short period which may be regarded as slight disturbances of waves of long period, is there a wave of longest period? If not, is there a trend? These questions are meaningless. They are not even properly formulated as a first step in considering whether there is anything more to say about longer scale processes, for such waves are, like the conceptual schemes of the physicists, partly constructions of our own minds that go beyond the facts. There is perhaps nothing more to say except the obvious remark that long ago there seems to have been no human activity on the earth and that lately there has been what we regard as rather too much. However, most social processes seem to be more or less undulatory—or are so conceivable. And in many instances what we may take as the trends of these processes appear to be segments of undulatory processes of longer period.

What can be said of other general aspects of social change? Auguste Comte distinguished three stages—the theological, the metaphysical, and the positive—in the growth of human societies. It is perhaps psychologically significant, though logically irrelevant, to note that in the end Comte tried to found a new religion of his own invention, which seems inconsistent, and that he was a philosopher rather than an observer. Little survives of Comte's philosophy of social change. No doubt he was right in his belief that the social importance of science, both pure and applied, had on the whole increased. It seems to have increased enormously since his time.

Herbert Spencer conceived social change as a predominantly orthogenetical evolution from the simple to the complex. He held that the evolution is largely determined by what he supposed to be a law of the instability of the homogeneous. The meaninglessness of all this was long ago demonstrated by the physicist Tait in a forgotten controversy with Spencer. Perhaps a remark of Clerk Maxwell's on a postcard addressed to Tait will suggest the natural attitude of a man of science in these premises. Maxwell wrote:[6] "Have you (read) Willard Gibbs on Equilibrium of Heterogeneous Substances? . . . Refreshing after H. Spencer on the Instability of the Homogeneous." Of course many things in human societies have in many respects greatly increased in complexity, for example, in technological complexity and in organization. But there seem to be other things in which the movement has been, even over long periods, the reverse. This is held to be the case of the grammatical structure of language. Moreover, it seems that what may

<hr>

[6]   C. G. Knott, *Life and Scientific Work of P. G. Tait*, Cambridge, England, 1911, p. 284.

be called the rituals and routines of European societies have run a parallel course with grammar. Sir Henry Maine's views[7] on the replacement of status by contract bear on this point.

Ends and Means

In what I have just said I have tried to select fair specimens of descriptions of social changes and to suggest their limited utility for our present purpose. We may now turn to opinions about what social changes are desirable. Nothing is more familiar than Jeremy Bentham's "greatest happiness of the greatest number." Of this Edgeworth once said:[8] ". . . is this more intelligible than 'greatest illumination with the greatest number of lamps'?" And Edgeworth was right, for two superlatives make the solution of the problem indeterminate, and the phrase is accordingly meaningless. Yet how much stronger is the emotional appeal of two superlatives! And who among us has ever noticed the obvious fallacy that Edgeworth noticed? And why has Edgeworth's remark been generally forgotten while Bentham's phrase is nowhere forgotten? Well, the reasons for all this are many, complex, and tolerably obscure. Let us talk about them.

To begin with, there is no logical or scientific test of desirability, except in relation to an end or purpose, and then desire is a poor word; we had better talk about utility. For instance, a boy may just want to go swimming. In that event the means to his end become problems that admit of something like logical or scientific study, and we may even safely speak of progress toward that *given* end. But unless the desire in question comes into conflict with other desires, experience shows that it is ordinarily a waste of breath to reason about going swimming. On the other hand, this boy may want to go swimming because another boy is going swimming, because he wants company. Then the question of other means to this end may arise and is, in principle, within the range of logical and scientific analysis. Let us accordingly speak of

7   *Ancient Law*, Chapter V.
8   *Mathematical Psychics*, London, 1881, p. 117.

utility as relative to an end or purpose and in principle determinate. Let us also note that statements about the ultimate ends
of society are expressions of wishes that are in general as meaningless as Bentham's "greatest happiness of the greatest number."

Utilities are heterogeneous. There are present utilities and
future utilities; for instance, spending and saving. There are material utilities like food and psychological utilities like music or
poetry or philosophy. And there are utilities of the individual and
utilities of society. Being heterogeneous, utilities are likely to conflict. One of the commonest kinds of conflict is that between individual and social utilities. In such conflicts we hear of egotism and
altruism, private interest and public welfare, the good of the service and self-seeking.

Such are our present difficulties. There is, however, one ultimate social end, survival, that seems to be different from the others,
for unlike progress or justice it can be observed. The Roman
Catholic church survives; Nineveh and Tyre do not. These facts
can be verified on April 12, 1939. Moreover, survival, both of the
individual and of society, is a widely accepted end in all societies.
If, then, we define, *arbitrarily* define, the survival of a society as
an end, it is possible to investigate what is vaguely called the survival value of certain things for that society. And then in this
sense we may speak of their social utility. Of course, this task is
difficult, not to say in general fruitless. For the social sciences are
not yet very helpful in a dispassionate inquiry.

There is also, perhaps, some slight possibility of judging the
total state of a society in relation to its survival. Thus in, say, 1910
there was a general feeling that the Austro-Hungarian empire had
small powers of resistance, the British Empire great powers of resistance. As we vaguely say, the one empire seemed to lack, the
other to have stability. Many historians were prepared to give reasons—not very sound scientific reasons, to be sure—in support
of these opinions.

Science and Social Progress

One has lately grown accustomed to hearing from distinguished men of science assertions addressed to the general public that the effects of science, especially the effects upon society, are altogether good or progressive, or useful. I can see no grounds whatever for such an opinion. In the first place, referring to what I have already said, I assert that the question is meaningless. In the second place, I assert that if, by means of arbitrary definitions, the question were given meaning, the answer could be found at best only after years of research.

Let us consider two specific questions. At the moment one of the most conspicuous effects of science is the development of military aviation. According to what and to whose emotional judgments does this constitute social progress? According to what arbitrary definitions, and for whom, does this today or will this ten years hence make for the stability of what societies? Surely the only possible answer is, we do not know; or rather this correct answer is an impossible answer for nearly everybody, because the passions, and fear above all, intervene.

Now consider population. There are grounds for thinking that the present state of most human societies is unstable, that this instability is largely associated with the growth of population, that this growth of population is largely due to applications of science and to a decline in the rate of infant mortality and that this decline also is largely a result of applications of science. Of course, we do not know all this. But in the face of such considerations and in view of our obvious ignorance, who shall say that the applications of medical science *may* not some day play a large part in bringing about the destruction of many societies? Again I say, we do not know. And I suggest that men of science may well consider the question whether they wish to assert what nobody can know. In this way they might at least avoid the risk of making such statements as the following: "It is science and its applications that . . . have knit the whole world together into a unity that makes war an anachronism."[9]

One thing seems clear; among the innumerable effects of sci-

[9]   Robert A. Millikan, *Science and the New Civilization*, New York, 1930, pp. 68–69.

ence on society, some must be harmful according to any definition, now or hereafter, to many individuals and to some societies.

It is also worthy of note that sometimes the effects of science upon society may well be only implicit functions of the state of science, but explicit functions of the *rate* of scientific development. In other words, the same scientific development proceeding rapidly might have one effect, proceeding slowly another quite different effect. It is a curious theorem that, regardless of such differences, the effects are desirable—or undesirable. But, however strange theorems of this type may be, dogmas of this type are very familiar.

Let us look again at the problem of stability. In the beginning of Morley's essay *On Compromise* you may read[10] (as many Victorians did with satisfaction and approval): "The right of thinking freely and acting independently, of using our minds without excessive awe of authority, and shaping our lives without unquestioning obedience to custom, is now a finally accepted principle in some sense or other with every school of thought that has the smallest chance of commanding the future." To such nonsense a simple faith in progress may bring a man like Morley. I hope that his false prophecy needs no further remark, but the phrase 'obedience to custom,' which is perhaps the worst nonsense of all,[11] must now be examined, for it may lead us to one final and positive conclusion.

Morley was in many ways a thoroughly typical Englishman of his period. His behavior was faithful, conscientious, decorous, decent, seemly, congruous with all standards of good breeding, suitable to his orderly occasions, becoming in a high-minded citizen, befitting a man of his standing and integrity. He was kindly, honorable, upright, fair-minded, just, truthful, law-abiding, scrupulous, and trustworthy. His unblemished conduct and equitable demeanor unfailingly and with regularity observed the proprieties in all things. Was this *obedience* to custom? Certainly not. And it was neither unquestioning nor questioning obedience. It was some-

---

[10]   2nd ed., London, 1886, p. 1.
[11]   Except possibly the notion that schools of thought command the future.

thing like the *li* of Confucius,[12] the manifestation, in general unconscious, of a need as strong as the need for food, or stronger. Had he learned this behavior intellectually? Again, certainly not; neither he nor any other man. And such behavior did not even occur to him when he wrote of "unquestioning obedience to custom." But it was deeper than intellectual processes in his nervous system, for it was largely constituted (in the widest sense of Pavlov's school) of conditioned reflexes. If it had been interfered with, an experimental neurosis might have resulted.

Machiavelli once said[13] that the ancient religion "was one of the chief causes of the prosperity of Rome; for this religion gave rise to well-regulated conduct, and such conduct brings good fortune, and from good fortune results the happy success of undertakings." This was also the opinion of Polybius,[14] who had observed the Romans. Again the conditioned reflex, together with ritual and routine, predominates, for the Roman religion was an all pervasive cult, and it was little more. Polybius speaks of it as maintaining the cohesion of the state.

Le Play's great study of European working-class families tells the same tale.[15] He found that those families were coherent in which respect for parental authority and for the Decalogue persisted, and his whole work clearly shows that regular conduct was again the important factor, as it had been in the Romans two thousand years earlier—regular conduct arising largely from conditioned reflexes associated with routines and rituals of the family and of religion.

Le Play's unsound families lacked a harmonious pattern of conditioned reflexes. With continuing industrial development the number of such families has probably increased, for about the end of last century Durkheim recognized and described a specific path-

---

[12]   "The Master said . . . 'It is by the Rules of Propriety [li] that the character is established.'" Confucius: *Analects*, Book VIII, Chapter VIII, § 2. Translation by James Legge.
[13]   *Discourses on the First Decade of Titus Livius*, Book I, Chapter XI.
[14]   *Histories*, VI, 56, 6–13.
[15]   *Les Ouvriers Européens*, passim.

ological state[16] which he called *anomie*. It seems to be due to an intensification and enlargement of the very conditions described by Le Play in his unsound families. Its differentia is extreme lack of cohesion. Durkheim speaks of an incoherent dust of individuals.

Still later Pareto, in his taxonomic studies of the residues, found the same thing.[17] The residues are widely current manifestations of sentiments, chiefly observable in nonlogical conduct. One class of residues, those of the so-called persistent aggregates, are plainly a product—in the main—of conditioned reflexes, rituals, and routines. In Pareto's considered opinion the persistent aggregates are the chief cohesive factor that binds societies together.

Here is a body of evidence and of carefully formed inductions. It points to a clear conclusion, to a conclusion that has been almost completely obscured by the European intellectual tradition. This conclusion has been obscured because the makers of the intellectual tradition, and still more its transmitters, like the political scientists of whom Aristotle speaks,[18] have rarely known human societies intimately at first hand. And when the facts have obtruded themselves, "intellectuals" have too often regarded them as expressions of ignorant prejudice or superstition, unworthy of their notice, and as an impertinent intrusion of nonsense into their more serious concerns. The conclusion, greatly over-simplified, is this: The acquired characters of men are of two kinds. One kind is chiefly intellectual, the other arises chiefly from conditioning, and from rituals and routines. This it is that has been neglected by intellectuals; yet this is the older, the more primitive, and in many respects by far the more important of the two. Men share it, in modified form, with dogs and other animals.

A suitable dose, neither too much nor too little,[19] of such ac-

16   *Le Suicide*, Paris, 1897, passim.
17   *The Mind and Society*, New York, 1935, Vol. II.
18   *Nicomachean Ethics*, Everyman's Edition, X, pp. 260–261: ". . . in all other cases those who impart the faculties and themselves exert them are identical (physicians and painters for instance) ; matters of Statesmanship the Sophists profess to teach, but not one of them practises it . . .

". . . they [the Sophists] have no knowledge at all of its nature and objects . . ."
19   I suggest that there may have been too much, for various ends,

quired characters, harmoniously interrelated, seems necessary to the stability of individuals and of societies, and as a foundation for orderly change. When social change is too rapid, a suitable dose is less often acquired. Without a very great deal of the resulting regular conduct, what we call liberty is impossible. Men will not *obey* custom, but if they feel a need to do right, that is if, like Morley, they are suitably adapted by conditioning to the ways of their own folk, they may often, at least in many circumstances, safely do as they please.

When societies are too unstable, individuals suffer. It seems probable that the psychoneuroses are most common in Durkheim's anomic people and that, for instance, disease of the coronary arteries, gastric ulcer and duodenal ulcer are most frequent in unstable societies. An index formed by adding appropriate measures of the incidence of these diseases and of divorce, and subtracting a measure of attendance at church, might sometimes run more or less parallel with an index of industrial development. Then would both—or neither—measure social progress? They would measure —what they measure.

Conclusion

It seems probable that, in a given place, at a given time, for a given end, there may be an optimum rate of change of a given thing. Some day this will be a subject ripe for careful study. Then the conditioned reflexes of men, as they are at any given time and in any given place, will be seldom negligible. More often than not, I suggest, when the end is survival, they will be again, as they have been so often in the forms that we name loyalty, the bonds of family, the sense of kinship, love of country, and religious devotion, powerful social forces, and dangerously lacking when in default. For note well that humanitarian sensibilities, liberal opinions, and social philosophies, in this respect like scientific attainments, are not the equivalent of the sentiments that accompany conditioned

---

about five centuries ago in China, and that there may be too little today in our own society.

reflexes. In origin and in function they are different things. Sentiments of the first kind, arising more or less directly out of concrete experiences, hardly at all related to the intellect, closely related to what we call in some men breeding, in others discipline, in still others decency, act as cohesive forces. Sentiments of the second kind, much less a result of concrete experience and of conditioning, much more closely associated with intellectual activity, seem to have other functions, and not this one. Both kinds of sentiments will probably be powerful social forces in the future.

The cohesive forces, though neglected and despised by "intellectuals," though weakened by rapid social change, might even save us from disaster. This we can only surmise, but that they will continue to operate is certain, "car il faut cultiver notre jardin," and they arise spontaneously, by conditioning, from this cultivation.

Meanwhile a meaningless word will still be meaningless. And yet we need not hate progress, unless, like Holmes, we do so in self-defense. That a meaningless word should have had for two centuries the fortunes of this word is no small thing.

Bibliography

The Social Science Writings of L. J. Henderson

The Fitness of the Environment. New York: The Macmillan Company, 1913.

The Order of Nature: An Essay. Cambridge, Mass.: Harvard University Press, 1917.

Pareto's General Sociology: A Physiologist's Interpretation. Cambridge, Mass.: Harvard Univesrity Press, 1937.

Sociology 23 Lectures, 1941–42 edition, previously unpublished.

Introduction to Claude Bernard. *An Introduction to the Study of Experimental Medicine.* Translated by H. C. Greene. Originally published in translation in 1927. New York: Henry Schuman, 1949, v–xii.

"An Approximate Definition of Fact." *University of California Publications in Philosophy* 14 (1932) : 179–99.

"Science, Logic, and Human Intercourse." *Harvard Business Review* April 1934, pp. 317–27.

"Pareto's Science of Society." *Saturday Review of Literature*, 25 May 1935, pp. 3–4, 10.

"The Relation of Medicine to the Fundamental Sciences." *Science* 82- (1935) : 477–81.

"Physician and Patient as a Social System." *New England Journal of Medicine* 212 (1935) : 819–23.

"The Practice of Medicine as Applied Sociology." *Transactions of the Association of American Physicians* 51 (1936) : 8–15.

[With Elton Mayo] "The Effects of Social Environment." *Journal of Industrial Hygiene and Toxicology* 18 (1936) : 401–16.

"Aphorisms on the Advertising of Alkalies." *Harvard Business Review*, Autumn 1937, pp. 17–23.

"What Is Social Progress?" *Proceedings of the American Academy of Arts and Sciences* 73 (1941) : 457–63.

"The Study of Man." *Science* 94 (1941) : 1–10.